Do I Stand Alone?

Also by Jesse Ventura

I Ain't Got Time to Bleed: Reworking
the Body Politic from the Bottom Up

Do I Stand Alone?

GOING TO THE MAT AGAINST POLITICAL PAWNS AND MEDIA JACKALS

MINNESOTA GOVERNOR
JESSE VENTURA

with Julie Mooney

POCKET BOOKS
New York   London   Toronto   Sydney   Singapore

POCKET BOOKS, a division of Simon & Schuster, Inc.
1230 Avenue of the Americas, New York, NY 10020

ISBN: 0-7434-0586-2

First Pocket Books hardcover printing September 2000

10 9 8 7 6 5 4 3 2 1

POCKET and colophon are registered trademarks of
Simon and Schuster, Inc.

Designed by Helene Berinsky

Printed in the U.S.A.

QM/✶

to the American voter—
I hope that includes you

ACKNOWLEDGMENTS

I wish to thank my family, Terry, Tyrel, and Jade; all my staff and commissioners at my office and at the state capitol in Saint Paul, including Senior Staff, Steve Rosacker, John Wodele, Wendy Wustenberg, and the others; AEI's Julie Ann Mooney, who put all this into a readable order, and Ken and Vincent Atchity; all the folks at Pocket Books, but especially my editor, Emily Bestler, and Kip Hakala; my attorney, David Bradley Olsen; Mike Braverman and Barry Bloom; and the people of Minnesota who voted for me and gave me an experience beyond belief. Together we will not fail.

Either you think, or else others have to think for you and take power from you, pervert and discipline your natural tastes, civilize and sterilize you.

—F. Scott Fitzgerald

CONTENTS

INTRODUCTION
My Wake-Up Call to America

*W*e will have to repent In this generation not merely for the *hateful words and actions of the bad people but for the appalling silence of the good people.*
—Martin Luther King, Jr.

I'm not writing this book to convince you of anything. I'm writing it to ask for your help. I need you to help me wake up America.

We have a problem. We Americans are in danger of losing something very precious, something that many who came before us risked their lives to make sure that we had. It won't be suddenly snatched away. It's simply slipping away little by little each day. And it's slipping away because we're letting it go.

I'm looking at television and newspapers that seem to carry nothing but bad news about our candidates, our political system, and our political future. I'm looking at politicians who look like they all came off the same assembly line, fully equipped with opinions that don't really mean anything. I'm looking at rabid special interest hustlers and agenda-driven extremists, grinding their way deeper and deeper into our political system. And I'm looking at dismal turnouts at the polls that seem to get smaller every year.

We're allowing our government to be manipulated away from us by people who want to use it to serve their own ends. By not demanding higher standards from our public servants, we're allowing our leaders to degenerate into a bunch of bickering imbeciles, ignorant of the issues that are important to us, and too wrapped up in their own partisan quarrels to pay attention to the jobs we elected them to do. By choosing to be mindlessly entertained by the news, we've allowed it to become a circus. We're losing our passion for democracy and free speech. We may even be losing our understanding of what these principles mean. At worst, we are at risk of losing the ability to make the real choices that define political freedom.

We're supposed to be a nation whose government is of, for, and by the people, yet the people seem to have fallen asleep at the switch.

The Problem As I See It

The problem, as I see it, is that too many people are trying to tell us what to think . . . and we're letting them! Sometimes it seems as though the majority of us have forgotten how to make up our own minds. We have more educational opportunities than any other country in the world. We've got access to a mind-boggling amount of information now that the Internet has come along. We have the freest press, and constitutionally protected rights to express whatever opinions we want. There's never been a better opportunity for freethinking. So what gives? Why aren't we thinking anymore?

Can it be because we've got so many people volunteering to do it for us? Or is it just because we don't give a damn? Take the public's relationship with the media.

> *Those who would give up essential liberty to purchase a little temporary safety deserve neither liberty nor safety.*
> —Benjamin Franklin

Until a few decades ago, the media served *us:* they were our source of information about what was happening in our government, in our nation, and in the world around us. Today, the media serve only themselves. They're driven by whatever makes them the most money. They compete with entertainment programming for ratings and advertising dollars, so in order to steal readers and viewers, the news media have become a form of entertainment themselves. The media are abdicating their role as informers in favor of becoming cheap entertainers.

What's worse, we want them to. We have to have fast-paced, blood-pumping, action news, and bold-faced, juicy headlines. We want high-speed chases and disasters and fights—we really love the fights. Nobody wants to watch a boring story about new legislation being passed when *Extra*'s top story for the night is two transvestites slugging it out. So, political debates are being portrayed like action films, with candidates sniping at each other from their opposite corners. Critique of public officials is starting to look more like a daytime soap opera, packed with scandals and dark secrets, than like an intelligent debate. Elections are covered with all the hoopla of game shows: it's not who's got the best grasp of the issues, but who's got what it takes to win, win, win!

Our media, which are supposed to be our citizens' eyes and ears, have become a travesty. But the sad part is that we've encouraged them every step of the way. We're only getting what we asked for.

Our media aren't the only ones who have failed to serve us as intended. Our political leaders have become so obsessed with raising money and squabbling with each other, they no longer bother with the genuine issues at hand. Bipartisan government was supposed to work as a system of checks and balances to help keep our government centered. But the two parties have gotten so wrapped up in trying to stay in power that they no longer have any time for us and our concerns. If we were truly involved in our government, the two parties would have to be more responsive to the people who *elected* them. But when we aren't involved, we give Republicans and Democrats license to misbehave.

We've also given too much of our collective political voice to special interest groups and activists with narrow agendas, who don't have the public's best interests in mind. Our Founding Fathers warned us in every way they could that if we took our eyes off our government for too long, extremists and fanatics would creep in and start bending the government to their will. Well, guess what happened?

There's a whole class of specialists out there, the spin doctors, PR people, and image consultants, who make a career out of making up our minds for us. As Republican leader Dick Armey once said, "In Washington, you can torture the data until it confesses to anything." If politicians are there to serve us and listen to us, why does the spin industry even exist? Nobody who truly intends to represent the people needs to hire somebody to "fix" the public's perceptions—unless, of course, the media are creating distorted perceptions to begin with.

Politicians lie. The media distort. The spin doctors spin. No wonder we're discouraged. We don't know who to believe anymore. Nobody seems to speak our language anymore. Nobody seems to be listening to us. Political duty has become an ugly chore, like cleaning out the cat box. The temptation to neglect it is huge, and the longer it's neglected, the worse it smells.

But this is the kind of nation we get if we don't stay on top of the issues and pay attention to what our elected leaders are doing. How many people even know who their city councilman is, let alone where he or she stands on the local issues that most directly affect their lives? This is the kind of distrustful social climate we get when we don't know how to think through the issues for ourselves and depend on the spin doctors and the news/entertainment media to do it for us.

If we don't act now, it's going to get even worse in the next generation, because we aren't teaching our children how to think for themselves either. We're not even teaching them why it matters. What wisdom will they have to pass on to their children about civic duty, when we haven't given them anything to pass along?

The Founding Fathers tried to warn us. Back in 1789, when Ben Franklin was asked what kind of government the Continental Congress had created for the new United States of America, he replied, "A Republic, if you can keep it." Franklin knew it would be an uphill battle. He and the other Founding Fathers were aware that every government in the world is highly susceptible to corruption. They knew that a government that truly served the people was extremely rare. And they believed that without the public's constant vigilance, extremists and tyrants would work their way into the system, and bend the system to their own will, so that it served their own ends instead of the people's. Well, guess what? The Founding Fathers were right.

The Purpose of This Book

Consider this book your instruction manual. Its purpose is to alert you to the political and social problems we're facing, to encourage you to reexamine the way we think about social issues and political processes, and to help us get centered again on the constitutional ideals that have served us for over two hundred years. We need to strip off all the layers of spin and rhetoric and BS

Every time we try to lift a problem off of our own shoulders and shift the problem to the hands of the government, we are sacrificing the liberties of the people.

—Jack D. Douglas
The Myth of the Welfare State

that have accumulated over the past several decades and get a fresh perspective on the issues that affect us all.

We also need to examine the way we form our opinions and start building a more efficient "tool kit" for thinking on our own, so that we don't get tempted to rely on spin doctors and PR gurus and media sensationalists to make up our minds for us. Only then can we begin to reintroduce common sense to the American political process; only then can we start building a solid new strategy for moving America forward.

Why You're Hearing This from Me

Why are you hearing this from me? Because I care. Because I was raised to be proud of my country, and to do my part to make sure it remains a country to be proud of. Also, because in the time I've spent serving as Minnesota's governor, dealing with the state of America's politics every day, I've gained a unique perspective on the problems facing our country.

I came into this job from a very different background than most politicians. For one thing, I'm a private citizen, not a career politician. My life is in the private sector, not in poli-

> *Nothing astonishes men so much as common sense and plain dealing.*
> —Ralph Waldo Emerson

tics. My point of view is that of a working family man, not a political "favorite son." And as a member of the Minnesota Independence Party, I'm an outsider to the good-old-boy networks that the two traditional parties have carefully woven into every aspect of our government.

The reason I'm not a Democrat or a Republican, or a leftist or a rightist, or any other kind of an "ist" is because I believe that every issue needs to be considered on its own merit, not glossed over with some kind of prefab rhetoric. The issues that we're facing today have to be dealt with on their own terms, not squeezed into a single ideology. Do people who vote a straight Republican ticket or a straight Democratic ticket honestly believe in everything their party's candidates stand for? Of course not. But it's a lot easier to vote for a label than to vote for an individual. You might as well be choosing between Coke and Pepsi.

I have never let myself become beholden to special interest groups or PACs. I've never accepted money from them, so I don't owe them any favors. And I haven't bought into any political ideology whipped up by some fanatical group. The only "special interest" I represent is the interest of the working man and woman. I believe that the citizens of this country are fully capable of deciding for themselves what's best for them. And I believe that it's government's job to support them in those choices, not to make those choices for them.

I've actually come under criticism for representing the common people. Kris Berggren, a writer for the *National Catholic Reporter,* said in February 1999 that I "clearly respect Joe and Jane Sixpack." Other reporters have run with that notion and used it to insult me, as though I should be ashamed to speak for the ordinary people who don't have million-dollar bank accounts or ten different diplomas on their walls.

Joe and Jane aren't stupid. If you talk with them about the issues that matter, they understand. A lot of what needs to be discussed in politics is complex, but it isn't impossible to understand. It doesn't require a specialist. Much of it does take careful examination, thought, and discussion, but there's nothing that's so difficult to understand that the average person can't grasp it. Anybody who tells you you're not competent to handle these issues by yourself is just feeding you more propaganda from the people who want to be in control.

This country was founded on the philosophy that people have the best quality lives when they get to decide for themselves what makes them happy, and when they can speak their minds without worrying that the government is going to swoop down on them. A nation is most free when people are encouraged to be diverse in their thinking. That's what leads to the greatest number of opportunities for all of us.

That's why it's so important for us to resist letting others tell us what to think. Diversity of thought and free thinking are the enemies of partisan rhetoric and political spin.

You've probably noticed by now that I come without a spin doctor. I don't have an army of image consultants who tell me what to say to get the highest ratings, and to mop up after me if I say the wrong things. I call it as I see it, even when it gets me in trouble. And it does, believe me. It gets me in trouble all the time.

From the beginning, I promised you I'd speak my mind, and I'll keep on doing that, no matter how tough it gets. But it's not the easiest thing to do in today's social climate. These days, if you speak out, you make yourself a target. People come out of the woodwork to hound, berate, and misinterpret. This is not a very comfortable time in our nation's history for free thinkers and free speakers. But we have to have the courage to speak our minds anyway. We can't have a democratic society without doing that.

When *Time* magazine interviewed me at the end of my first year as governor, they said I was "more candid than 99 percent of politicians." That's a great compliment to me, but it makes me wonder why the other 99 percent of politicians out there are less candid. If they're going to call themselves leaders, they owe it to us to make their real opinions known. That's what leadership is.

I believe that anybody who offers themselves for public office owes it to the people to be straightforward with them. The public needs to know how their elected leaders truly think and feel, even when it's not popular. Honesty is vital to getting our nation back on track. How will we ever be able to face our problems, and understand them, if we're not willing to be honest about them? How will we ever learn how to recognize the truth, if the only messages we hear from our leaders and our media are packaged, polished, and carefully worded so that we automatically come to the conclusions that they've chosen for us?

The underhandedness, the manipulation, the wheeling and dealing I've run into from the folks who have a death grip on America's political power base is astonishing. I've seen more than enough to fill this book in my first year in office. I'm going to share with you what I'm seeing, so we can talk about what's wrong with our political system and what we need to do about it.

When those who are to be governed abdicate their influence by not getting involved, do you know what happens? Somebody else steps in to fill that void. The real danger in a democratic society is that the fanatical extremes will rush in to fill that gap, and they are able to do so only because they're a lot more vocal than the passive mainstream populace. By refusing to take advantage of the opportunity to be involved, we allow people with agendas and extremists—those way out there on the fringe—to bend our government to their will.

I know I'm probably going to get attacked again in the media for writing this book. But honestly, I can't wait to see what kind of nonsense they come up with to try to bring me down. I'll be quoted out of context—that's a given. And of course somebody will try to say that I neglected my duties as governor in order to write this book, which you know isn't true. But ultimately, the worst they can do to me is tell me I have no right to speak my mind, which is BS, of course.

I've got every right to speak freely, and I'm going to ask you to do the same. I don't care whether or not we agree on every issue. Frankly, I'd be a little worried about you if we did. But the point is that we have a right to form our own opinions, and we have the right to expect our elected officials to take those opinions seriously. Somebody's got to have the guts to start exercising those rights, for all of our sakes.

I know what you're thinking: No good deed goes unpunished. Speak up, and you make yourself a target. Give the world the best you have, and the world will kick you in the ass. Well, let's have the courage to get kicked in the ass anyway. Let your school board, your councilmembers, and your legislators know what you think. The will of the people is still the most powerful force in America.

That Silent Majority

My first trip to the White House was a humbling experience. Terry and I had flown into Washington for the annual Governors' Association conference, which included a dinner at the White House. When we walked in that enormous front door, we just stood there for a moment, in awe. I remember thinking to myself, my God, this is where it all happened. This is where Abraham Lincoln and John Kennedy made history.

When you arrive at the White House, you go through a receiving line to meet the President. Then you go into the dining room, where they have place cards that tell you where to sit. To help mix things up socially, you don't sit with your spouse. That makes it kind of fun. After dinner you go into the next room for the entertainment and dancing.

When we were there, a swing band was playing. The President and First Lady were dancing all by themselves, because everybody else was giving them a wide berth. So I took Terry by the hand and said, "Put your champagne glass down. We're going to go dance." We went up and started dancing right next to the President and First Lady. We were the only other couple out on the dance floor!

I thought, who cares? I may never get this chance again!

At one point I leaned toward Terry and said, "You dare me to cut in?" She gritted her teeth and gave me a look that said "Don't even think about it!" But in hindsight now, I bet she wishes I had. The Clintons are very gracious hosts; I think they would have gotten a charge out of it!

After the song was over, the Clintons immediately engaged us in conversation. They're great to talk to. I told them about my very first proclamation as governor, declaring February 15 Rolling Stones Day. They thought that was great. I had them both autograph my menu that night. Hillary Clinton signed it, "With deep admiration and respect." I believe she was sincere. That's coming a long way from the time she arrived in Minnesota during the gubernatorial campaign and told Minnesotans to put aside the "circus side show act," which was how she referred to my campaign, "and get down to the business of electing Skip Humphrey."

I don't hold that against her. She was brought in as a hired gun to stump for Humphrey, so of course she had to say something like that. There are all kinds of things that are said in the heat of battle, but when the election is over, you have to move on. That's the way it is in politics.

Hillary's got a phenomenal memory for personal details. This year, Terry wasn't able to go, but when Hillary Clinton greeted me, the first thing she asked was, "How are Terry and the horses?" Of all the people she has to remember, she held on to details like that about me and Terry. She had only met Terry once, a year earlier. I leaned in and asked her at one point, "Madam First Lady, are you sure you want to run for the Senate? Are you positive you wanna do this?" She just laughed and said, "Yeah!"

It's incredible to me that less than two years ago I was more or less a political nobody, and now I'm rubbing elbows with people in America's highest offices. In February of 2000, Vice-President Al Gore's people called to let me know that he was going to be visiting the state, and that he would be calling me at home to set up a meeting. The day he was supposed to call, Terry was just walking in the door with an armload of groceries when the phone rang. You know how sometimes when the phone rings, you get a premonition of who's on the other end of the line? I just had a feeling that it was Al Gore, so I sat tight and let it ring so that Terry would pick it up.

I heard her answer in the other room, then a pause. Then she said *"Really?"* in an incredulous voice. She thought it was just one of my friends pulling a prank.

But it was the Vice-President all right. He canceled his meeting with party caucuses that morning so that he could have a breakfast meeting with me. Our first meeting was just the two of us in a room together for fifty minutes. I talked to him about the fact that even though the federal government had mandated special ed programs for all the states, it had never delivered most of the money it promised to help fund those programs. Special ed kids are usually in competition with regular ed kids for funding, and they've traditionally been so dramatically underfunded that my daughter has actually had to go to classes in a broom closet. The Vice-President made me a promise that during his time as president he would get special ed kids the funding that they should have.

Vice-President Gore made it clear that he would love an endorsement from me, but he didn't ask for one. Of course, before I would even consider giving an endorsement, being the good politician that I'm learning to be, I'd feel it was only fair to give George Bush the same opportunity to be heard. And then I'd probably get away with not endorsing either of them! My excuse would be that I'm a third-party guy, and I don't endorse Democrats or Republicans.

This is amazing, when I think of where I came from, and that a little over a year ago I had virtually no political connections. Now the Vice-President is seeking me out! It boggles my mind that I'm now seen as some kind of political expert. Political science majors want to hear what I have to say. I was the keynote political speaker at Harvard last year. A year and a half ago I had hardly any political experience, and now I'm giving a talk in front of Harvard's political best and brightest. Me, with a high school education, talking to Ph.D. candidates. And these kids were hanging on every word I said. Alan Dershowitz, who was in the audience, told my literary manager that my "performance was most impressive."

It was great. First they introduced me and I gave a speech with the media present. Then they kicked the media out and I got to sit down and eat pizza with the students and just talk. Now I've got an invitation to go do the same thing at Yale, Harvard's natural rival. They told me in the invitation, "If you had fun at Harvard, come to Yale!"

I'm so flattered by the response I've gotten from the public. It's phenomenal. A few months ago Terry and I went out to a little bar and burger joint for a quick lunch. We could hear people whispering as we walked in, but they left us alone and waited until we were almost done eating before they started coming up with their kids and asking for autographs. And then as we were getting ready to leave, they all stood up and applauded. And all I did was eat a burger!

Once when the first lady and I drove from downtown to our house in Maple Grove, people kept driving by, smiling and waving and giving us the thumbs-up. We were laughing so hard in the car, it was getting borderline ridiculous! Then we started looking at who was doing it, and it was truly across the board: African Americans, elderly couples, young teenagers. It crossed all boundaries of ethnicity, age, and gender. It's stuff like that that makes me feel that I've gotta keep fighting the fight. They're the ones I'm doing it for.

To what can I attribute this phenomenal outpouring of public support? I have to think it's simply that the public sees my winning the election as a victory for them. They're not showering me with all this support because I'm special, but because I'm an ordinary guy. I'm one of them. And they know I represent them in everything I do.

My strength out there is in that silent majority. They don't necessarily speak out, but they're listening. The media, the legislature, and the behind-the-scenes power brokers give me a lot of grief. But I get exactly the opposite from the people of Minnesota. Their encouragement and support is what keeps me going.

Every month I do a bus tour to a different part of Minnesota, to see what's going on and to talk to the people. I get a lot of positive energy from those tours, because the people are always so supportive. When I leave the Twin Cities and get into the outstate areas, the people's support is especially strong. And yet the mayors and councilpeople in greater Minneapolis–St. Paul recently gave me an unsatisfactory rating. Maybe it's simply that they don't want to have to take the blame for things being crappy in their area. It's easier to blame me.

The first lady keeps telling me, "Don't even worry about these politicians. The people love you." When my security people call up the local police in these little towns and tell them I'm coming, they ask, "What type of protection do you need?" And my security people say, "Rock star!" Meaning, when I come to town, you're going to get a response like you would if I was a rock star. The kids will be going nuts. Everybody is going to be trying to shake my hand and touch me.

I'm so flattered by that! It's remarkable. And I think that response from the people, too, may contribute to the unsatisfactory rating the mayors in the outlying towns give me. Maybe there's some bitterness there. I think when these representatives see me go out to their districts, and they see their constituents come out and treat me like that, maybe they feel a little jealous. They live there, and they're not treated that way. I'd probably be jealous too. So maybe that adds to the friction between us.

I'm an anomaly on the American political scene: I'm a private sector guy through and through, and I'm not a member of either of the two traditional parties. I have no aspirations to build a political career, so I'm not interested in swapping favors or garnering influence. I answer only to the people. I don't think very many other political figures in high office can say that. It gives me a unique perspective into the state of American politics today.

But isn't that what politicians are supposed to be, in a government of, by, and for the people? Aren't they supposed to come from the public, identify with the public, serve the public? How can they claim to serve the people if they're beholden to anyone else?

Within the next several chapters of this book, I'm going to be talking a great deal about the snags in our political system that keep it from working the way it should. But as you're reading, I want you to keep one thing in mind: The greatest threat to our political freedom is not the career politicians, the partisan gang wars, or the power-hungry lobbyists. It's the apathetic public that allows them to flourish!

I'd like to be able to take the people's enthusiasm as a sign that public apathy isn't necessarily a permanent condition. I hope it means that when the people believe they're being heard, they will come back into the system and participate. I dearly hope that that's so. I want to believe that my public service has made a difference. Because I'll let you in on a secret: Being in public office is tough!

Starting from the moment I threw my hat into the gubernatorial ring, the traditional political power brokers have been doing everything they can think of to knock me out of power. I truly believe that I have gotten more harassment than any other governor, because I'm independent, and because I'm powerful. I'm a threat. And they have to take me down.

At least the politicians' hatred of me is understandable: I'm jeopardizing their comfortable careers. But the media have no excuse for the way they've treated me. They smelled blood in the water and they've been circling ever since, ready to go on the attack whenever they see an opening. Why? Because sordid headlines make money. If anyone says something derogatory about me, whether it's true or not, whether the source is even remotely credible, they're all too eager to print it. There's big money in character assassination.

But it's not just the politicians and the media that make this job difficult. The average American has no idea what kinds of things you have to endure today to serve in public office. Did you know, for example, that I average about one death threat a week? Even my family gets threatened. My sixteen-year-old special ed daughter has been threatened, in vile, horrible ways. And she hasn't ever harmed a soul. She's as innocent as anybody on earth.

I don't know if the people who do this are just trying to get back at me, or if it's just that bad people tend to focus on someone innocent. But I have to assume that if these wackos are capable of making threats, they're capable of carrying them out.

I may or may not seek a second term as governor. Of course, I don't plan on even thinking about making that decision for another couple of years. But the further I go in this job, with the never-ending media beatings and the continuous hassle I get from the legislature, I'm feeling less and less inclined to sign up for another four years of it. I'm probably about fifty–fifty right now; I could go either way. But I was more enthusiastic even six months ago than I am now.

Even though there are times when I get depressed and I think, "This isn't worth it. I'm not running again," I wouldn't trade the experience and the education I've had for anything. And I hope I've done some good, if only to shake up the tired old status quo of public office. Whatever else they say about me, nobody can say I'm your run-of-the-mill politician!

My security people, who are a truly outstanding bunch of guys, told me that the first time we went to Washington for the governor's conference, when we were there with fifty governors and fifty sets of security, the other security people were coming up to them saying, "What's Governor Ventura like?" My people said, "He's great!" And they all said, "I knew it!"

They like working for me because I do stuff that no other governor will do. They never know what to expect. Once, Terry and I went to a Warren Zevon concert—that was unusual enough as it is; usually governors and first ladies go to see *Swan Lake* or something like that. But I'm strictly a rock-and-roll governor.

Warren Zevon is one of my favorite artists. But one of his songs has a lyric that goes, "My shit's fucked up." While we were at the concert, Warren Zevon sang this lyric. Terry's security person turned to my security person and said, "What did he say?"

If I ever were to become president (which will probably never happen) and it comes time for me to host the National Governors' Association, instead of having the entertainment for the evening be a swing band like they had the first time we went, or Kenny G, whom they had this year, I'm going to have Warren Zevon play. And I'm going to tell him beforehand, "Don't change a single lyric!"

I can just imagine all the governors in their tuxes and the first ladies in their ball gowns, hearing, "My shit's fucked up," and then turning to each other, whispering, "*What* did he say?"

2

What's Keeping the American Political System from Working As Well As It Should?

The last two years' legislative sessions here in Minnesota have been marked with a bizarre spate of name-calling and stupid accusations. In a very unkind article, Senator Dean Johnson accused me of leaving the state too often. But do you know what he did the very next day? He himself left the state to go play golf in Alabama! When he got back I called him on the carpet. I said, "How dare you accuse me of leaving the state when you yourself are doing it? You left right during the session to go play golf in Alabama—with lobbyists! Why shouldn't I go public with that?" He backed off real quick on that one. Now he's trying to smooth things over.

Representative Gregory Davids also made some strong comments to the press, in which he called me a moron and a fraud. The interesting thing about Representative Davids is that he initially applied to be my Commissioner of Commerce, and I didn't choose him. So you be the judge of why he feels it's necessary to call me a moron and the biggest fraud he's ever seen. Those are strong words; they're not the kind I can just let fly over my head. I won't necessarily retaliate, but I won't forget.

I'm volatile that way, and I admit it's a fault that I have. It's just not in my nature to walk away from a fight. If they're going to call me names, they shouldn't expect me to forget about it later when they want something from me.

Notice, too, that Davids called me a moron, even though I was smart enough to win an election that his party couldn't! I can't be that dumb, can I? He later said he apologized to "all the morons out there" whom he had offended. Who is he calling a moron? Everybody who voted for me? Is that what he thinks of the voting public?

The name-calling has all pretty much started this session. I think it's partly because of what happened last session as we were finishing up. We were putting together an emergency bonding bill for things that had come up since the regular bill had gone into effect a year earlier. I told the legislators they could have about $100 million for emergency bonding, and they came in with a request for $150 million. I line-item-vetoed about $50 million out of it, because there were all kinds of add-ons in their bill that I didn't consider emergencies: plans for constructing highways and rebuilding bridges. I took that stuff out, because that's the kind of thing that belongs on this year's bonding bill.

I took some heavy hits for that veto. I was accused of neglecting the rural areas. But I called up my Commissioner of Transportation and asked him, "Do highways and bridges deteriorate to an emergency status in less than a year?" He said, "No, absolutely not." And I said, "So these weren't real emergencies." If they weren't in bad enough shape to go on the regular bill just a few months earlier, then they weren't in such terrible condition that they couldn't wait a few months more to go on the next bill. So that's where I put them.

But the people in the legislature who were pushing for more money were blind to the fact that I did get their money for them, just in a different form. They started screeching about how I'd taken away their funding. That's par for the course for today's career politicians: They twist the truth; they don't give you the whole picture. They give you only the portion that suits their particular agenda, the same way the media do. It's far more common than the public realizes.

The legislature has worked hard to put me in my place this year, to show that they can override my veto if they want to. But what they don't realize is, I don't care! If they override my veto, then I've done all I can to change things, and I go home at night with a clear conscience.

Strangely enough, after all the grief they've given me, the legislature came out this year with a bill that would give me a pay raise from $120,000 a year to $150,000. I didn't even ask for it! They came up with it all on their own. The moment the thing crossed my desk, I smelled a rat. I'm politically savvy enough by now to be suspicious any time the legislature appears to be doing me a favor.

Sure enough, when I looked at the bill a little closer, I noticed that it also had a provision that would cut a bunch of my communications staff. Maybe, too, they wanted to see if I would take the pay raise, so they could turn around and call me greedy.

At first I indicated that I would veto the bill. I told them, "Rather than giving the governor a pay raise, why don't you give that extra money to the first lady?" The first lady puts in a lot of hours for the state of Minnesota, and she doesn't get paid for any of it. But now I think what I'll do, as long as there's not too much baggage attached to it and I won't have to cut any of my staff, is accept it, and donate the extra $30,000 to the Jade Foundation and the Roosevelt Scholarship, the two childrens' charities I started last year. Because if I take the raise, it means that other state officials and commissioners could also get pay raises. There's a law that says that no other officer can make more than 85 percent of the governor's salary. That law makes sense to me, because the governor is the CEO of the state. But if I can draw a higher salary, then so can my commissioners. I think higher salaries will generally make it easier for people who are doing well in the private sector to try their hand at public service.

But rest assured, if I take the raise they're offering me, it will come back around to bite me in the ass. That's just the nature of the ugliness that's developed between me and many of the legislators. I have to admit I've been part of it, too. In the spring of 2000 I caused a big hoo-ra when I called every senator that wouldn't agree to put a uni-cameral legislature (which would condense the Senate and House into one unit) on the ballot a gutless coward. That was no casual comment; I truly believe that they are cowardly, because they don't have the courage to let the people decide how they want to be governed.

Well, when I called them cowards, they all got bent out of shape and cried foul. But only a month earlier, Representative Davids wrote that article in his local paper calling me a moron. And nobody took exception to that. They get upset when I say something about them, but they feel it's open season on me. I think if you're going to give it, you've got to be able to take it.

But now that they've gotten on my case for name-calling, I'm going to switch tactics on them. I'm going to shine a light where they don't want it shone, and focus on some issues they'd rather not have the public thinking about.

People will say I'm paranoid, but I really don't think so. I came into this job with an open mind, not looking to do battle with any-body. Yet a huge part of my job has become fending off petty attacks. I truly believe that there's an element on the political scene that is determined not to let me succeed. Because if I do, it will set a prece-dent for other independents and third-party people, or any indepen-dent thinkers, to succeed. It's very much in the back of their minds that if they can make me fail, then they can turn to the public and say, "See? We told you so. Don't ever make that mistake again. You need to elect either a Democrat or a Republican, or this is what will happen."

But it's not going to work. I believe that philosophically their own differences are so far to the left and right of each other that they'll never be able to move close enough to the center to get rid of me. That's why they end up resorting to this meaningless crap of name-calling, doing little things to irritate me, trying to get the public's mind off the issues, and trying to sell this whole notion of me being corrupt and self-serving.

For the most part, I think it's the system that's fraudulent, not nec-essarily the people in it. On the one hand there's a small number of corrupt people who are using the system to their advantage. But the vast majority are well-meaning people who just get swept along in it. Our political system has a way of bringing out the worst in people.

On the other hand, I have a number of people who go out of their way to work with me and help me. But they have to be very careful, because they don't want to lose their party support. I never mention their names because I don't want to get them in trouble.

It reminds me of the night I had dinner over at Judge Rosenbaum's house with Supreme Court Justice Kathleen Blatz and federal Judge Jack Tunnheim. Judge Tunnheim was on the commission that released all of the JFK assassination documents. The JFK murder conspiracy is one of my passions, and I was thrilled that I got to spend three or four hours grilling him on it.

He told me that there were names of CIA people involved in the investigation that he couldn't mention because they were still alive, and he didn't want to get them in trouble. Every document got released except those that posed a security risk to individuals who are still alive. But that leads me to another question: Why would there even be this massive amount of JFK documents held in the archives under national security protection if it was just Oswald, this little private who was nuts, who took a gun and assassinated a president?

At any rate, just as Judge Tunnheim was protecting those CIA agents, I feel obligated to protect the legislators and officials who are willing to work with me. I understand that it takes courage on their part. They're pulled in two different directions: Their conscience is tugging on them to do what's right, but often as not, their party caucuses are yanking them in the opposite direction.

There's very little respect for public office these days. My opinion is that you can dislike the person in office all you want, but you still show respect to the office itself. Recently, I was giving a speech to the Minnesota Chamber of Commerce, and I started talking about unicameral legislation. A lot of legislators vehemently oppose this idea, because if it were to pass, they'd lose their jobs. It doesn't seem to matter to them that it's a much better deal for the public, who they are supposed to serve. They don't like it because it's not good for them. But when I mentioned it, Senator Steve Novak and Representative Dave Bishop actually started catcalling from the audience. I later got a letter from the head of the chamber apologizing for their bad behavior.

For the most part, I think the bad behavior is just a symptom. The real flaw in the system runs far deeper than mere name-calling. The way our system works, it encourages public servants to compete with each other. And when the stakes are high, that competition naturally gets ugly. A large part of the problem is that legislators tend to see people in the party opposite from theirs as natural enemies—and people outside the two parties as an even greater threat.

Another flaw in our system is the fact that it encourages public servants to view their jobs as an endless quest to bring more pork home to their districts. I think that's another reason why they hate me, aside from the fact that I don't belong to either of their parties: I'm always cutting pork out of their bills. My goal is to keep taxpayers' money from being wasted; I'm not interested in doling out political favors. But by making less pork available for them to bring home, I'm thwarting their power.

The legislators are used to governors who will offer them pork in exchange for their support at voting time. Rest assured, pork is never handed out for free. And usually the votes bought with that pork are for projects that require even more spending. When political leaders are only out to grab up as much of the political pie as they can, it's not surprising that government growth keeps spiraling out of control.

Pork-Barrel Politics

When I put out my new transportation plan and bonding bill, the mayors and city councils of towns outside the metropolitan area took a look at it and gave me an unsatisfactory grade. They were looking at it purely in terms of dollar amounts, and they complained that 53 percent of my bonding money went to the metro area, and only 47 percent went to outlying areas.

But if you look at those amounts per capita, the plan works out to $102 a person in the metro area and $108 a person in the rest of the state. I'm actually spending *more* on the people in the outlying areas. How these mayors and councils came to the conclusion that I'm being unfair to outstate Minnesotans is beyond me.

We mailed all sixty-three of these mayors and councils a copy of what they said about the bonding (borrowing money for state projects) and transportation plans and a letter explaining what it actually is. And we asked them to read it and consider retracting what they said. But I'm not holding my breath on that one.

I suspect they're also mad at me because I followed the law. During the 1999 legislative session, the legislature passed a law stating that any bonding projects had to have a statewide significance in order to be included in the bill. Well, for years, whenever a city had a project, they'd send their local state representative to take it over to the capitol and have it put on the state bonding bill. They viewed the bonding bill as a source of free money from the state; they could get their projects built with state money, and they got to take credit for it.

When they passed this law, I decided to hold everyone to it. I cut out tremendous amounts of these local bonding projects. I said, "No, let them bond locally for it. If they want to do it, let them handle it. If it doesn't have a statewide significance, then it goes against the law they passed last year." Well, I think that may also be the reason they gave me an unsatisfactory rating. Since so many public servants have come to see their job description as "bring home the pork," they're going to oppose anyone who cuts off the amount of tax dollars they can get a hold of. And if we uphold this new law, there won't be as much pork going home anymore.

But under the pork-grabbing system, taxpayers often end up paying for things that they don't benefit from at all. Here's a standard example: The city of New Ulm, Minnesota, has a big park with a gazebo and a statue of a guy they call Herman the German. The town has a lot of German-Americans, and Herman the German was a famous town father. Herman's probably very important to the folks of New Ulm, but he has no state significance. And yet New Ulm's representatives got $50,000 out of the state bonding bill to renovate his statue.

Now, I have nothing personally against Herman, or against New Ulm. But that isn't what state money is supposed to be about. I don't get why taxpayers in, say, Duluth or Blaine should be forced to give up some of their money to fix another town's statue. If the leaders of New Ulm want to renovate the town's monument, they should take responsibility for the project and find the funding on their own.

But that's exactly the kind of thing that goes on in pork-barrel politics: If your local representative can bring home $50,000 to renovate Herman, that looks very good on his resume come election time. He got his piece of the pie for his region. But the real question is, how did he get his piece of the pie? Chances are, in the bicameral system, he had to trade something for it. That's the way it works: To get something, you have to have something to give to somebody else.

Chances are the people of New Ulm will only see the newly renovated Herman glittering in the sun and they'll be happy. They'll probably never realize what went on behind the scenes to get him that way. They'll probably never know what they, and the rest of the people all across the state, are sacrificing in order to pay for Herman's face-lift with state dollars.

Here's a classic scenario of the way pork-barrel politics operates. Usually Minnesota's annual bonding bill ends up being between $400 million and $600 million each year—except for 1998, when it shot up over a billion. It was steady for years, then suddenly, a gigantic blip on the screen. You know what happened that year? The mayor of Saint Paul and a bunch of his cronies decided they wanted to build a new hockey arena. Now, in order to do that, they needed to garner support from all their constituents. How do you garner support? You got it. You start passing out the pork.

They used the 1998 bonding bill to dole out favors. That's how they got enough people on board to vote for the new stadium. All those little towns got to sneak their pet projects into the bonding bill in exchange for voting for the arena. That's the way the bicameral system works. Their votes may have nothing whatsoever to do with the will of the people, or with whether the issue at hand is good for their constituents. It's all about which side of the vote gets them the most pork.

And so, the 1998 bonding bill amounted to a billion dollars worth of credit, paid for by the people. People don't generally understand that a bonding bill works in much the same way as charging up a credit card. Sure, you can buy what you want now, but then the bills start coming to your house, and you have to make payments with interest. And, just like with a credit card, it ends up costing you a lot more than if you'd paid cash.

In the past few years, bonding has been a reasonable thing to do, because interest rates have been good. But now interest rates are climbing again. I don't think this is a good time to incur a lot of debt. But that's the problem with pork-barrel politics: Good sense and fiscal responsibility aren't part of the strategy.

Another by-product of pork-barreling is that it encourages public servants to make a lifetime career out of politics. Pet projects aren't the only things that can be bought with pork. Politicians also use pork to purchase power, influence, and votes. A long career of garnering favors can make a politician very powerful—and very hard to budge.

Take state senator Roger Moe, our senate majority leader, for example. I have nothing against Roger personally; he's a good senator. But consider for a moment that Roger Moe has been in the senate since one month before I deployed to Southeast Asia. I deployed in February of 1971. Roger Moe took office in January of 1971. He's been there almost thirty years.

If you look at what the Founding Fathers had in mind, that our government was supposed to be of and by the citizens, it seems a little contrary to that spirit that someone should try to hang on to an office and a power base the way Senator Moe, and many others like him, are doing.

Like many other powerful, long-term legislators, Roger Moe is a big-time opponent of a unicameral legislature, because he doesn't want to lose his power source. The bicameral system is very much pro–career politician. Roger carries so much power because he's been there so long. If they took him out of office and put in a new senator, the district that new senator represented would fall behind, because the new senator wouldn't have any power. He or she couldn't deliver the goods. Senator Moe has been garnering power and influence for all those decades. He's built up a strong network of support to help him bring home the pork. A new senator wouldn't have any of that, so if his constituents vote Roger out, they know their district will fall behind.

The bicameral system works to keep career politicians in office because it favors politicians who think it's their job to surround themselves with webs of influence.

It's not supposed to be that way. Each representative ought to be relatively equal—why should one group of people have more representation than another? But because the bicameral system favors the career politician and the power broker, it behooves the city or the district to reelect its career politicians, because it doesn't want to lose its meal ticket.

That's why career politicians don't like dealing with me. I don't play those games. Political power is gained by playing the trading game, and I won't negotiate tradeoffs. No matter how important something is to me, I won't allow the "you give me this and I'll give you that" game that's become the mainstay of American politics. I'm a firm believer that every bill and every thought ought to stand on its own merits, or not at all. I would rather get nothing and keep my integrity than swap one thing for another. That's just a personal value that I have. But it's very difficult for old-fashioned partisan politicians to grasp that idea.

Governmental Bloat

Our political system as it now stands encourages government growth, which is why we in Minnesota are facing a huge surplus of legislators. With a population of just over 4 million, we have about 201 legislators—more than California, whose population tops 33 million. We're only a middle-sized state in terms of population, yet we have the largest senate in the United States.

We don't need that many legislators. If legislators were really doing their jobs and serving the people, I think we could do just fine with about a quarter of that number. I want to see us go to one house with about 65 legislators.

The ironic thing is that even though we've got this huge bloat in our legislative branch, the legislators aren't willing to streamline their operation. Instead, they're trying to carve up my executive branch of government. They're trying now to get rid of three of my government relations people. Yet I've already voluntarily trimmed down my branch of government: I combined the departments of Administration and Technology, and I tried to combine the departments of Commerce and Public Service.

As if it weren't bad enough that Minnesotans have to pay the salaries of all those extra legislators, they also have to pay for them to keep caucus staffs. In my opinion, caucus staffs should be paid for by the parties. But believe it or not, they're paid for by the public, even though 60 to 70 percent of the people don't consider themselves affiliated with either party.

I've talked about this on my radio show, and I've gotten blasted for attacking people. The legislators don't like the light shone on that issue. They say, "This is our staff, just as you have a staff." But the legislators aren't involved in the full-time running of the government, as my staff is. And their appointments are strictly by party affiliation. I would never allow my staff to be partisan. I have people on my staff from all parties.

When Public Service Becomes Public Careerism

When public servants think of their jobs as lifetime careers, they tend to make decisions in terms of what will serve *them*, rather than what will serve the people. No matter how good something might be for the people, if it's not good for them, they don't even want it discussed, let alone put on the ballot.

> *There are two distinct classes of men in the nation: those who pay taxes, and those who receive and live upon taxes.*
>
> —Thomas Paine

Here in Minnesota, 80 percent of the people say they want a chance to vote on unicameral (one house) legislation. Whether they're for or against it, the people want the opportunity to have their say. But it's one of those things, like term limits, that's all but impossible to get on the ballot. Because even though the vast majority of the public may want it, the people ensconced in power don't.

To give you a simple example of how impractical the bicameral system can be, let me tell you about what happened to the 1998 bonding bill. Every year, both houses have to submit a dollar amount that they want to put into a bonding bill for state projects. The actual amount that gets bonded is a function of what the two houses and the governor finally agree on. The year before I got here, the 1998 bonding bill came out of one house at one particular dollar amount, and out of the other house at a slightly higher figure. Now you'd assume that where the two houses don't agree, they'd thrash it out and eventually arrive at a number that was somewhere in between the two figures, right? Nope. It came out higher. It comes down to this: The more levels of government you allow to get involved in spending your money, the more of your money will be spent.

Between scoring pork handouts and trying to get reelected, it's no wonder career politicians have no time to worry about serving the public. Many politicians today spend a huge amount of their time in office revving up for the next job. There are those who see a seat in the house as just a step up to a seat in the senate.

Many of these career politicians are so far removed from the average working American, they probably couldn't even carry on a five-minute conversation with one of us. Besides, how interested do you think they are in what we have to say? They have their careers to think of. They're too busy trying to figure out the best way to bring down their opponents. When politics becomes their life and their livelihood, they're naturally going to focus on self-preservation. They don't have time for us.

The Founding Fathers warned us about career politicians. They tried to tell us that if the people in public office were too far removed from the average citizens, they couldn't possibly do a fair job of representing them. As far as I can tell, the Founding Fathers meant for public offices to be filled by butchers, bakers, and candlestick makers, who would do their duty to their country for a few years, then go quietly back to their life's work. Our system encourages career politicians to build their nests in public offices and settle in.

Bipartisanism Is Out of Control

The two-party system has given this country the war of Lyndon Johnson, the Watergate of Nixon, and the incompetence of Carter. Saying we should keep the two-party system simply because it is working is like saying the Titanic voyage was a success because a few people survived on life rafts.
—Eugene J. McCarthy

I think a lot of the mischief in politics today comes not so much from individual legislators as it does from the two parties. It's a lot like going to a school where there are two prominent gangs. If you're somebody like me, coming in without an affiliation to one gang or the other, you're put under pressure to join one or the other, just to survive. And if you remain independent, both gangs will try to destroy you.

Of course, the analogy doesn't go much further than that, because with gangs we're talking about real violence; people can literally lose their lives. Gangs will go after you with knives and guns, whereas in politics the weapons are merely words and votes. It's not violence, but it's still warfare. When I was doing talk radio I loved to refer to the two parties as the Demo-Crips and the Re-Blood-licans. I'd say they're really no different than street gangs, except that they wear Brooks Brothers suits.

Bipartisan warfare is what's behind most of the gridlock that plagues our government. Many people think that government should support gridlock; they think gridlock is good. Maybe they're confusing gridlock with checks and balances, or they think that legislation that's held up in the legislature for a while will get all of the flaws shaken out of it before it passes. But really, with a bicameral system, the situation is not so much gridlock as it is grid*iron*. It becomes a fight, a competition to see who can rise through the ranks and grab the most power. And it's a fight that generally divides itself along party lines. That is, unless an independent or a third-party person comes in from the outside. Then these two blood enemies will join forces to try to tear the outsider apart.

This election has made me think that I must have reinvented the word *centrist*. All of today's candidates saw how well it worked for me in 1998, and now they're trying to convince the voters that they're centrists. Why? Because that's who wins the election. Here in Minnesota, where 15 to 20 percent of the voters are hard-core Democrats and 15 to 20 percent are hard-core Republicans, a huge majority sits, undecided, in the middle. Whoever captures that middle majority wins the election.

I don't know what the numbers are for the rest of the country, but

I bet it's not vastly different. When you get a solid third-party candidate in the middle, that 60 to 70 percent feel that they have someone to rally to. The people who run the elections aren't stupid. They know that the centrist vote is what sways the election, and that if a solid third-party candidate comes along, that candidate can upset the whole balance. The hard-core left and right are a constant. It's the middle that can change.

And yet, the party system remains a candidate's best ticket into power, because parties are the way to get around every campaign finance law there is. We've got very strict laws on the books limiting the amount of money an individual can give directly to a candidate. Otherwise, for example, Donald Trump could give me hundreds of millions of dollars and virtually elect me by himself. But there's no limit to what an individual can contribute to a party, which can then turn around and dole out what it gets to its candidate.

The same goes for foreign donations. No candidate can take contributions from foreign sources, otherwise foreign countries could control who is in power in the United States, and the American people would lose their representation. But both parties have taken contributions from other countries, and then handed that money over to their candidates.

Those laws that were put on the books to protect our electoral system from unfair advantage and inappropriate influence are easily sidestepped by going through the party system. The effect is just the same as if the laws weren't even on the books.

If you still have any doubts that partisan politicians serve their parties and not the people, let me tell you about the Republican attitude about getting light-rail service (like the commuter rail systems Washington, D.C. and Denver have) through the Phillips neighborhood of South Minneapolis. Phillips is a very poor district that's been falling apart for years; it's just now starting to get renovated. The people who live in Phillips told me how important light-rail would be to connect them to jobs and downtown.

But when I told the leadership of the Republican party how much light-rail was going to help transform that neighborhood, their response was, "We don't care. We don't have anyone elected down there." I thought for a moment, "Wait a minute. Aren't you elected to serve all of Minnesota? Or are you truly elected just to serve your party?"

That's what it's become today. Many people truly are elected only to serve their party, and they base their decisions accordingly. Their rule of thumb is to vote for whatever gives their party more power. And they know that nobody in the Republican party is going to get elected in the inner city. Traditionally, inner cities are Democratic strongholds. Sure, there are Republicans down there, but they don't have much of a chance to get elected, so the whole area is simply over-looked by the Republican party, because there's no power to be had.

People within the two parties literally don't have the luxury of voting their conscience. They have to vote the way the party leaders tell them to, or they get into trouble. They know that without their party's support they're nowhere—or at least that's what they believe.

The party leaders aren't making their decisions based on their consciences, either. Their platform is made up of political deals, favors, and influence. Does that sound to you like they're serving the people?

That's why you so often see a politician talking one way and voting another. A lot of the opponents of light-rail ended up having to vote for it because they were made to by their party leaders. When we put our budget together last year, it had the money for light-rail in it, and even people like Representative Carol Molnau, who has been one of light-rail's most vocal opponents, ended up having to vote for it. She was made to get in line by the speaker. Molnau and others told their constituents they would never support light-rail. That's why they're coming back this year and attacking, because it's an election year and they have to save face, and because their constituents are going to say, "Hey wait a minute! You promised you wouldn't vote for it and you did!"

Now they're trying to get the light-rail program repealed by saying that we were untruthful about how much it was going to cost. When we submitted the amount, we noted that the estimate was in 1997 dollars, and that the actual amount would be higher when it finally came through. We made it very clear. That's what normally happens on any project of this kind. But they're ignoring that part and pointing to the higher numbers, making all this noise about how we duped the public. There's plenty of plausible deniability out there, and that's the way they usually get around having to be accountable. There it is again: that selective truth-telling. But I believe that a half-truth told in order to deceive is the same thing as a lie.

That's what I think has happened: They're embarrassed over their vote, which they had to cast the way they did in order to keep their party's support, so now they're trying to save face. They're allowed their individualism on the unimportant stuff, but when it comes time to vote on the things that count they have to do what they're told.

And of course, they will never *ever* reveal to the public that they were made to get in line. Because then the public would sit back and say, "Well then, why does it matter *who* we vote for? If this little core group of leaders is calling the shots, then who is truly representing us?"

There's only one way I know in today's political world to be able to vote your conscience, and that's if you're outside the two traditional parties. Maine's governor, Angus King, is the only other independent governor in the nation, and he's able to vote his conscience. I consult with him a lot. He warned me early on about the way it would be: "One week the Republicans will love you and the Democrats will hate you, and a week later they'll reverse."

I don't know if Angus has gotten to the point that I'm at, where both sides are after him. He's probably a better diplomat than I am. His personality is not as abrasive as mine; he's smoother and more of a soft-talker. But he's told me he's seen them do a full 360-degree turn in forty-eight hours: The legislators that loved him yesterday suddenly start hating him, and the ones that hated him will suddenly love him; then twenty-four hours later, it will be back to the way it was again.

I've seen it too; people who will argue vehemently on one issue will be completely in agreement with me on another. I think for the most part that's healthy—that's the way it's supposed to be when people are really debating the issues on their own merits. But the trick is to keep each issue separate and not hold over bad feelings from one issue to another.

The most ironic issue was not even an issue—it was my interview with *Playboy*. Last year, when my popularity was riding high, it was terrifying for the legislators. They didn't dare mess with me. I was polling in the seventies. Then, in the fall, I did that controversial interview with *Playboy*, and they thought they saw a chink in my armor.

Keep in mind that the whole interview was just my personal opinion; none of what I told them had any bearing on the way I govern. And when you take a *Playboy* interview, where they pump sound bites into the media, it all sounds much harsher than you intended. Anybody who's an avid reader of *Playboy* and knows their approach would probably not even have been concerned about that interview. But to those people who don't read *Playboy*, and don't realize the provocative questions that are asked in an interview like that, it can seem offensive. And apparently, a good many people were offended.

Right after the article came out, in the midst of the media frenzy, my popularity took a nosedive to 54 percent, which is still hugely popular. Most elected officials, if they're maintaining a favorable rating of over 50 percent, are in great shape. And when you consider that I'm a third-party candidate, it's even more phenomenal. If I was polling that way in an electoral race, I'd have it in the bag.

But when my opponents saw me go from 70 to 54, it gave them courage. They saw it as an opportunity to move in for the kill while I was down: "He's offended the public. We can get him now." Unfortunately for them, I wasn't down for long. Within only a few months, my approval rating rebounded to around 68 percent. Now I'm even more of a terror to them than before, because I can survive the crucible of public displeasure. I'm stronger than ever.

So now they're looking to snipe at me any way they can. When I appointed Reform party member Steve Minn as Commissioner of Commerce and Public Service, they voted him out. It was a retaliatory move. It wasn't a strike at Steve Minn, it was a strike at me through him. It was their way of telling me, early in the session, "When we all get together, we carry the power."

And I know they do. They can override any one of my vetoes. But remember that both they and I ultimately answer to the same authority: the voting public. Every single one of them is up for election this year. I'm not. And rest assured when we get out of session, I won't forget—the Navy SEAL in me doesn't get mad, he gets even. When it gets close to election time, the public's going to hear some things about them that they don't want the public to know about.

If you still need more convincing, look at the way the legislature has handled spending on crime. Recently here in Minnesota, a young girl was allegedly abducted out of a convenience store by a former sexual offender. Her mother joined together with a few other mothers whose children had been abducted. They're now trying to pass more stringent sexual offense laws, and they're advocating putting in a system that would connect every county by computer, so that no matter where an offender goes to court, the judge will have access to all his records.

I think this is a fine idea. But the problem is, the equipment in our Bureau of Criminal Apprehension building is outdated. It couldn't handle that kind of data. It's an old, crappy building that isn't up to par with the new technology.

I put in a bid for $58 million for a new BCA building. The Democrats put the same amount in, but the House Republicans first refused to put in any, then—kicking and screaming the whole way— they agreed to put in $30 million.

Republicans love to pass tough new laws, but if they really want to get tough on crime, why are they fighting me over building a new BCA building? What point are the laws if we don't have the tools to enforce them properly? Are the laws just for show? Just to make us feel good? Or are they there to stop repeat offenders?

I did my radio show from the building one day. I asked my listeners, "Why is government always so shortsighted? They'll build a road, and by the time they open it, it's already outdated. Why don't they ever build for the future?"

The Republicans want to cut-rate this BCA building at $30 million. But if we do that, by the time it's built it will already be at capacity and we'll need more, bigger, and better. Why don't we build the $58 million building that we can grow into? In five years, we'd need it, if not immediately.

The Republicans, who are supposed to be the big law-and-order people, are pushing to pass all these crime laws, and yet on the flip side they won't spend the money to support their own legislation. And that's what people truly need to understand: If you want to be tough on crime, you *will* pay a price for it. Because you can't be tough on crime without opening your wallets. But many of the politicians don't want it that way. They want to look good by passing the laws, but they don't want to have to be responsible for getting behind the money it costs.

Since this writing, the bill has now flip-flopped: The Republicans fully fund it; the Democrats fund only half. They want to use it as a bargaining chip on the bonding bill.

Cleaning "House"

So how do we stop the politicians from sniping at each other long enough to get them to do their jobs? Frankly, I don't know how much hope there is for reforming

> **C**onstantly choosing the lesser of two evils is still choosing evil.
>
> —Jerry Garcia

the hard-core mudslingers we have in office right now. It's what many of them were raised on. It's status quo for them; they know no other way. Plus, the way things are done now benefits them personally, and that's what matters most to them. We can police them, and we can write them angry letters when they misbehave. But don't count on any of that being too effective.

I think we need to concentrate on getting new blood into office, both at the state and the federal level. We could start paying closer attention to who's doing the mudslinging, and when election times come around, we can vote 'em out of there. Maybe it's time to send the more belligerent legislators a message. And the best way to get that message across to them is with our vote—for someone else.

I believe our best bet for turning the tide of this nonsense is to go looking for talented people from the private sector, people who are not hanging on the extreme fringes of either party. In fact, today's hyperpartisan political climate makes a good argument for giving folks outside the two traditional parties a shot at political leadership. If we want the bipartisan bad behavior to stop, we may have to do some vigorous "House" cleaning and Senate-sweeping.

Should Political Campaigns Be Popularity Contests?

When the leaders choose to make themselves bidders at an auction of popularity, their talents, in the construction of the state, will be of no service. They will become flatterers instead of legislators; the instruments, not the guides, of the people.

—Edmund Burke

In January of 2000 I turned on the TV to watch the coverage of the Iowa caucuses, and for half a second, I wasn't sure if I was watching coverage of a political event or a horse race. The reporters covering the caucuses even used some of the same terminology used in horse racing: They talked about candidates distancing themselves from the "pack," and of two closely matched candidates running "neck-and-neck." They dazzled us with lightning-fast statistics and percentages and projections, all kinds of shiny, high-tech graphics, live up-to-the-minute coverage . . . and not one word about what any of the candidates stood for.

We've come to think of our elections the same way we think about sports. We focus on competition and winning. How many of us actually know what the most popular candidates stand for in any given election? Why isn't anybody asking what these candidates plan to do if they get elected? Doesn't it matter?

When elections turn into horse races and popularity contests, the candidates who end up rising to the top are not necessarily the ones who have the brightest ideas about how to govern our nation. Sometimes they're the ones who will do anything to win. And as you can see from the way most recent elections have gone, that focus on winning leads candidates to try to sabotage each other and bring each other down.

In the past few decades, the politicians who want to hedge their bets in an election—and don't care what it takes to do it—have put together an impressive tool kit of dirty tricks to use against each other. They'll maneuver a candidate into having to make a statement on so-called "wedge issues," like abortion or the death penalty, the kinds of issues that get voters off the fence. Then they'll jump all over the candidate for that one comment. Watch, for example, the way George W. Bush is playing the immigration card against his opponents.

Or they'll call up voters, pretending to be doing a poll, and they'll say something like, "Would you vote for Senator X, if you knew that she misappropriated funds from . . ." and so forth. Of course, Senator X never misappropriated any funds, but look how carefully they word it. And even if the senator can prove she didn't do it, the damage is done. Is this how the people who are supposed to represent us should behave?

Corruption and politics just naturally seem to go together. There has probably been some amount of dirty dealing in just about every election in history. But in the last few decades, it's become more common for candidates to look for ways to destroy each other. If I had to point to one incident that told us the "dirty tricks" era was here to stay, I'd blame it on the "Willie Horton" ads George Bush launched against Michael Dukakis. Remember that? It was pure manipulation. Bush's people tried to frighten white voters into thinking that if they elected Dukakis, the streets would be crawling with violent black convicts! The program that released Horton wasn't even a Dukakis program. It was a blatant distortion of fact, a stupid, vicious, racist tactic . . . and it worked.

And that's what we create when we get political campaigns confused with sports. Campaigns are not sports competitions; they're job interviews. Candidates are applying for jobs as public servants, and we, the voters, are the ones doing the hiring. If we're going to hire the right person for the job, we need to focus on the candidates' qualifications, their understanding of the issues that matter to us, and their plans for handling those issues. If any given candidate is too busy trashing his or her opponents to focus on the issues, then they've just told us they're not qualified for the job.

Today it's common for politicians to be obsessed with elections. For many, it's gotten to the point now where campaigns are never ending. The first day those newly elected leaders take office, the next campaign is up and running. The new officials have hardly gotten their chairs warmed up before people are asking them whether they'll seek reelection when their first term is over. It's not fair to us, and it's not fair to them. First of all, it's yet another distraction from the job they got elected to do; second, how are they supposed to know that far in advance?

How fair is our campaign system in terms of who gets to run? Ideally, everybody who wants to run would have a chance to be heard, and if the public likes what they hear from a candidate, then that candidate should be given a chance to run. But as our system now stands, only a handful of would-be candidates make it that far. I can tell you from experience that the odds are stacked against a candidate outside the two traditional parties. Third-party candidates have little chance of even being heard, let alone being taken seriously. Democrats and Republicans, over the decades they've been in office, have engineered it that way.

The irony is that, as destructive as the system is to outside candidates, it's also destructive to the two big parties. Before candidates even go up against their opponents in the other party, they have to face off against candidates within their own party. Many of them launch the same arsenal of dirty tricks against their fellow party members, and then when the smoke clears, they wonder why there's such a lack of trust within the party! I always thought it was pretty stupid that candidates within a party fight like cats before the primaries, then afterwards they're expected to make up, and even pick a running mate from among the enemies they just made!

Even those candidates who rise to prominence within their parties have to watch their step. They are beholden to their party's leaders; they're dependent on them for their support. They can't be too far off the party's platform, or they get their support yanked out from under them. When you're focused on what's popular and what's politically expedient, it's easy to lose track of what you really believe in.

Our election system as it now stands puts incumbents in a vastly superior position to challengers. The incumbents in the parties make it a very unlevel playing field for the new candidate. I saw a great example of that when I was running for mayor of Brooklyn Park. Every year Brooklyn Park has a big festival called 'Tater Days. The whole town turns out for the big 'Tater Day Parade. And all the seated officials get to ride in the parade and pass out campaign literature. The people get to see the names of their council members; they get to see them waving. It's great exposure for a candidate. But it's only available to incumbents: The official filing date for challengers is a month later, so even if they've announced they're running, they're not allowed to pass out literature. It's little things like that that help keep incumbents in place and keep challengers out.

Incumbents, too, usually take advantage of their government paychecks during campaign time, whereas the challenger from the private sector seldom has that option. When I ran for governor, I was made to give up my job as a radio show host in order to campaign, because it was deemed a conflict of interest. I went without income for six months while I campaigned, yet my two opponents, Skip Humphrey and Norm Coleman, both public employees, kept their jobs and their incomes the whole time, even though they were campaigning ten and twelve hours a day just as I was. The taxpayers footed the bill for them to do a job they weren't even doing!

The taxpayers essentially funded their campaign. They didn't fund mine. Now, why shouldn't they have had to take a leave of absence if they weren't performing the duties of their office? If they're really able to campaign full time and still do their jobs, then their jobs must not be as tough as they say they are!

I want to try to pass a law at some point that says if you're in public office, you're not allowed to campaign from 8:00 A.M. to 4:30 P.M. Monday through Friday. If you want to campaign, you can campaign at night and on the weekends. This wouldn't affect legislators because they're only in session in the spring. But it would keep incumbents from forcing taxpayers to pay them salaries for work they're not doing.

And if we need a law like that in Minnesota, don't we need it just as much nationally? Look at the way it's going right now for the two presidential candidates: How can George Bush be governing Texas? He's traveling all around the country campaigning for president. That's not an indictment of Bush, it's an indictment of the system that allows it. Al Gore is doing the same thing: He's campaigning full time. Maybe there's not all that much for the Vice-President to do. But surely there's more to the job than breaking ties in the Senate, going to funerals, and being a heartbeat away from the presidency.

But if you're not an incumbent, and you're not independently wealthy, your chances in an election are almost nil. I don't think people truly realize the sacrifice I made to run for this job. I went from July to January without a paycheck. Put that in the lap of the average wage earner and ask him or her, "Would you be capable of going without an income for six months?" Fortunately, I had enough put aside that I could do it. But I'd be willing to bet that most people in this country couldn't manage it.

But to the person in office, it's not an obstacle. If I decided to run for a second term, I could spend six months doing nothing but campaigning if I wanted to, and I'd collect my check just the same as if I was putting in ten to twelve hours of state's business every day the way I do now.

The incumbent also gets the benefit of all the media attention. There's not a day that goes by that my name isn't in the paper, whether the coverage is good or bad. I remember in the world of pro wrestling we used to say, "There is no bad publicity. Just make sure they spell your name right." Incumbents have the benefit of name recognition.

If I do run again, my campaign is going to be very simple. I'm going to spend less than I did the first time around. And I'm going to focus all my effort on the last month before the election. I'll go on radio and TV and say very simply, "Look, if you want me to do this job for four more years, I'm willing, able, and will give my utmost effort to do it. If you don't, elect someone else." And if they don't reelect me, I'll go back to the private sector with no regrets. I'm a firm believer that that's what a public servant is supposed to do: You serve your time, then you go back to what you were doing before.

Campaign Spending Is off the Charts

It's bad enough that campaigns have turned into mudslinging contests. But they have also become entirely too expensive. Today, money dominates political campaigns. When people say they want to run for office, often the first thing anyone asks is not "Where do you stand on the issues?" but "How much money can you come up with?"

Even a modest campaign takes millions. A lot of talented political leaders have decided not to run, or have dropped out of the campaign earlier than they needed to, because they didn't have the cash.

As of today, there is effectively no limit to the amount of money a candidate can spend on a campaign. And as a general rule, the best-funded candidate is the one who wins. Not the one with the strongest leadership skills, but the one with the biggest bankroll. Just look at the war chest George W. Bush amassed and spent to get his party's nomination.

When campaigns are that expensive, it takes a huge amount of effort to pull together the money required to keep a campaign going. When candidates have to focus so much effort on raising money, they don't have as much time left to devote to the issues.

But once they're voted in, they finally get to concentrate on doing their jobs, right? Not necessarily. If they want to keep their jobs for another term, incumbents have to start thinking about getting funded for the next election, sometimes from the day they arrive in office. Many are effectively campaigning all through their term. A lot of politicians spend a pretty big chunk of their time in office drumming up supposed "grassroots" support for themselves. Do you ever read the "informational" letters you get from your congressperson—mailed at the taxpayers' expense? They're usually nothing more than slick advertisements for why you should reelect him or her.

And here again, members of the two traditional parties have a vast advantage over any third-party candidates. They have much greater funding available to them from their party's coffers. And as I learned when I ran for governor, in some cases the two parties have rigged the system to deny public funds to third-party candidates. There are all kind of strings they can pull behind the scenes to keep outsiders from getting the money they need, everything from making sure they don't get access to the government funds they qualify for until after the election, to subtly influencing bank managers to say no to third-party candidates' requests for loans.

Making matters worse, these days campaigns are so costly that sometimes even party funds aren't enough to do the trick. That's why many of our would-be political leaders sell their souls to special interest organizations, political action committees (PACs), and big corporations: That's where the big bucks really come from. There's no end to the number of special interest groups out there who are hungry for a slice of the political pie. Sadly, that's the way it sometimes works: PACs purchase their own pet candidates by funding their elections. And once those candidates are in office, they return the favor by making policies and passing legislation that helps out their financial patrons. It doesn't sound like there's much room for "we, the people" in that scheme, does there?

As long as political campaigns measure their success in dollars, politicians will find a way to top each other in campaign spending. And if we don't decide to do something about our campaign system, it isn't likely to get any better. In fact, now that it's common knowledge that bigger bucks mean a better shot at winning, the price tag of the average campaign is probably going to keep going up.

Now, most of the time in a free capitalist society, you get what you pay for. The more you spend on something, the better the quality of the product. But all those millions that are being spent on campaigns aren't giving us higher-caliber candidates. A lot of the time, it looks to me like exactly the opposite. Voters are getting turned off to the political system in record numbers. In every election candidates spend more money, and in every election, fewer people vote. You'll often hear candidates say they spend that money to reach the people, but how successfully are they reaching us if fewer of us vote each time there's an election?

When Are We Going to Get Serious about Campaign Reform?

So what do we need to do to break this cycle? How can we get the dollar signs out of our politicians' eyes so they can see clearly to focus on the issues? That's the tricky part: In order to effect change in our political system, we have to get the attention of the politicians themselves. And don't forget, if they managed to get into office, they benefited from the system as it is. How excited do you think they're going to be about changing it?

Whenever the people get a chance to say something on the issue of campaign reform, most of us are for it. We know how badly it's needed. In fact, plenty of ambitious candidates know how strongly much of the public feels about campaign reform; that's why so many of them trot out some tired line about how important reform is to them. But once we get them into office, they very quickly develop a form of postelectoral amnesia. The reform never happens.

Next time you hear a politician say he or she is for campaign reform, watch closely and see what happens when an actual plan for reform is proposed. Likely as not, they'll fight it tooth and nail. Any time somebody even whispers about limiting the amount spent on campaigns, some politician always blows the First Amendment whistle and starts screeching about how we're trying to limit his or her free speech. Actually, it's the dollar-driven campaign process that's limiting free speech, by shutting out any candidate who can't afford to buy into the game.

Should Campaign Funds Be Limited?

We are probably going to have to take some extreme measures if we want to fix our campaign system and make our candidates behave. I think we need to be talking about making PAC contributions illegal.

Candidates tend to pay attention to whoever coughs up the cash. If the only sources of funding they have are the people, then candidates will have no choice but to listen to us.

We also need to fix the loopholes that exist in the campaign funding system. There's already a cap on donations to an individual candidate, but no limit to the amount you can donate to a party. This so-called soft money is then funneled to individual candidates in the form of "issue ads." See how easy that law is to get around?

I think we also ought to talk about capping the amount that each candidate is allowed to spend on a given campaign. If we did that, it would go a long way toward leveling the field.

Some people have tossed around the idea of providing all candidates with equal chunks of free air time, free print space, and free Internet access, which they could use to state their positions, hold debates, and conduct question-and-answer sessions. I'm all for ideas that get candidates to spend more time talking with the voters, answering questions, and getting to hear what their constituents actually sound like. That's a healthy habit for politicians to get into: being answerable to the people!

We just have to be careful with the term *free*. In some circumstances, *free* might not necessarily mean what it appears to. Who exactly will pay for the free air time? These are the kinds of questions we need to be talking out.

We have a great political system, but it's got some weak spots that need fixing. I believe that all of the problems that we see in our campaign system today are a result, directly or indirectly, of lack of public participation. If we want to make political campaigns work the way they're supposed to, we need to understand the way the system works, we need to get involved in the system firsthand, by voting and volunteering, and we need to give our political leaders the message, loud and clear, that we expect them to help us fix the process, not perpetuate the abuses. We reinforce the status quo by not demanding reform.

If we fail to educate ourselves about the way the electoral system works, then we leave ourselves open for politicians to reinvent it to suit their own needs. That's how campaigns became popularity contests in the first place, with people casting their votes not for the candidate they want but for the one they think is most likely to win.

If we want our politicians to answer to us, the people, we've got to participate in elections. Many people get onto the ballots and into office by default, because voter turnout is so low that their own little cadre of supporters is all it takes. Here's a little-known secret: Career politicians *love* low voter turnouts! Statistically speaking, the lower the number of voters, the more likely the incumbent is to stay put. That's why many career politicians hated the Motor Voter bill, which allowed people to register to vote at the Department of Motor Vehicles at the same time they renewed their driver's licenses. These people were put into power by a small constituency; if a whole bunch of new people registered to vote, then there's a chance they might vote them out! See how that works? When the people vote in great numbers, they are political corruption's worst enemy.

There are plenty of good ideas out there about how to make campaign reform happen. The problem is, the best ideas in the world are going to be futile if we don't get behind them—and push! It's pretty unlikely that the bulk of politicians are going to take it upon themselves to reform our campaign system. It's only going to happen if we demand it.

The beauty of it is, just as we allowed all of these problems to flourish by our lack of involvement, we can also solve all of them by getting involved again. We can educate people about the system by emphasizing it in public school curricula and in public service announcements, and by encouraging parents to teach their kids about the system and its importance. We can do a powerful amount of good just by voting—in every election, not just in the big ones— and encouraging others to vote. We can support programs that encourage voter registration. And finally, we can, and we *must*, write to our representatives and demand campaign reform.

We will have to get very united and very vocal about this. We're going to have to fight for it, or it's not going to happen. We need to be willing to commit to it for the long haul, because it's going to take a while. All worthwhile reform takes time.

Special Interest Bullies

We have two self-proclaimed citizens' groups here in Minnesota, the Taxpayers League and Common Cause, who have gone after me with a vengeance. They portray themselves as nonprofit groups, but you never know where they're getting their funding, because they don't report it. These two groups and others similar to them don't like me because I'm outside the traditional power base. So they're always on the lookout for things they can say to knock holes in my credibility.

Common Cause recently went after me because of a fund-raiser we were putting together for the Jade Foundation, an umbrella organization Terry and I launched in 1999 to help disadvantaged kids, whether they be mentally, emotionally, or physically disabled. We tend to give our money to smaller charities, so we can really see the donations at work. The larger organizations are great; they do a lot of good work. But when you contribute to them, it's often hard to know what your money really went for.

Recently the Jade Foundation gave $5,000 to an organization that was losing its music program. That money is going to carry their program now for another year, so the kids will have an opportunity to play music.

We have to continually raise money for our foundation, which is named after my daughter, Jade, who is a special ed kid. We decided to hold a fund-raiser featuring Minnesota pianist Lori Line. She's phenomenal. She started out playing the piano at the Dayton's store. She's so good, she's worked her way up to the point where she and her husband Tim are completely independent. They own their own record label, they sell records out of their own office, and do tours all over the country.

But as much in demand as she is, she was willing to go to the historic State Theater in downtown Minneapolis and give a free concert to benefit the Jade Foundation. Terry had heard some of her music, and she dragged me to one of her concerts one night, even though it's really not my thing. I'm strictly a rock-and-roll kind of guy. I was afraid I'd fall asleep in the middle of the concert and be an embarrassment.

I was pleasantly surprised. Her concert was so full of energy and fun. Her musicians are all Minnesotans, including a gospel singer who's absolutely amazing. When she left the stage I borrowed a lighter from one of my security guys, lit it, and held it up for an encore, the way everybody does at a rock concert. She came back onstage for her encore laughing—she said nobody had ever done that for her before. She said she'd always remember me because of that!

So when the first lady approached her about the charity concert, the idea was that we'd have it at the residence, just a small gathering. But Lori said, "No, let's do it large. We'll raise more money that way." So we had it at the State Theater in May. She played at the end of her tour for free.

But here's where it gets ugly: When we announced the concert, the news media went to Common Cause for a quote about it. Now, why would the media go to a group like that for a quote? They give these groups credibility because they know they're going to play devil's advocate. They know they're going to throw some water on the party. They'll figure out a way to create controversy. That's why the media seeks them out, because controversy sells. Do you know what Common Cause's response was? They said, "We think this is a front so that rich lobbyists can buy the expensive tickets and have access to the governor."

I went ballistic. I called the paper and told them, "That's despicable, that you would print this in your paper and try to cast a shadow over a totally charitable event." The story had nothing to do with Common Cause, yet the media sought them out. The whole concert was nothing but a great opportunity to help disadvantaged kids. Corporations bought boxes and brought disabled kids to the concert. We raised tons of money for local charities. And yet they had to find some way to make it ugly. I'd like to know how they sleep at night.

Lobbyists can also affect the system in other, sometimes very sneaky, ways. The other lobby group that has taken a dislike to me, the Taxpayers League of Minnesota, calls itself a watchdog group, but they're not watchdogging anything; they're too busy trying to make trouble for me.

It's one thing for a citizens' group to look for corruption, and expose it whenever they do find it. It's another thing to do what these two groups have done: to go out with their own agenda and try to destroy someone. It's their agenda to take me down, so they won't allow anything I do to look good. No matter how benign it might be in reality, they'll find a way to put an ugly spin on it.

Both Common Cause and the Taxpayers League have been after me constantly about my money-making activities. It's as if they think I don't have a right to make money. I've been very careful to keep my job as governor separate from my other profit-making activities. I usually go outside the state of Minnesota so that there's never a conflict of interest.

The night I refereed wrestling at the Target Center in Minneapolis, the Taxpayers League had fits, saying I had disgraced the office and used it for profit. But I was working for Vince McMahon, a former employer of mine from long before I had any dealings in politics. He has no interest in Minnesota, other than selling his pay-per-view shows or renting the Target Center. So what difference does it make if I go referee for him one night, and start two charities with the money I earned? Who does it hurt? It isn't like it's something I haven't done before. They might have a legitimate concern if the National Football League came to me and wanted me to do something like that, because I'm not qualified. But I'm certainly qualified, by virtue of a career that spanned three decades, to referee a wrestling match.

Why does the media feel that they have to report things about a political figure that have nothing to do with the regular public? The night I refereed at the Target Center didn't affect any Minnesotan. On the other hand, if I make money, I'm going to pay some of it in income tax, which benefits the state. Also, the two charities I started with the money I made, the Jade Foundation and the Roosevelt Scholarship, are going to be legitimately benefiting Minnesotans, I hope, for years to come. Yet, they would have preferred that I hadn't had that income or paid that tax or started those charities. That's how you can tell that it's politically motivated—when the outcome would have harmed no one and maybe even helped someone, yet they still complain.

The Taxpayers League is vehemently opposed to the light-rail system we're trying to build here in Minneapolis, so they're always trying to make it look as if something underhanded is going on. It's ridiculous. But groups like these are very powerful on the American political scene today. They say they're nonprofit, but don't forget that the people who work for them are getting paid. They're making money for the work they do. How exactly is that nonprofit? They don't have to say where they get their money from. They may be getting it from a political opponent for all the public knows.

But if the media are going to use them as a credible source, as a "conscience," which they do all the time, how come they've never done a story on who they are? Doesn't that sound like the responsible thing to do, to give the public some information about them, so that they can show why they're worthy of being a credible, legitimate source? But they never have. The public is just expected to assume that they're credible.

I knew these groups were around even before I took office, and I've seen them do similar things to other public figures. But I'm under the microscope much more than anyone else I've ever seen. When Governor Carlson was here, he would leave on numerous trips out of state, and they never even publicized it. When I leave the state, I have to account for everything I do.

I'm sure there are other groups like them, in other states and nationally, but those two groups have been the main thorns in my side. They're working so hard to put it in people's minds that I'm some sort of bad person with sinister motives, and that I'm just trying to use my position. I truly hope that when Minnesotans read the things they write that they'll realize these people are not what they say they are.

Here's how I know they have an agenda: They contradict themselves. Common Cause recently criticized my Department of Revenue for being technologically out of date, which is true. They're on thirty-year-old computers over there. But when we tried to get more funding to advance our technology and bring it into the new millennium, Common Cause opposed the spending of that money. So tell me they don't have an agenda. They'll criticize me on the one hand, but then they won't give me the tools I need to do the job correctly. Then they'll come around on the backside to criticize me for not doing my job.

And this is the kind of behavior you get from activist groups when political power comes to mean more to them than their cause does. A political enemy is always an enemy, even when that supposed enemy is championing the group's cause.

Take, for example, my position that first ladies (and first gentlemen) should receive a salary for the work they do for the state. When I become a lame duck, I'm going to work very hard to set that up, starting with the next first spouse after Terry. It doesn't necessarily have to be a big salary, but there should be at least some compensation. It would help future governors' spouses pay for the expense of getting their hair done or buying clothes for official functions when they're expected to represent the state of Minnesota.

I think it's an atrocity that first spouses are expected to work for free. It's sexist. It's ridiculous that you have someone who represents the state and works on behalf of it, but doesn't get paid for her time. The real irony is that the first lady has an assistant who does get paid! How do you justify that?

Some day Minnesota will have a female governor, and I'll be curious to see if the first gentleman will leave his job, as Terry has had to leave hers, in order to look after the residence and take on all the smiling-and-waving duties that are expected of a first lady.

When I first came out with that, I took a bunch of hits from the newspapers, calling me greedy. But interestingly enough, I got a bunch of praise from first ladies and first gentlemen all across the country, applauding me for having the courage to come out with it. A lot of people feel that way but have been afraid to say anything.

And yet, interestingly enough, no feminist groups had anything to say about it. Do you know why? Because the feminist organizations are in league with the Democrats, and I'm an independent. That's the way politics works. You stick with your political allegiance, even when it holds back your cause. That's the politics of deal-making and influence-peddling at work. Who cares about the original issue, the actual cause, when there's political power to be had?

It's just like when I ran for governor, and Mae Schunk and I were the only vested union members running, yet we couldn't get one union endorsement because all the union leaders were in league with the Democrats. We had tons of union members supporting us, but union leaders would have nothing to do with us. This web runs far deeper than meets the eye. The people generally have no idea how deep it goes, or how many areas of their lives it touches.

Lobbyists, political action committees, and other groups with narrow agendas are now exerting more influence than ever on our political system. Many of them don't stop at straight-out campaign contributions. Behind-the-scenes manipulation of politicians is in vogue today among Washington's influence-peddlers. And as we've seen, politics has become increasingly driven by dollars. As a result, time that Congress could be spending on the issues that concern us all gets spent on nuzzling the hands that hold the feed bag.

The concerns of these special interest groups seldom have much in common with the concerns of the mainstream public. So when politicians become beholden to special interest groups instead of to us, odds are pretty good they're not concentrating on the job we need them to do.

Lots of these groups not only "buy" politicians by making big campaign contributions, they also cash in on prevailing public sentiment. They make an awful lot of noise in the media, and often bend politicians to their will simply by putting artificially created public pressure on them. Many politicians these days are in the habit of doing what's "publicly expedient," if only to shut up their critics. Doing the expedient thing has become, of necessity, more important to them than doing the right or the sensible thing. This is not the way we should be making policy.

I'm not opposed to lobbyists on principle; I just don't want their money. I'll take their ideas, though. When lobbyists come to the capitol building with something to say, my government relations team meets with them and brings me a report. I always give their ideas consideration. But I draw the line at taking contributions from them. The way it works all too often is that lobbyists contribute to politicians' campaign funds in order to get their ear. But then the politician who's taken their contribution feels obligated to them, and that's an unfair advantage. So I tell them I have a very clear policy: I'm happy as ever to take their ideas, but I don't want their money!

Special interest groups have a habit of tuning out everyone else's cause but their own. Typically, these groups start out with at least a kernel of a valid complaint, but they become so focused on their single issue that they can't hear anyone else's point of view. They're not interested in what is best for the people in general. They're only interested in what serves their cause.

They tend to latch on so hard to their point of view that they end up taking it to ridiculous extremes. That may be one reason why many of them resort to manipulation tactics and political warfare: They know they can't win converts by quietly stating their position.

Special interests become a bane to free speech when they try to silence anybody who disagrees with them. Some special interest groups out there today are so vicious that any other group that disagrees with their position—including the American public—is fair game. They're not above disseminating false information or launching smear campaigns to destroy an opponent's reputation. They do whatever it takes to shut 'em down.

Corporate Bullies

Everything I've said about special interest groups goes for corporations too. During political campaigns, corrupt corporate leaders will try to use their financial muscle to squeeze out the candidates they don't like. They'll pull any strings necessary to keep out someone who threatens their interests.

Even outside the political realm, corrupt corporations exert their power in ways that ultimately harm the average citizen. They understand supply and demand as well as anybody, but they're only willing to play by those rules as long as they're good for them. When they're not, free market be damned!

These days a lot of what's going on in Congress has very little to do with the average citizen. We don't have the money to compete with mega-corporations, and we don't have the influence to compete with special interests. Come campaign time, who will career politicians be more likely to answer to: the people or whoever's paying their campaign bills?

Morality Brokers: Religious Fundamentalists and Extreme Liberal Agendas

We've looked at partisan warriors, career self-promoters, special interest hustlers, and corporate bullies. But there are other groups out there trying to wrestle control of our government away from us. I'm talking about the fanatics, ideologues, and zealots, all across the political spectrum, who are so obsessively married to their vision of what's right for humankind that they want to convert us all.

> *Conservative: A statesman who is enamored of existing evils, as distinguished from a Liberal, who wishes to replace them with others.*
>
> —Ambrose Bierce
> *The Devil's Dictionary*

These people don't want us to be free to choose what's right for ourselves. They believe that they have the answers that will save humankind, and they've got to force us into compliance for our own good. These "morality brokers" influence our system in subtle ways. They try to co-opt our legal system to make it channel their value system, and they get themselves into public office by whatever means necessary, then bend public policy to their will. They're masters of spin; they influence our culture insidiously by misrepresenting their opponents' position and disseminating propaganda.

You could argue that many of them mean well: They have a system that they believe in. But anybody who tries to legislate their beliefs is going against the fundamental tenet of American society: We are all free to choose for ourselves what "right" living is. Our Constitution guarantees us that freedom.

There are countries where legislated beliefs are the norm. Take Iran, for example. The national religion is Islam; the national standard of behavior is what the Koran teaches. It's all very carefully prescribed. I'm sure a lot of faithful Iranian Muslims hear about us and our separation of church and state, and they think that's the worst thing they've ever heard. Shouldn't the government answer to Allah?

It makes sense if you look at it that way. Unless, of course, you happen to be a Christian. Or a Jew, or a Baha'i, or of any other faith than Islam. Then you're out of luck. In America, we don't coerce people into religious beliefs.

Numerous groups out there are trying to do this, but basically, morality brokers come in two sets of extremes: "religious fundamentalists" who try to legislate morality, and "extreme liberals," many of whom seem to be so against any form of civil constraint that they even want to do away with laws that are there to protect everyone. The extreme Right tends to focus too much on ideology and not enough on ideas; the extreme Left tends to focus too much on rights and not enough on responsibilities. Ironically, both extremes can pose threats to our freedom. Fundamentalists threaten our freedom to practice the belief system that's the most meaningful for us by trying to impose their own beliefs onto our social, legal, and political systems. And those who advocate making even heinous crimes "value free" threaten our safety by failing to hold criminals accountable for their actions.

THE RELIGIOUS RIGHT

In the fevered state of our country, no good can ever result from any attempt to set one of these fiery zealots to rights, either in fact or principle. They are determined as to the facts they will believe, and the opinions on which they will act. Get by them, therefore, as you would by an angry bull; it is not for a man of sense to dispute the road with such an animal.
                                              —Thomas Jefferson

Since the mid-1990s, the Religious Right has been conducting a sort of "hostile takeover" of American politics. The Religious Right is notorious for claiming that it represents mainstream America, when in fact it doesn't. The Christian Coalition is a prime example of what I'm talking about. The name would make you think they stand for all Christians, right? They don't. Even though 58 percent of Americans claim to be strongly religious, only 18 percent of these feel that the Coalition represents them. An overwhelming number of people seem to think it's wrong for the Christian Coalition to co-opt Jesus Christ for their own political ends.

Many folks in the Religious Right claim that theirs is the only political group that promotes morals, family life, and religious values. But plenty of folks all across the political spectrum believe in law and order, hard work, and devotion to God and family. No one group owns these ideals. Most Americans, regardless of their political persuasion, believe in the principles that founded this country. But the Religious Right wants us to believe that a particular candidate has to subscribe to their particular brand of Christianity to be morally acceptable.

A lot of right-wingers love to throw around the term *welfare state* because it hits a nerve. You know I'm not crazy about welfare, but welfare spending in this country is hardly the burning issue the Right tries to make it into. Only 1 percent of the country's budget goes to welfare, and the vast majority of welfare recipients are off the rolls within two years. Now granted, welfare does need reform, and we particularly need to look at the attitudes we hold toward welfare, minus the political spin. But it's nowhere near the catastrophe the more vocal segments of the Right want you to believe it is.

The same goes for immigration. Because they're opposed to immigration, many of the folks on the far Right would like for you to believe that our country is being overrun with indigent Mexicans and Haitians, which is simply not true. America has always been a nation of immigrants. Yes, we do have to uphold a fair and sensible policy where immigration is concerned. But immigration is an integral part of who we are.

There are dangerously racist overtones in a lot of what the

extreme Right has to say. They know that much of America still has a sore spot where race is concerned, and many of them like to peddle their agenda by picking at that sore spot. One example is the way they encourage racism by distorting crime statistics in minority communities, especially statistics dealing with drugs and violent crime. Many folks on the far Right love to play off the public paranoia they help create.

WHERE THE FAR RIGHT IS WAY WRONG: YOU CAN'T LEGISLATE MORALITY

Anybody on the far Right—or anybody else for that matter— who thinks that we can legislate our way to a more moral America is misunderstanding something about the nature of legislation. Legislation can't create morality. Morals are about character and core beliefs. No amount of lawmaking can affect them. The law might be able to deter you from certain behavior, but it can't make you believe that the behavior is immoral. That seems self-evident to me. But apparently there are still those in our society who can't seem to understand this, and who insist on imposing their beliefs on others. The perfect example of this is the perpetual introduction of anti-flag-burning legislation.

We need to separate in our collective minds the difference between laws and morals so that everyone's freedom is protected.

THE ANTICAPITALIST, ANTIGOVERNMENT, AND SPENDTHRIFT LEFT

Oddly enough, while much of the extreme Right was busy co-opting the Republican party, the mainstream Left remained strangely silent. Maybe a lot of the silence is due to the fact that it doesn't have the same cohesion as the Right. At least the Right is able to give the appearance of a united front.

When I look at the left-most reaches of the political spectrum, I see three distinct branches of overly zealous leftist thought: the "mega-libertarians," as you could call them, who get bent out of shape over just about any kind of government-based social control; the "welfare rights" people, who see the government as a bottomless feeding trough; and that sad last hurrah of failed political philosophy, the Communists and Socialists, who still can't let go of the belief that government should micro-manage our economy and provide for all.

I don't think I need to say much about America's few remaining Socialists and Communists. Time and time again, all over the world, it's been proven that their system doesn't work. We have yet to see a prosperous Communist state. It's pretty clear that the more a government controls a nation's economy, the more it kills the people's motive for productivity.

We have more to worry about from the folks on the Left, the "undeclared socialists," who think you solve every social problem by throwing money at it. I'm talking about the welfare rights advocates and the people who push for ever larger NEA grants and free college funds and government-sponsored day care. There's no way this group is anywhere near the threat that the Right wants you to believe they are, but they do advance a policy that we need to steer clear of. The government is not a bottomless pit of wealth. Where do you think every penny of government money comes from? The taxpayers. You and me.

Any time government has money to give away, it's because it was taken from somebody else. That's why I'm fundamentally opposed to government programs that simply hand out cash to anybody who whines loudly enough. The danger is that these kinds of programs invariably grow bigger and more costly without addressing the root of the problem: the reason that people are in need of a handout in the first place. Dependence on the government tends to encourage more dependence on the government.

Don't get me wrong. I'm all for a government-funded social safety net. What kind of a nation would we be if we weren't able to help people when they were genuinely in need? But we've got to make sure our government programs remain safety nets and not hammocks.

Less dangerous are those on the extreme Left who are so anti-government and so anti–social control of almost any kind, that they take the concept of civil liberty to ridiculous extremes, to where they're defending children's "rights" to access pornography, pedophiles' "rights" to have sexual relationships with "consenting" children, and parents' "rights" to euthanize newborns whose medical care threatens to be prohibitively expensive. You think I'm kidding? These people do exist. They're out there. But they don't pose that much of a threat, contrary to what the Right would have you believe, because their ideas are so far out of the mainstream that they're unlikely to ever affect social policy or legislation.

Now, you know that I consider myself a libertarian. I support minimal government interference in people's lives. But what sets me, and most other moderate libertarians, apart from the folks on the extreme Left is that I do believe that government has a role to play in controlling antisocial behavior.

The arguments I hear from many people on the far Left is that they don't believe human behavior can be judged—at all. They're the ones who will quote you one tiny fragment of Jesus' "Judge not" sermon without bothering to read the rest of it, which is all about your duty to judge yourself, *and others,* carefully. In order for us to maintain a civilized society, we do have to judge, to an extent. I believe that government's proper role is limited to judging behavior that is harmful to people and property. Invariably, where the mega-libertarians screw up is carrying their argument for the rights of one person or group so far that they end up trampling on the rights of another. The right to swing your fist must end where your neighbor's nose begins.

WHY AN OVERDOSE OF LIBERTY LEADS TO
A HEMORRHAGE OF FREEDOM

The problem with getting too wrapped up in arguing for our rights is that we seldom argue as loudly for our responsibilities. There's not one right that you and I can claim that isn't somehow tied to a responsibility. My right to own a gun is limited by my responsibility not to shoot a person with it. If you start arguing that your liberty to do whatever you want extends to behaviors that threaten my life, your liberty robs me of my freedom. In a civilized society, we uphold each others' rights by upholding our own responsibilities. There is only one kind of society in which you can demand all of your rights, without limitations, and accept none of the responsibilities: a society of one.

Most Damaging of All:
A Lazy American Public

You can see that we've got a lot of diverse forces working to dilute the power of the average working people: corrupt career politicians, bipartisan pit bulls, corporate and special interest bullies, morality brokers, spin doctors, and extremists of all kinds. But the most insidious and damaging force by far is an apathetic public. That's the one ingredient without which political corruption couldn't flourish. We can't afford to let ourselves become lazy in our political habits, or we're the ones who'll pay the price.

It starts when we get lazy about forming our opinions. It's just easier to criticize mindlessly than to take the trouble to think things through. That's often encouraged in today's cultural climate; sadly enough, it's particularly prevalent among young people. These days, cynicism is considered hip. But the trouble with cynicism is that it doesn't do anything constructive. Blind cynicism can only destroy.

We're supposed to critique our government; the Founding Fathers designed it that way. We're supposed to be skeptical of our elected officials, and we're supposed to keep a close eye on them. That's healthy and necessary for a democratic society. But there's a huge difference between skepticism and cynicism. We cross the line when we relentlessly tear our leaders down, when we literally go hunting for stories to ruin them. That kind of behavior doesn't serve anybody.

Airing everyone's dirty laundry is a poor substitute for good, old-fashioned civic duty. It may be easier and even more entertaining. But it's a pretty shortsighted form of entertainment. It's undermining our country's government. Statistics show a steady decline in voter turnout. Fewer people volunteer for political work than they did just a few decades ago. We often tend to let TV "candy news" shows tell us what to think about a given issue, rather than studying the issues in a variety of newspapers and other sources, so that we can develop an intelligent opinion for ourselves. Whenever we let someone think for us and act for us, we implicitly agree to go along with their agenda. Whenever the public isn't involved with its government, it creates a climate where abuse of power can flourish.

We Americans are also lazy about offering ourselves for public service. Many of us don't bother to vote, even in presidential elections. We often don't bother to stay informed on the issues, let alone to seek out diverse viewpoints on them. We seldom do volunteer work for the candidates we like. And most of us never consider running for civic office, even though plenty of local government positions are part-time and flexible, to accommodate private-sector working people.

In recent years, I think we've gotten lazier about building the strong personal characters, principles, and morals that a democratic society requires of its citizens. We live in a very permissive society today, one in which it's widely accepted that the right thing to do is whatever makes you "feel good" at the moment. We're a culture that, to an extent, rejects all guilt as bad without admitting that there might be times when guilt is appropriate. We tend to fall back on pop psych excuses for our faults by blaming our personal history, although we're often very quick to point out the faults of others. Yet if anybody dares to point out ours, we tend to accuse them of judging us, as though judgment, like guilt, is an inherently bad thing. In a cultural climate like this, it's not all that hard for political corruption to find a place to flourish.

WE MAKE CONTRADICTORY DEMANDS OF OUR PUBLIC FIGURES

It's tough to be a politician in today's social climate, because we have become very hypocritical about the demands we make of public figures. We yell that we want honesty from them, but when they give it to us, we crucify them. We've become very good at digging up dirt; we're so good at it, we sometimes even manufacture dirt where there is none. When we do this, we hamstring our political leaders. They're damned if they do and damned if they don't.

This is a sign of the times. In Kennedy's day, if a politician was less than discreet, we turned a blind eye. You've heard all the rumors about Kennedy: indiscretions that make Clinton look like a monk by comparison. But the attitude of the day was to quietly sweep it under the rug. Obviously, that extreme doesn't work either. But nowadays we tend to go around vindictively turning over every rug we can find, until we find something we can gloat over. Obviously, we should expect decent behavior from our leaders. But there's a difference between holding our leaders to a standard, and deliberately, even gleefully, trying to find ways to bring them down. Everyone has had youthful indiscretions. We seem to demand leaders who have never committed a sin. Yet when somebody like Al Gore comes along, polls say he's too boring.

WE DON'T GIVE PUBLIC FIGURES A
WAY BACK FROM THEIR MISTAKES

We've effectively taught politicians that they're not allowed to make mistakes. It seems as though if they've ever done something obnoxious—or even questionable—no matter how many decades ago they did it, we hold it against them forever. We will lose out on a lot of good leadership if we refuse to accept anyone who doesn't have a spotless record—as if any of us has such a thing. I'm far more suspicious of the people who claim to have a squeaky clean past than those who honestly, openly admit that they've been wrong.

> *The politician who never made a mistake never made a decision.*
>
> —John Major

I know, you're thinking of one particular president who only admitted he was wrong when he got caught. You're suspicious of public apologies, because you've heard some pretty insincere ones from your leaders in recent years. So how do you sort sincerity from insincerity? How can you tell when somebody has truly reformed? There is no foolproof way to do that. But if a public figure owns up to his or her past mistakes, can clearly explain why what he or she did was wrong, has made retribution, and has built up a long track record of doing things right, that's a pretty good indicator that that person has learned from his or her mistakes.

A person who has honestly learned from his or her mistakes is potentially a very effective leader. It takes true character to admit you're wrong. It takes real moral fiber to turn yourself around and do things differently. And people who have learned something the hard way have absolute confidence in their convictions: They've been on both sides of the issue, and they *know* which one is wrong and which is right. They're in a position to lead powerfully on that issue.

DO WE AMERICANS NEED TO GET A LIFE?

Ironically, what our society has become is a direct result of our prosperity. The petty whining, the mean-spirited criticism, and the endless obsession with scandal are the hallmarks of a society with a lot of free time on its collective hands. Only the well-off truly have the luxury of being self-absorbed. We tend to imagine that we have huge problems. We don't. We hardly even know what real problems look like.

You don't hear this kind of petty whining from the Irish, or the Polish, or the Russians, or the Somalis. They all have genuine suffering in their recent histories; it's still very much in their collective memory. They know what it's like to go hungry, to have nowhere to turn for relief. They know what it's like not to be safe, to face violent death every day. They know what it means to have no political voice, to not be allowed to vote. We Americans, on the other hand, take a lot for granted.

Even in our own country, in more troubled times, you didn't hear the kind of whining that you hear now. In the whole first half of this century, Americans were struggling to get through the Great Depression, two world wars, and a hell of a lot of racist and sexist oppression. Character, honor, and optimism were tools that came in handy during those times.

Does relative peace and prosperity have to mean that we become trivial and self-absorbed? I hope not. We still have free will. We can choose to become whatever we wish. We can make better choices in our lives and in our politics. The same principles that laid the foundation for the peace and prosperity that we now enjoy also made certain that our government would forever belong to us, the American people. If we don't like what we see in politics, we have all the tools we need to change it. All we have to do is make up our minds.

3

Our Irresponsible Media

*T**he men with the muck-rake are often indispensable to the
well-being of society, but only if they know when to stop
raking the muck.*
                                          —Theodore Roosevelt

When I was mayor of Brooklyn Park back in the early 1990s, I was a
speaker for D.A.R.E. (Drug Abuse Resistance Education), the antidrug
program for teens. I liked to talk to the kids not only about illegal
drugs, but also about one of the worst legal ones: chewing tobacco. I'd
tell them, "Are you prepared to chew it your whole life? Because you
will become addicted. It's not something you chew today and then not
chew tomorrow."

I could speak with authority about the stuff because I used to
chew Copenhagen. I stopped cold turkey the day a dentist friend
showed me the lesion on the inside of my lower lip that all tobacco
chewers get. He told me, "As long as that lesion's benign, you're fine.
But if it's malignant, they'll cut a third of your face away in less than
three weeks." Now, I hope to have grandkids some day, and I don't
want them to think of me as a monster. So I quit. That speech goes
over very effectively with the kids.

But one Sunday, a huge headline popped up in a local paper,

accusing me of having been seen smoking a cigarette at Target Center Auditorium, a smoke-free building. The article even claimed that when somebody asked me to put it out, I got belligerent and ground the cigarette into the carpet. The writer accused me of being hypocritical for my antitobacco stance. Her article used words like *idiot* and *musclehead* to describe me. Her headline read, "Maybe We Should Call Him Jesse the Butt!"

Well, I don't know who she might have been talking about, but it wasn't me. I was at a horse show with Terry in Cannon Falls that night. I had dozens of witnesses who saw me in Cannon Falls. And here's the real kicker: I don't even smoke cigarettes! I never have!

This reporter hadn't bothered to check her sources. All she needed was to hear the same gossip over the phone from three different witnesses, each of whom supposedly saw a large man wearing a bandana and smoking a cigarette. I got her to retract her statement in her regular column. But she never did personally apologize, publicly or privately. And of all the kids who saw that headline and thought I was a hypocrite, how many actually saw her retraction?

We thought about suing to get her to reveal her sources. A judge might have decided that she had to reveal their names. And who knows—it may have turned out that she didn't have any real sources. She could just as easily have made them up! But in the end, we decided not to go after the sources, because the retraction was what we really wanted.

That same journalist also published an article about a prominent Minneapolis businessman getting arrested in Colorado on cocaine charges. It turned out it wasn't even him, but a totally unrelated guy with the same last name. She didn't even bother to check. After that, her column did not appear for a while. But how will that businessman ever fully restore his reputation?

That's all it takes. Journalists can ruin a public figure's credibility with stories like these. And they do, and go home to dinner without a worry in the world. They think the First Amendment makes them immune to responsibility and liberates them from conscience. This kind of thing happens all of the time, all across the country.

In the summer of 1999, when I gave out a $1.3 billion tax rebate, a local reporter went out and hunted around until she found one confused old guy who didn't understand the rebate and somehow thought he'd get more. That way, this reporter was able to print the headline she wanted: "Not Everyone Happy With Their Rebate." The writer even admitted she had to search hard for somebody who wasn't happy.

A similar thing happened in February of 2000, just before I announced that I was leaving the Reform party. Somebody in the local media reported that there were a bunch of people picketing outside the governor's residence, with signs that read, "Jesse, Quit the Reform Party!" In truth, there was only one guy with a sign. But if a mob makes a better story, the media will turn one guy into a mob.

It really makes you wonder about the motives of some of these people. Bill Press of *Crossfire* recently accused me of trashing every presidential candidate except John McCain. *Trashed* was the word he used. I haven't trashed anybody! Dean Barkley was on with him recently, and Press was saying, "I'm sick and tired of these people who keep saying they're taken out of context." Then he flashed up on a huge screen my quote about Tailhook, where I said I understood how it could have happened among a group of warriors. But of course, he left out the very first sentence that had come out of my mouth, which was, "I don't condone it." Dean tried to defend me, but Press wouldn't let him speak.

Our media today are accountable to no one. And they know it. But it seems that the more arrogant they get, the higher their ratings go, and the more papers they sell. They've got no incentive to report only reliable, unbiased news.

Because I'm skeptical of just about all media in general, I don't rely heavily on any single news source. My staff provides me with clippings and briefings from all the major news outlets, which I digest daily. But I realize that most people have to get their local news from one or two sources at most. They're in the position of having to assume that what they're being told is factual.

Here's a case in point. We have two major newspapers here in the Twin Cities: the *Saint Paul Pioneer Press* and the Minneapolis *Star Tribune*. I think the *Star Tribune* is the better of the two, but as far as credibility goes, both papers are only a notch above the *National Enquirer*. If the metropolitan area's two major newspapers can't be trusted to provide the people of the Twin Cities with reliable news, where else can they turn for information?

The Media's Obsession with Scandal

In December of 1999, the Minnesota Timberwolves were scheduled to play an international basketball game in Tokyo. I had been planning a trade mission to Japan, and being the die-hard Timberwolves fan that I am, I thought it would be a great idea to schedule my trip to coincide with the game, so I could be on hand to support them. Having the governor of the state there in attendance would be a great tie in, make a big event even bigger, and focus that much more attention on Minnesota. We thought it was a good business move.

The event was a huge success. The game went over extremely well, and by the time I got on the plane to come home, Minnesota had a new multimillion-dollar pork export deal with Japan, an even bigger beef export deal in the works, and a heightened Japanese interest in Minnesota tourism.

But guess what kind of headlines I came home to? Reporters were squealing that I had treated myself and a bunch of my buddies to a Japanese vacation at the taxpayers' expense! They cited the Timberwolves game as the ultimate boondoggle, as though I had spent the whole trip indulging myself. They demanded that I reimburse the taxpayers for the whole trip.

This is a classic example of the way the media can create scandal where there isn't any. The only newsworthy aspects of the story were its value as a trade mission. Because that's what it was, from top to bottom. Those "buddies" I treated to the game were all state employees. And most nights, after the day's business was done, I just sat in my hotel room, responding to calls from Minnesota officials. But the media put their own ugly spin on the trip and turned the whole thing into something it wasn't.

They crossed the line even farther with the scandal they invented over my security spending. At the end of 1999, the heads of Capitol Security submitted to the legislature the amount of money they had calculated it would take to provide security for me and my family. Well, for whatever reason, the legislature only allocated half of what they asked for, which left me in the awkward position of either having to scrape that amount out of some other part of the budget, or go without the full amount of protection they recommended.

Now, if the media had wanted to shine an honest light on this story, they might have taken the legislature to task for being unwilling to budget the money for their governor's protection. That would have been a useful thing to do. It would have been beneficial for the public to know that Minnesota's legislature was playing these kinds of games. But instead, the local media decided to twist the facts around, and use the story as a chance to go after me. They decided to make it sound like I was spending way too much on security: Jesse's bilking the taxpayers again with his indulgent life-style!

Well, the facts tell a different story. According to a recent study, I'm one of the least expensive governors around when it comes to security. I cost taxpayers about $800,000 less in security than the average governor, whose security runs state taxpayers about $1.9 million a year. But there's no story in that. Which headline would you pick up, "The Governor Spends Less on Security" or "The Governor's Overspending His Limit"?

The press doesn't mind omitting facts in order to create a scandal. Just before the legislature went into session in February, the press printed a big headline, "Governor Has Taken Thirty-two Days of Vacation!" They made sure to print it the day I got on a plane to leave town, so I couldn't even respond.

But what they didn't tell the public was that they were counting 1999 and the new year as a single year. I took nineteen days total in 1999. Less than three weeks. Then I took thirteen days in February to get rested before the legislature started up again. In a calendar year, if I get three weeks each year, then when the new year starts, I get a fresh three weeks. But they didn't bother to take that into account. They also counted weekend days in their tallies, too, when all the government offices were closed.

I knew that when the legislature convened, it would be a knock-down, drag-out fight for four months. So I rested, and I trained, to get in better shape for the battle. But there's nothing anywhere saying that three weeks is all I'm allowed to take. It's just a number I set for myself. My security people said, "Governor, you're on duty twenty-four hours a day; you can take as much vacation as you like. You could take ninety days a year if you wanted." Ultimately, my boss is the voters. If they think I'm out of line taking three weeks of vacation a year, they can vote me out.

Today's media are obsessed with portraying the ugliest side of humanity: dishonesty, hypocrisy, ego battles, and fights. It's not enough anymore just to report the news. They've got to make the news sexy. Their main criteria for the stories they write are not what's newsworthy, but whatever gets the public's attention. Scandal sells, so that's what they write.

Many of them don't care if they have to make it up; they can always hide beneath the umbrella of "protecting their sources." They always have a way out. In fact, why should they bother to go through the trouble of writing a credible, carefully researched story, when they have a deadline coming up and their editor will probably just tell them to "punch it up" anyway? Nobody's holding them accountable for the stuff they write. As long as they're selling lots of papers, they know they'll have a job.

The media today are all about making money. They say they're not, but they are. They do whatever it takes to get the juicy stuff, because the juicy stuff makes them richer. They'll try to scoop stories that haven't happened yet. They don't respect "no comment" anymore; they'll just badger people until they get something. I've had journalists tell me, "We have leaks from your administration who have told us . . ." when I know they haven't. They go out of their way to tear down, to ridicule, and to criticize.

Don't get me wrong. The press is supposed to criticize our political leaders. That's the main reason the Founding Fathers gave us a free press. It's the press's job to help us keep politicians in line by keeping our actions in the public eye. In monarchies and dictatorships, if you criticize your political leaders, you quickly find yourself being marched up a long ladder and down a short rope. So we should be thankful as hell that we live in a country where the press is free to criticize government officials.

But criticism is not the same thing as a personal attack. My dictionary says criticism is an art; it's the art of making discriminating judgments. It's an evaluating tool. It doesn't even necessarily mean that in the end you'll come up with something negative. An attack, on the other hand, is a malevolent act, especially when it's unverified. It's hostile in intent. When you criticize, you're on an objective search for the facts; your goal is a sound opinion. When you attack, your goal is to do harm.

It's a lot easier to tear somebody down than it is to construct a solid argument in response to something someone has said or done. Intelligent debate takes a lot more work. To form a solid, fair criticism of someone's position, you first have to verify what the person actually said. People are misquoted and taken out of context every day. Then you have to make sure you understand what the person really meant (no fair intentionally misinterpreting them). Then you have to evaluate it, check the facts, and look at it from several points of view. And finally, you have to go through the same regimen with your own opinions to see how they stack up. Thinking takes work. That's why, as I once heard someone say, it's a lot easier to point the finger than it is to point the way. Besides, why do all that work when blatant attacks sell more papers?

The Media's Appetite for Fights

Journalists love to portray every story as a battle, because that's what gets the public's attention. The American public loves a good fight! Look how often the headlines describe two opposing viewpoints as a "war." They did that with me and Ross Perot. One reporter wrote a headline that declared, "Venturans vs. Perotbots: Open War in Reform Party!" Come on! I'm not at war with the man. We disagree on a few parts of the Reform party platform. But instead of debating the merits of each of our positions, which would be helpful, this reporter chose to make it sound like Perot and I are dukes-up in some stupid clash of egos.

This is a dangerous game, and the media play it all the time. In order to create a war, you have to create two opposing sides, right? So in the name of presenting "both" sides, they go looking for an opponent. Well, first of all, who says there are only two sides to every issue? And second, who says that every issue even has another side? Not every viewpoint is equal, but when the media go looking to match up every newsworthy figure or issue with an opponent, they can make it seem as though they are. When you pit so and so versus such and such, as you do in a wrestling ring, it's implied that the two opponents are a fair match. And I'm here to tell you, it ain't necessarily so.

The media's policy of turning every story into a fight is frustrating the hell out of public officials and civic leaders, because they feel that they can't get their information across to the public without it being twisted into a stupid showdown. And it's ultimately dumbing down the American public because when we're getting it reinforced to us day in and day out that there are only two sides to every story, after a while we start to believe it. We begin to assume that the issues really are as cut-and-dried as the media tell us they are. You're either for us or against us.

The Media Cop Out by Going for Character Assassination Instead of Concentrating on the Issues

The media seem to have this attitude that if you're in public office, you've forfeited all your individual rights. One Friday on my *Lunch With the Governor* radio show, I talked about the grossly inappropriate behavior of Representative Carol Molnau, who, during a forum, kept putting her hands on me. She grasped my arm, she patted my back, she even put her hand

> **R**esort is had to ridicule only when reason is against us.
>
> —Thomas Jefferson

on my thigh. I told her to stop. Can you imagine how that would have been perceived if she were male and I were female? If I had touched her that way, it would have ended up in court, guaranteed.

But you don't touch the governor that way, with that kind of familiarity. It shows disrespect for the office. I'd never touch the President that way! If you saw the videotape of her behavior, you'd see that what she was doing was far more than a single, simple hand on the shoulder. Yet my opponents criticized me for being overly sensitive.

Joe Soucheray, a local radio personality here in Minneapolis, and a regular columnist for the *Saint Paul Pioneer Press*, has been one of my most vocal critics. The day the Molnau story broke, a woman called in to his show to say that I had no right to complain about

Carole Molnau touching me because of the things I did when I was nineteen that I wrote about in *I Ain't Got Time to Bleed*. Now, I don't get that stretch. Because I had done something dumb when I was nineteen, now that I'm forty-nine years old and married, thirty years later, this woman should be allowed to touch me any way she wants? I was on Joe Soucheray's show, and I said that even though I've had a wild and woolly past, that doesn't mean that I've lost my rights not to be touched inappropriately.

I've come to believe the media don't want anyone to have heroes today, because whenever somebody gets to the status of hero, the media really go into search-and-destroy mode. It's almost as if they're saying, "This guy's human. He's not really a hero. We're going to prove he's not." Suppose it's a firefighter who pulled people from a burning building: They'd go looking for somebody who will say, "I knew that firefighter when he was a drunk and his wife left him." Then they'd splash that all over the headlines: "Hero Has Checkered Past." And the public may get so caught up in the intrigue, they'll forget all about the fact that the firefighter walked into a burning building and saved people's lives.

And it can go the other way, too. If there's anyone the media want to make a hero out of, they have plenty of power to do so. Look at the O.J. Simpson trial.

The media are constantly circling like sharks, waiting for you to drop your guard and leave something dangling. First they buddy up to you, and they write all these glowing stories about how refreshing and truthful you are, and they get you to open up to them. So you start believing what they're writing about you. You start trusting them. And you think, "Wow! They really do want to hear the truth! They really like me!" They keep feeding you more line and more line, and then suddenly, they yank on the hook.

All of a sudden, you're not refreshing anymore, you're abrasive. You're not telling the truth, you're an embarrassment. You're evil, you're stupid, you're a clown. And the real kicker is, it's the same people saying these things who used to be yodeling about how great you are!

That's why the first lady hardly ever talks to the media anymore. She saw me fall into the trap time and time again, and she wanted no part of it. These days any article you see about her says the same old thing: where she was born, how much she likes horses, and so forth. *George* magazine recently came to do an article on her. She kept asking, "Why would *George* want to do an article on the first lady of Minnesota?" I think it's because they were hoping to catch her in an off moment. They were hoping she'd say something stupid. Or they were going through her to try to get to me. Because the moment she got through with her *George* interview they asked me for one. I turned them down.

Terry says after every interview she does, when everybody's gone, she sits there and agonizes, "Okay, what could I have possibly said that they could take and make us look ridiculous?" She wakes up in the middle of the night, worrying. And this is what you go through when you're just trying to be honest.

We watched the same kind of thing happen to John McCain. That's one reason why John McCain enjoyed so much popularity for a time: He angered some people with the things he said, but he wasn't tiptoeing through the tulips the way the other candidates were. He wasn't afraid to take on Pat Robertson and Jerry Falwell, and call them on their control of the Republican party. I can almost guarantee you that McCain saw what I did in Minnesota, and a lot of the campaign formula he put together was based on it.

But here's what happened to John McCain: The press saw this open, honest, refreshing guy, and a little light bulb went off in their heads. Suddenly, after months of stories about how great he was, all these articles came flooding into the papers about his abrasiveness, his uncontrollable temper, and a hundred other stories about nasty run-ins people had had with him. The media did to him what they've done to me and to others. They tried to take him down.

The media hold a double standard about whose opinions they'll print. Whenever I say or do something, the media go looking for someone to counter it. They'll take any source as long as the source says something negative. Yet it doesn't work the other way around: When someone says something bad about me, they don't come to *me* for a statement. They don't give me the same opportunity to counter a false statement.

Joe Soucheray's colleague Patrick Reusse covers sports, but he recently wrote a column literally blaming me for every bad thing in Minnesota. Now keep in mind, I'd only been in office a little over a year—how much damage could I have done? He blamed me for all our current farm troubles. He even blamed me because Honeywell moved their corporate headquarters out of Minnesota. How could I have stopped them? When a corporation decides to move their headquarters, they don't make that decision within a two-month period. That's something that had to have been in the works for years. I didn't even learn of their intention to move until the night before they announced it. What was I supposed to do to stop it? And was it really my job to stop them? They're a private business; they can move wherever they want.

Reusse's entitled to his opinion, just as much as anyone else. But in this case he was setting himself up as some kind of political expert, giving this long-winded diatribe on the state of politics and the causes behind everything. He was passing judgment on things he wasn't qualified to judge.

I used to work with Reusse's producer, so I called him up and asked him to do me a favor: "When Reusse goes on the air today, just ask him who the Commissioner of Agriculture is in the state of Minnesota." He did, and of course, Reusse had no idea. Do you know why he didn't know? Because he's a sports writer. Maybe he didn't have any sports to write about that day, so he decided it would be a good idea to rip me apart.

Even journalists the public thinks of as credible and honest will occasionally stoop to character assassination. A prime example is Don Shelby, an anchorperson at a local CBS affiliate here in Minneapolis, who is perceived as honest and objective. But, where I am concerned, he doesn't always put a lot of effort into verifying his facts. He once complained that I only do things in government that affect me personally.

He was referring to the fact that I supported the repeal of the law that banned studs on snowmobile tracks. They had been banned a few years ago, because they tear up the roads. But without the studs, snowmobiles are difficult to control, so the existing law was actually contributing to accidents.

Shelby said the reason I supported the repeal of the law was because I own snowmobiles. He knew I owned personal watercraft, so he made the leap from there that I must also own snowmobiles. The truth is, I don't own a snowmobile. I've never owned a snowmobile. I've never even ridden on one! But if the story sounds good enough, even the best of them will fly with it.

Journalists go looking for the one piece of a story that will generate outrage, and they ignore the rest of the story, especially those parts that contradict the small piece they've chosen to focus on. For example, when they asked me to comment on the Tailhook scandal, the very first words out of my mouth were, "I don't condone it." I went on to explain the reasons why I thought a phenomenon like Tailhook happened, and that to an extent we brought it on ourselves by creating warriors who lived beyond the pale of societal norms. But the reporters simply ignored my first sentence, and my second, and my third, until they found something that made it sound like I was excusing the airmen's behavior. And that's what they ran with. How is it helpful to the public for the media to deliberately distort what I was saying?

And woe unto the public figure who tries to correct the press's statements. If we say that a particular headline was wrong, we get accused of waffling, or whining, or of trying to whitewash our comments. If we fight back, we get accused of being thin-skinned. But what are we supposed to do? Sit quietly while they destroy our reputations?

The alternative is to become scrupulously careful about what we say. In today's climate, public figures don't have the luxury of expressing opinions on extracurricular subjects. I learned that lesson the hard way after my interview with *Playboy* magazine in November of 1999. An unbelievable amount of fallout came from that one interview. I got called on the carpet by hundreds of reporters over half a dozen different issues. But the one that has been the most misinterpreted by far was my comment on organized religion.

I admit that when I said organized religion was a crutch for weak-minded people, I should have clarified that I think *some* religious people are weak-minded, not *all*. The ridiculous thing is that at the moment I made the comment, we weren't even talking about religion in general. We were talking about the way the Religious Right tries to push their beliefs on everybody else. To me that's a misuse of religion, and I believe it's the people who misuse religion who are weak and need strength in numbers.

Now, I'll fully own up to the fact that I didn't state myself very clearly during that interview. I abbreviated my point, when if I'd had the luxury of more time, I would have been more careful to clarify what I meant. The interview came at a time when I had a gazillion other things on my mind, and at a time when I was averaging about five interviews a day, all of which had to be squeezed in around the state's business, which often as not kept me busy until late in the evening.

I didn't mean to say that *all* religion is a sham, and I certainly don't think that *all* religious people are weak-minded. The truth is, I can see that the vast majority of religious people derive a lot of benefit from practicing their faith. And I'm fully aware that being openly religious takes strength, especially in today's intolerant social climate.

But I was commenting on the fact that organized religion gets misused a lot. In the hands of the corrupt, it can become a way of controlling people, when people with religious authority start to pretend they speak for God. Worse still is when corrupt people with religious authority also start courting political authority. The combination can be deadly. Do you know how many wars, all throughout history, have been fought for supposed religious reasons? I have heard so many stories about the misuse of religious power, I could probably write an entire book just about that one subject. But I didn't have time that day to write a book. I tried to express way too expansive an idea in that little span of time. The interviewer knew what the context of my comment was, but chose not to include it because the omission made the interview more sensational.

The media were overjoyed: Ventura's finally shot himself in both feet! It was pretty disgusting how gleefully they went to work plastering that comment all over the place, and extrapolating all kinds of things from it that I never meant. But worst of all was the way they went after Terry for the things that I had said. They cornered her when she was appearing at a horse show to raise money for a disabled children's riding therapy program. Terry's security literally got into a pushing match with one reporter.

The next day, they followed her into church and sat there through the whole service. She told them "No comment!" three or four times, but they don't take no for an answer anymore. They were so aggressive about going after what they wanted, they didn't care if they disrupted the service or if Terry was in tears; they were gonna get their interview!

The *Playboy* mess drove home a lesson that I've been learning all year: Don't hand the press ammunition! I'm under so much scrutiny these days that I can't talk freely. The media frenzies that result threaten to monopolize all my time. It's gotten to the point where, to counteract the situation, I only talk to the media about policy. I don't even talk about personal stuff anymore. But no matter how much I button my lip, and no matter how much I try to clarify what I meant, that misinformation from the *Playboy* interview is still out there.

Rest assured, if I run for reelection, I'm going to have to relive the whole hoo-ra all over again.

The media's fixation on fights and scandals is a gross misrepresentation of what they are supposed to be doing. Personally, I don't think they have any business at all reporting opinions. Their job is to report facts and events. I think they should leave opinions to the op-ed section. It's a principle of journalistic ethics to present a balanced perspective on the stories of the day. Journalists are supposed to go looking for more than one opinion on a given topic. But today's journalists have gotten hung up on the idea that stories are supposed to be "balanced" like a seesaw, not "balanced" like a nutritious diet.

I submit to you that the seesaw way of doing things is badly flawed, because it can only present a story in terms of two equal sides, even when there are more than two sides. Also, it assumes that the two sides are equal, when often they're not. Worse still, the seesaw method requires that reporters go looking for the two farthest extremes of an issue, because they're likely to be the ones that are the most opposite. But how well are the farthest extremes going to represent the majority of the people?

Imagine the difference in news coverage if reporters followed the "nutritious diet" idea of balanced news instead. You'd get a broad spectrum of views, from many angles and many voices. If they simply presented a range of views, instead of diametrically opposing the two most strident among them, they would leave us free to decide for ourselves the validity of each perspective.

And who says we even need to look at each perspective in terms of either buying it 100 percent or pitching it out 100 percent? Suppose only a crumb of person A's opinion makes sense to us, but we agree with a big chunk of person B's, and although we don't much like the particulars of person C's plan, we do like his or her overall approach. Who knows? Maybe the best solution of all would be to add A's crumb to B's chunk, and apply them to C's method. But if all we ever get are the extremely skewed views of Y and Z, and the only options we're offered are to choose one or another, how will we ever know?

So much of the media's current disrepute is a result of taking honorable journalistic principles to stupid extremes. Under the umbrella of presenting diverse views, many reporters seem to think they've got an obligation to report even the most unsupportable, most wacko points of view with the same effort as they do more sensible viewpoints. I think that in general, in the proper context, they should give everybody a chance to be heard. But that doesn't necessarily mean that every viewpoint has to be given equal emphasis.

Oftentimes reporters get harassed by people on the extreme fringes of an issue, who start howling about their First Amendment rights if the paper doesn't print their views. The people who represent more sensible, more widely accepted views aren't hollering as loudly, so the people on the fringe end up getting their views into print as often, or even more often, as the people who hold more valid views.

Now, I'm all for letting everybody have their say, whether I agree with them or not. Bile may creep up my throat every time I hear the Klan preaching their white supremacist garbage, but I wouldn't deny them the chance to say what they have to say. I think in a case like that, the most powerful weapon against the Klan's point of view is the Klan itself. When Klan members stand up there in plain sight and state their position, the public has a chance to consider the viewpoint along with its source.

But just because everybody's entitled to free speech doesn't mean they're entitled to use public media as their vehicle. Newspapers and television stations aren't obligated to disseminate the views of everybody who thinks they've got something to say. They've only got so many pages they can print, and so many minutes of air time they can broadcast. They all have to discriminate. They have to choose, from among limitless possibilities, what information is going to be the most useful to the greatest number of people. When the media give air time and print time to whoever demands it the loudest, they're making their choice based on who's the most obnoxious, not necessarily who's got the most legitimate opinions.

It's nothing new to see the media going on the attack. As long as the idea of a free press has been around, reporters have gone on the warpath. But there's a major difference between the way it's done today and the way it's been done throughout history. In the past, most of the time, when the media went after people it was because they truly believed that those people were in the wrong. There was passion behind their attacks; their hearts were in it. Today, the media's policy is attack now, figure out why you're attacking later.

I don't pretend to know exactly what caused the American media to get stuck in attack mode, but I bet it had a lot to do with Watergate. Remember, back then we were still deep in the "Question Authority" era, when every institution was suspect and every leader was assumed to be corrupt. Then along came this blatant breach of public trust at the highest levels of government. A lot of journalists made their fame and fortunes from exposing Watergate. It was a real coup for them, and it created a precedent: Where there's a scandal, there's a journalistic career waiting to be launched.

But what happens when there isn't a scandal waiting for a journalist to jump aboard and ride to fame and fortune? That's when we get into the era we now see all around us: If a scandal is what it takes to get the public's attention, you can build your own! Strip down that bland news story, dress it up as a scandal, and watch it take the country by storm!

This has had a devastating effect on our public leaders. Everybody's walking on eggshells because they know the slightest misstep is going to land them in a world of hurt. Back a few decades ago, it wasn't uncommon for public figures to feel relaxed around media people, and even spend time just hanging out with them casually. They had a chance to form bonds of trust and friendship, and in that atmosphere, a lot more genuine information could come across. But today, hanging out with the media would be kind of like taking a leisurely dip in a shark tank.

Because of the media feeding frenzy, I wouldn't wish public service on anyone today. When you go into public service today, you can rest assured that all of your background will be laid open, your privacy will be destroyed, and your reputation will be threatened by one set of lies after another . . . and all this just so you can do public service? Why bother? I know that we're losing out on a lot of top-quality people in public office these days because plenty of talented people decide it's just not worth all the pain and terror.

The attack media have also had a terrible effect on the public itself. If all we ever hear is scandal, we start to wonder if there's anybody we can trust. It makes humanity look bad. It just adds to the cynicism you see all around you these days. Of what benefit is that to society, to totally undermine the public's trust?

The Media Create the News Rather Than Reporting It

Our minister had been trying for a while to get us to develop some kind of relationship with the press. He had this well-intentioned idea that the harassment would stop if we could all just find a way to get along. He really wasn't all that aware of the state of things. He had never dealt with the media before, so he really didn't know the depths to which they'll stoop.

Then came that day, shortly after the *Playboy* interview was published and the media were going into a feeding frenzy over it, that a whole pack of media people literally chased Terry into the church, hounding her for a statement. Our minister went out to them to try to diffuse the situation. He said something to them like, "While I don't necessarily agree with what the governor said in that interview, I know the man, and I know the way he thinks about religion . . ." and he went on to defend me. Well, do you want to know the only part of his statement that they printed? "I don't agree with the governor!"

The minister was absolutely floored that they did that. He was furious. He called Terry right away and told her, "I didn't say that! There was a whole paragraph that went along with what they printed!" Terry simply said, "Welcome to our world, Pastor."

That's standard operating procedure in journalism today: The only facts worth reporting are those that back up your own opinion or that inflame the issue. And if you have to tweak those facts a little to support your opinion, if you have to misquote someone intentionally by taking their words out of context, so be it. And if you want to bolster your case further with a little nasty name-calling, so what? It's your right as a journalist, under the First Amendment.

Joe Soucheray, the KSTP radio personality and *Saint Paul Pioneer Press* columnist, always refers to me as Governor Turnbuckle. He's notorious for putting an ugly spin on the things I do. He's a prime example of the way journalists will report half-truths and skewed viewpoints in order to bolster their agenda.

Soucheray once said in his column that my radio show, *Lunch With the Governor,* is worthless because I don't have any adversaries on as guests, and I simply promote whatever it is I'm talking about. I explained to him that there's a reason for that: I feel that about 40 percent of the time the media provide misinformation to the public about what I've said and done. They stand between me and the public.

For example, when Soucheray wrote about my efforts to get a light-rail system built in Minneapolis, he quoted only part of what I'd said, and even that he got wrong. He wrote that I'd said opponents of light-rail are trying to put us all on the highway and make us drive. He responded in his column, "Where else are we supposed to drive, along riverbeds and windrows?"

The point I'd been making was that we don't have a viable transportation option besides our cars. But the reason I brought that up in the first place is because the government won't reduce our license tabs. Minnesota's license fees are some of the highest in the country. Because we have no alternative but to drive, we're stuck having to pay exorbitant license fees.

But Soucheray's goal obviously wasn't to make information available to the people of Minnesota so that they could make up their own minds about the issue. If that had been his intention, he would have presented my whole idea, not just the portion of it he quoted out of context. Journalists like Soucheray aren't disseminating facts; they're reporting their opinions as though they were fact. They promote their opinions by reporting the truth selectively, even if they have to take a tiny portion of what you said out of context in order to do it. Even if they have to get creative with the tiny portion they quote. To them, the end justifies the means.

Why would the press try to push their opinions as fact? Because that makes them powerful. There's political control to be had in the spin business. These days, the media are boldly trying to control our political process. They've gotten into the business of inserting themselves between government and the people. You'll hear some people saying the press has a liberal bias, and others saying it has a conservative bias. Well, the press definitely has a bias, but I think it varies from organization to organization.

The main point is that they try to bend public perceptions to their political preference through the news that they report, and that shouldn't be happening.

There are exceptions to the rule, of course. Not all journalists are out to manipulate the public. Plenty of capitol beat reporters do a terrific job. They're in the basement of the capitol building every day; they're virtually living in it. Most of the capitol reporters here were angry when a local gossip columnist who goes by the name C. J. broke a blatantly untrue story about my supposed misconduct in a Montana bar, because they realized that an article like that jeopardized their relationship with me. To have someone who doesn't even work in reporting do that made them furious.

But even many of the capitol beat reporters can't resist sticking little adjectives into everything they write. They once called me "the prickly governor," implying that I'm difficult to get along with. It's as though they can't resist the urge to editorialize. They can't be content with simply reporting the facts. They have to spin me. Why do they do that? Why don't they just call me Governor Ventura and say what their story is?

This kind of editorializing isn't always necessarily intended to do harm. In fact, a lot of the time, I doubt that they even mean it. We all do this kind of thing from time to time. But when somebody does it in a newspaper with a readership of millions—or worse, on live national television—the impact is exponentially large. When I was getting in the news a lot because of the *Playboy* interview, NBC anchor Katie Couric commented on the air that I was overexposed, that I didn't warrant all the attention I was getting in the media. But then a week later she called up my staff, wanting an interview. If she really felt that I was overexposed, why was she trying to give me more exposure?

The Media's Lack of Accountability

I don't think journalists today put any time into finding out what is factual. If it's an exciting story that their editors will splash out there, they could care less whether it's true. And, I believe, they could care less who gets hurt over it. I believe most journalists are that way. The only exceptions are some of the national media figures, a few of our capitol beat reporters, and young journalists fresh out of college— and these younger ones don't have enough seniority to get anything printed. Eventually they learn that if they write and print the truth, they probably won't get printed anyway, because it's not as exciting as a story that is less truthful.

In my opinion, 60 percent of what the media put out today is fact, and 40 percent isn't. People need to understand that when they listen to something the media have to say, there's maybe slightly better than a fifty-fifty chance that what they're hearing is true. Almost as likely as not, they'll throw out some flash-bang story because it sounds good. There's almost never a follow-up, even if the story is proven untrue. And even when there is a follow-up, the odds of it getting the same level of coverage are tiny. Many lies are perpetrated today by our own media, just for the sake of having a novel, titillating story, something that will grab ratings.

The public has very little recourse against the media's power, but public servants have even less. That's how NBC was able to make a movie about my life, with all kinds of falsehoods and misrepresentations, and I couldn't do a thing about it. The media have full rein to say anything they want to say about me, and because I'm a public figure, they can get away with it. But does that apply to my relatives, whom they grossly misrepresented? They're not public figures. It was completely legal for NBC to make a profit by misrepresenting me, but how does that extend to my family?

The media get away with all of this garbage because nobody is holding them accountable. Whose job is it to do that? It's not the government's job. The government should never get involved in policing the media, because the First Amendment forbids them from having any control over what the media say.

What about libel suits? Well, that's the problem. The media are allowed to protect their sources. You'd have a hell of a time proving that somebody intentionally committed libel if you can't even point out who made the statement.

Do you see how badly this can be abused? When the newspapers know they don't have to reveal their sources, they know they can get away with using sources that aren't credible. They can misquote their sources, if it serves them. There are probably times when they don't bother to use a source, they simply tell an out-and-out lie. There's nothing stopping them.

An Unreliable Media Is Particularly Hazardous to Our Political System

Information is crucial to a free society, in which every individual makes his or her own choices in life. A democratic republic requires an educated, well-informed society in order to function. Where do we get the information we use to make those choices? The media's job is to keep us informed. If the quality of the information they give us is flawed, how then will we be able to make sound decisions?

Who's to Blame?

I'm sure that the vast majority of young journalists start out with good intentions. They all go through journalism ethics classes in school, and in the beginning they may fight hard to verify their information and check their sources. But after a while, they probably get worn down by deadlines and the push for ratings and editors who keep hollering at them to "give it an edge." It's not easy to swim against the tide when you know they can replace you any time with somebody who's willing to play dirty. Especially when the only barrier to writing the irresponsible stuff is their own conscience.

But ultimately, I believe that if we want to find out who's really to blame for allowing our media to degenerate, we'd better look in the mirror. Nobody's walking into our living rooms, grabbing our remotes, and switching the TV from CNN to *Extra*.

We're the consumers. The only reason the media can make a profit off the scandals they generate is that we provide them with an audience! What's the matter with us? Are we so desperate for entertainment that we have to go looking to the evening news for it? We need to take responsibility for our choices, too.

It's bad enough that we consume this stuff, but we're setting up future generations to make the same bad choices we're making. Our kids come home from school and flip on *Jerry Springer*. That becomes their source of information. They're even more impressionable than we are. Why would we allow them to watch this stuff?

The news media have no business trying to entertain us. Their job is to provide us with reliable facts so we can make up our own minds about what's going on. They have no business telling us what to think. It's our responsibility to do the thinking. When we become passive consumers and allow them to do our thinking for us, we've agreed to let them lead us into any opinion they like. But don't forget, a sound opinion isn't their goal. Their goal is profit, no matter what the social cost. They're getting fat off our appetite for sleaze. If we don't speak up and tell them to knock it off, what's their incentive to stop?

How Can We Make the Media Behave?

I'm luckier than many other public figures because I have an effective weapon against the misinformation of the media: my own radio show. When *Lunch With the Governor* broadcasts on WCCO each Friday, I have a solid hour where there's no barrier between me and the public. The local media rail against the show, because they don't like it that I've found a way around them. They hate it that I have an opportunity to tell the people directly about the way the media have manipulated them on a given issue.

My opponents in the legislature now have a radio show called *Facts and Snacks* that comes on after mine for a half hour. They never do anything except try to deflect whatever issues I bring up. When they found out I was doing my show, they demanded that they be given equal time—as though the governor is somehow naturally in opposition to the legislature.

I use the radio show just to help me stay in touch with people. I try to offer positive messages. I end every show telling people not to drink and drive "because I have the best state troopers in the country and we'll get you, because it's our job, and we're good."

Joe Soucheray thinks all the people who call my show are boot-lickers. He and others have accused me of only taking positive callers. But we don't screen the calls, except to ask them to stay on topic. If you don't do that with a talk radio format, you get everybody who has a personal mission; if these people get an opportunity to air their personal agendas, they'll do it. Then you can't have a reasonable dis-cussion on anything. It breaks up the flow of the show.

I think my callers are just regular people who have the opportu-nity to call up and say, "Governor, we see what you're going through and we're with you all the way. Don't think you're standing alone. We're on to what they're trying to do to you and we support you."

That's why the media hate the show—they want to be the middle men. If I'm debunking things they've done, and exposing their tac-tics, that makes them look bad. Since I've been doing my show, I've had people call in and confirm what I'm saying—people who have talked to the media and then seen how mangled and misleading their quote comes out looking. They tell me, "God, they didn't even print the point that I was trying to make." And when they realize that I have to go through that day in and day out, these people become very sympathetic with me.

So what's the best way to keep the media from getting out of hand? Should the media be policed by a government committee? Absolutely not! Because who would police the committee? We'd be in for another type of McCarthyism. If the government starts to gain too much power over what the media can and can't say, we're getting too close to the situation the Founding Fathers were trying to avoid.

Should the media be made to police itself, the way lawyers police themselves through state bars? I doubt it would work, because the media have the First Amendment to hide behind.

Would it work to come up with some kind of citizens' watchdog organization designed to hold the media responsible? If we can't trust them to police themselves, and if we can't allow the government to have that large a measure of control over them, then we the consumers are the only ones left in that triangle. A citizens' watchdog group wouldn't be immune to corruption, either, but it would be less susceptible to it than the other two alternatives. A group like that could speak out whenever a journalist or news organization began to get out of line. It could keep the public informed of the various media's misbehavior. And it could relay the public's expectations to the media. I don't know how effective a group like that might be. But it might be worth a try.

It's a shame that the necessity exists for private citizens to use their personal time this way, but sometimes we do have to step in and perform this kind of chore. This is an example of what Jefferson meant by "eternal vigilance."

PICK YOUR NEWS

There's only one sure power that we have over the media, and that's our power of choice. Television, radio, newspapers, and magazines are all capitalist ventures; they only survive if they supply something the public wants. If we don't want our news to degenerate into soap operas, we've got to vote with our pocketbooks. We've got to be responsible news consumers, and pick the news outlets that behave responsibly.

As a society, we have to become much clearer on what is and is not newsworthy. News is the stuff that affects the public at large. If it affects only me and my family, it's not news. My personal life is nobody's business but mine. I'm a governor, that's the reason I'm in the public eye. All I ask is that you judge me on the things that affect my ability to govern. Any time the media start concentrating on something other than the issues that affect the public, they've overstepped their bounds, and it's up to us to nip it in the bud.

LET 'EM HAVE IT

We can also influence the media's output by speaking up and making our expectations clear. When they focus on scandal instead of the news, when they report intrigue instead of facts, we need to voice our disapproval. We need to call and write, even threaten to cancel our subscriptions and switch to competitors' programs if need be. They're a commercial enterprise; it behooves them to listen to their customers. If enough of us speak our minds, they'll pay attention.

Of course, I can't say all these negative things about the media without also acknowledging the people who are doing a good job. There are a few outstanding exceptions. The national press doesn't go in for nearly as much of the sensationalism and character assassination as the local media do. Chris Matthews (whose show, *Hardball,* is one of the better programs out there) and Geraldo Rivera have always treated me fairly. They ask good questions. They don't take cheap shots. They don't seem to be saying, the way the local media do, "Let's take this guy down. He must have a skeleton in his closet, and by God we're gonna find it!"

I have the utmost respect for Sam Donaldson, Cokie Roberts, and George Will. Their show's people complimented me off camera once. They said, "We love to have you on because you're the only one who can make George Will back up and take a breath." I think they find me refreshing because when they ask me a question, they're not going to get the typical politician's dance around the issues. With most politicians, when you ask them a question, they go right into the Tiny Tim routine, tiptoeing through the tulips.

Tim Russert of *Meet the Press* has been a good sport. I've had some fun with him. You've probably seen how often the media like to get me on their shows, and then they put up some bizarre picture of me from my wrestling days, where I'm wearing a pink boa, and they say, "Look, there's the *Governor of Minnesota!* "

Well, I couldn't pass up the opportunity to turn the tables, just once. One of Tim's old college classmates sent us a photo of Tim from back in his college days. In this photo, Tim could be the twin brother to the Meathead, Rob Reiner's character in *All in the Family.* The same beard. The same hair to the shoulders.

So the next time I went on *Meet the Press* with Tim, I came prepared. He just happened to start talking at one point about some photo of me, and I said, "Speaking of photos, Tim . . ." and I whipped out this college photo and asked the camera guys to zoom in on it. I said, "I want people to see the real Tim Russert!" I could tell he was really embarrassed. But he handled it like the good sport he is.

4

Getting Back to Constitutional Principles

*T*_he cause of America is in great measure the cause of all mankind._

—Thomas Paine

A paper in Billings, Montana, recently put a vile story about me on the Internet. An elderly man and woman who own a bar out there swear that I was there in 1987. They were positive it was me. They said I was there with three or four hunting buddies from Minnesota. They said we came in the bar, and I yanked a dancer off the stage and was harassing her. They said they were forced to go get her husband, who came in and stuck a gun in my crotch.

Now, this story made me especially angry, first of all, because I view that as a crime. That's assault. And, number two: I didn't do it! I've never hunted in Montana. They were sure it was me, because I was a great big hulking guy with a shaved head. They recognized me.

Well, there's a problem there, because in 1987, I had hair. I didn't start shaving my head until the early nineties, when I shaved everything except the ponytail in the back. I didn't start going completely clean-shaven until I decided to run for governor, because I knew the ponytail wouldn't fly.

That shows you how fraudulent the story was. Yet they printed it and put it on the Internet. The writer defended it, because he said he could tell the people weren't lying. And then the story made its way here, where a local gossip columnist known as C. J. put it in her column.

I had a very high-octane meeting with the people behind the article, in which they tried to blame us for letting them print it. They said they had called my press office, and had been told that I had things to do and didn't have time to meet with them over it. So without any further corroboration, they ran with the story.

Their other line was, "Well, it's been on the Internet for three days now and you didn't have anything to say about it." I said, "Anyone can put anything on the Internet. It's not my job to police the Internet and verify everything that's said. If you put something on there, it's your job to make sure it's sound."

I'd had my first taste of how fraudulent information in the Internet can be when I put my Porsche up for sale on one of the big Web auction houses. I got bids of $100,000 for it—and they turned out to be phony. And the people at the newspaper reported those bids, too, as though they were truthful. I called them on it: "So you've allowed people to believe that I sold a ten-year-old Porsche for $100,000 when it isn't true?"

They apologized in the paper the next day. But I always wonder, out of all those people who read the original article, how many also happened to read the apology? Retractions are nice to get because they prove your innocence. But there's no guarantee when you get them that irreversible damage hasn't already been done.

To keep myself from getting too mad at stuff like this, which happens just about every day, I always remember what my friend Arnold Schwarzenegger told me: "If you're making the tabloids with all their lies, that's when you know you've made it big."

Whenever I challenge journalists for not verifying their stories, or for the way they stick in their opinions as though they were fact, they almost always defend themselves under the premise of freedom of the press. They interpret the First Amendment as giving them the right to say anything they want and present it as the truth. To me, that's a symptom that we as a society, and maybe journalists in particular, have lost sight of what the writers of the Constitution intended. Do you really believe that the Founding Fathers meant the First Amendment to be a license to lie?

When our Founding Fathers sat down to create a government for our new country, they were still fresh from battle. It had only been a handful of years since they fought with King George over their basic rights to freedom. They were still stinging from the slap in the face of tyranny. They didn't want to see the same thing happen to their brand-new nation that had happened under British rule. So they decided to put together a system of government that would be as tyranny-proof and corruption-resistant as they could possibly make it. The Founding Fathers knew they were part of a great experiment that, if it worked, could point the way for all human societies.

The Constitution they wrote is pure genius. It reads more like a mission statement than an instruction manual. It's full of "majestic generalities," as Judge Robert H. Jackson put it; it sketches the broad principles and leaves the details up to us. That way, it's flexible enough to adapt to changing times. And it has: More than two hundred years later, it's still working. It works as well for today's high-tech America, with our hundreds of millions of people, as it did for postcolonial America with a few hundred thousand.

We're still part of that great experiment today. Two hundred years is not that long when you consider how big an innovation the Constitution is. We are still perfecting our union, by trial and error.

You'll often hear politicians and lawyers talking about interpreting the Constitution in terms of "getting back to the Founding Fathers' original intent." But you know what? We can't. The Constitution is such an open-ended framework that even in their time it had to be interpreted. Maybe that's why they wrote it that way: because even back then, there was a lot of argument going on over the meaning of lofty principles like "free speech" and "due process."

The Constitution is constantly being interpreted, mostly by the judges of the Supreme Court. We're always looking to it for answers. But the truth is, it can't answer all of our questions, it can only inform our decisions. That's what it was really meant to do.

The philosophical ideas that led to the Constitution were radical for their day. In the centuries before the American Revolution, people were taught to believe that kings were appointed by God. Can you imagine what kind of guts it took to go up against that? But the Founding Fathers believed that even a king didn't have the right to take away people's basic freedom. And even more radically, they believed that if a king did begin robbing people of their rights, it was the people's job to pitch him out!

The Founding Fathers were deeply suspicious of government. They viewed it as a necessary evil, which was meant to put everyone under a small amount of constraint so that they could enjoy a large amount of freedom. You think we're negative about government today? Our Founding Fathers were so cynical about government that they only wanted enough of it to do what was necessary, and not an inch more. They understood that the only reason we needed government was because morality alone wasn't enough to do the trick.

It was a new and radical way of thinking at that time in history to say that the kind of government that served humankind the best was whatever gave them the most freedom and security. In a short span of time, we went from a system that believed in a king appointed by God to a system that said that people had a right to choose for themselves whatever brings them the most happiness, and that the only limit to that pursuit is where it interferes with someone else's right to happiness.

WHAT'S A RIGHT?

I think we need to spend some time talking about what the authors of the Constitution meant by rights, because today more than ever before, people make a lot of noise about their rights without having a good understanding of what that term means in the Constitution.

According to the Declaration of Independence, we are entitled to life, liberty, and the pursuit of happiness. Those are "natural rights." Our rights are automatic simply because we're human; they're not "granted" by the government. Government's job is to protect the rights we already have.

But does that mean our rights are guaranteed no matter what? Not exactly. To a large extent, they're conditional upon our behavior. If you start messing with somebody else's rights, the government will come in and take away some of yours. In order for rights to be meaningful at all, they have to be viewed as a hierarchy, with the right to be alive at the top. Your right to breathe, for example, takes precedence over my right to smoke. Our rights are constrained to an extent by their effect on others. They're not absolute.

THE PRICE OF FREEDOM

Most of the talk about rights in the Constitution is in the context of our right to be protected from the government. The Founding Fathers knew that a true government of the people was rare. History makes it look like the most natural form of government is dominance and subordination. They were sure that any government they created was going to tend toward corruption. So they built into the Constitution a series of checks and balances to keep government under tight restraint.

The authority of our government is limited very strictly. The Constitution states clearly that it has authority only so long as it serves the people. If at any time the people determine that it's not serving us anymore, we have a right—you might even read it as saying we have an *obligation*—to amend it. The original Constitution, which is the source of our government's authority, was ratified by the people, who are still considered the source of its authority.

The Constitution is still the direct and ultimate operations manual in our government. All elected officials are directly responsible to the Constitution. Article 6 of the Constitution declares that "all holders of public office must swear first and foremost to support and protect the Constitution." I took that oath when I became governor of Minnesota, and so did every other public servant elected to office. It's our most sacred duty.

Amendment Number One: Freedom of Speech and Thought

Amendment I:
Congress shall make no law respecting an establishment of religion, or prohibiting the free exercise thereof; or abridging the freedom of speech, or of the press; or the right of the people peaceably to assemble, and to petition the Government for a redress of grievances.

The Founding Fathers made it very clear that free speech was a necessary part of a true democratic republic. The people had to be free to critique their government and their society, even if their views were unpopular. Without free speech, how would we recognize the truth if we heard it?

Free speech and a diverse range of available opinion makes for a higher quality, more tyranny-proof government, because it gives us a chance to engage our thinking skills. In a society in which the public is told what to think—a dictatorship, for example—people soon begin to stop questioning authority. Hitler used the control of information to his advantage in Nazi Germany. He gave a troubled public a scapegoat for all their problems, and he reinforced his message daily, until it became much easier for the public to go

The first principle of a free society is an untrammeled flow of words in an open forum.

—Adlai Stevenson

along with it than it was to swim against the tide. That's how a whole society of otherwise ordinary people came to accept and participate in the most horrible atrocities of the last century.

The Khmer Rouge also used the same technique. They tried to replace their society's history with their own revised version. To do so, they exterminated artists, scholars, and anyone else whose knowledge contradicted them. As long as the public had no access to any other version of history, they wouldn't have the means to challenge it. That's why it's so important for us to protect diversity of opinion: because it's the best way for us to hang on to our autonomy of thought.

And there's another reason why free speech is important to our nation: It makes room for individualism. Individualism is a huge asset to a society: It's what makes visionaries and scientists and problem-solvers. Societies that have only narrow, restrictive roles for their citizens to fit themselves into don't generally produce great people. Where individualism is encouraged, it creates a world where geniuses and artists can grow. And free speech, by giving individuals a means to express themselves, encourages that individuality.

The First Amendment protects everybody's opinion, no matter how brilliant or how stupid. The honorable and the obnoxious alike have the right to speak. That's the ironic thing about democracy: It goes out of its way to protect everyone's right to slam it, no matter how ridiculously or undeservedly.

One of the few times the government is allowed to limit free speech is when that speech specifically creates a "clear and present danger." You could stand on the top of Target Center and yell, "All left-handed blondes with freckles should be shot!" And the government will stand behind your right to say that. But if you say, "Go get an Uzi, find a left-handed, freckled blonde, aim at the heart, and pull the trigger," your days of public oratory are going to be over for a while!

Another limitation on speech has to do with what is known as commercial speech. For example, false and misleading advertising is illegal, because the harm to the consuming public is greater than any benefit to be gained by protecting the right to lie. Also, you can be sued for making false and defamatory statements about other people that damage their reputation.

THE DIFFERENCE BETWEEN FREEDOM AND LIBERTY

But don't forget that just because we're free to say just about whatever we want, it doesn't mean we're at liberty to say it no matter what the consequences to anyone else. Freedom and liberty are often used to mean the same thing, but there's a connotative difference. Freedom means you are allowed to act autonomously. Liberty means your actions are without restraint of any kind. The difference I see there is the difference between self-control and no control.

The First Amendment can be abused, just as any part of the Constitution can be. Don't forget, as you're arguing for your right to say whatever you want wherever you want, that the Founding Fathers didn't say we had *liberty of speech*. They specifically said "freedom." The word *liberty* doesn't carry any implied responsibility; the word *freedom* does. The way I interpret their choice is that there is control implied, but that it's supposed to come from us, and not from the government. The Founding Fathers trusted us to govern ourselves when it came to the issue of responsible free speech.

Free speech can be abused, and it often is. But the government is severely limited in its ability to do anything about free speech abuse, because it's constitutionally forbidden to get into the business of telling us what we can and cannot say. Obviously, the more the government controls our speech, the less free it's going to get. There's a conflict of interest any time the government gets into that realm.

HOW CAN FREE SPEECH HURT ANYBODY?

The Founding Fathers, Jefferson in particular, were very clear that the government had no jurisdiction over speech and thought, only over actions. After all, how can words hurt anybody? But even the Founding Fathers understood that words can trigger reactions, and over the decades and centuries since the Constitution was written, our legislature has found that there are times when it has to step in and control speech that produces harmful reactions. You're not allowed to verbally threaten, or directly advocate, bodily harm to anyone. And you don't have the right to say things that cause people to panic, unless there's an immediate reason to do so. The classic example of this is yelling "fire" in a crowded theater. You won't find too many people who will argue with controlling these kinds of speech.

But what about pornography? Does the government have any business controlling so-called obscene speech and images? You could argue that pornography is offensive, but is it harmful?

Now here's where things get particularly dicey. You can make a great case that pornography is *potentially* harmful, because of the fact that it encourages people to think of sex in ways that are degrading to other people's dignity and discouraging to personal responsibility. And any time people head down that road, the quality of our society suffers. But should the government step in any time there's *potential* harm? Do you realize how much government regulation that could lead to, if anything that *might* be harmful had to be controlled by the government? Jefferson made it clear that the government can only step in when there's action involved. We have to stay focused on prosecuting the harmful action, not the potential harm.

Now, I'm no fan of pornography, but the way I see it, it's an issue of free will. You could throw pornographic images at me all day long and it wouldn't change the values that I hold about sex. On the other hand, someone else could be completely deprived of pornography, and be fed all the right social messages about self-control and responsibility and respecting the dignity of others, and would still forever choose to see other people as nothing but objects for his or her own sexual gratification. I'm not saying we have some kind of "right" to pornography. But we do have a right to keep the government from making choices that we, as responsible, free adults, should be making for ourselves.

But the minute we switch the scenario from adults and start talking about pornography and children, it's a whole different ball game. I absolutely draw the line at making pornography available to children. Why? Because they're children! They haven't yet developed the skills and maturity and self-control to make choices about a thing like pornography. That's what parents are for: to help them develop those skills. Children are very impressionable. Parents who want to teach their children to respect their sexuality and the sexuality of others shouldn't have to be undermined by the allure of pornography.

So even though I think the government has no business banning pornography, I think it's perfectly reasonable to limit the outlets of pornographic speech and images. It shouldn't be on billboards or in public areas, and it shouldn't be anywhere where it could be made available to children. Children don't have a "right" to pornography, because rights carry responsibilities, and they're not ready for the responsibilities inherent in that right.

WHEN FREE SPEECH GETS TAKEN TO STUPID EXTREMES

Does the First Amendment's guarantee of free speech mean that you have the right to speak your mind anywhere you want? If you submit an op-ed piece to a newspaper and they don't want to print it, are they stomping on your rights? Obviously they're not. If you want to, you're free to start up your own newspaper and print whatever you want. With the advent of the Internet, a lot of people are doing just that. The Constitution doesn't guarantee you an outlet for what you have to say.

A prime example of what I'm talking about is the way a lot of people have come to view the National Endowment for the Arts and other programs that use taxpayers' money to pay artists to create different kinds of "symbolic speech." I don't think the government has any business using our money that way. If we want to patronize the arts, we can do that any day of the week, but why should we be forced to pay for it?

Artists who sell their work commercially or who work under private grants are beholden to the public and to their patrons. Their work has to be meaningful to its intended audience or the artist doesn't make a living. Now, don't get confused between being paid to do it and being *allowed* to do it: There's nothing stopping any of us from painting or composing or indulging in whatever creative expression we want in our own free time. But if an artist wants to make a living out of his or her art, it has to be of meaning or value to someone who is willing to pay for it.

Not so with the NEA. As an arm of the government, the NEA is in the awkward position of handing out the cash without being able to place any conditions on what it gets for that money, because for the government to limit what an artist can "say," verbally or symbolically, is a breach of the First Amendment. And so you often get government-sponsored art that would probably never make it in a commercial venue.

Now the thing is, I know that public arts endowments also give us things like *Sesame Street,* which are educational in nature, and might not be able to survive in a purely commercial market. But when we allow taxpayers' money to be spent on the arts, we inevitably get into a tangle over what art serves the public good and what doesn't. And eventually, there's the inevitable yahoo that sticks a cross in a jar of urine, calls it art, and demands that the taxpayers pay him for it. And if the government says no, he starts squealing about censorship, claiming that we've taken away his free speech.

You have a right to say whatever you want, verbally or symbolically, but that doesn't mean you have a right to get a government handout for it. It also doesn't mean you have a right to speak through any particular medium. The First Amendment only guarantees your right to speak, not your right to be financially compensated for your speech, and not your right to speak through whatever medium you choose. The First Amendment only gives us the right to speak our minds. It leaves the avenue for that speech up to us.

YES, YOU'RE ENTITLED TO YOURS, BUT . . .

There's a very dangerous idea kicking around out there that because the First Amendment gives us all equal rights to free speech, all viewpoints are equally valid. That's an incredibly dangerous line of thinking, and it threatens to undermine the main benefit that free speech was supposed to give us: the opportunity to decide for ourselves what opinion to hold.

Not all opinions are equal. Not all opinions are valid. Some people form their opinions by an objective search for facts; others may form them by deciding what opinion makes them look good, then go looking for "evidence" that they can use, or misinterpret, or even outright lie about, to shore up their point of view. That's why it's so important for us to consider the source, and to examine the motives that might be driving somebody to choose a particular opinion.

The First Amendment was never intended to say that all opinions are equal. In fact, you could even argue that it was intended to do the opposite. By allowing all viewpoints to be exposed to the light, it was meant to reveal which ones had no legs to stand on.

Sometimes these days you'll hear someone casually toss off the idea that truth is in the eye of the beholder, as though there were no ultimate reality. This is a dangerous idea, because if there is no objective truth, then all viewpoints are equivalent. You'll occasionally hear a well-meaning person say that we mustn't call Hitler evil, because he was entitled to his views and we certainly don't want to pass judgment on him. You tell me where thinking like that will lead us!

Now, there's a part of that idea that makes sense: None of us has a direct line to the truth. All of our viewpoints are flawed to one extent or another. But that's our problem, it's not reality's problem. It means we need to work hard to improve our thinking skills and we need to become conscious of our biases. It doesn't mean we abandon the search for truth.

THOU SHALT NOT OFFEND: POLITICAL CORRECTNESS HAS GOTTEN OUT OF HAND

I remember back in the mid-eighties when I first started hearing the term *politically correct*. It was usually considered a good thing. It forced us to take a look at the way we were using language, and it shone a new light on some of the bad stereotypes we were unintentionally reinforcing. Remember that? Suddenly we were looking at words like *handicapped* and realizing that it sounded like we were saying people with disabilities went around looking for a handout!

But over time, the concept got out of hand. It got co-opted by groups that were going beyond just raising the public's awareness, who started using the concept for shock value, to try to get a rise out of people. That's when we started getting Native American groups protesting Disney's *Pocahontas* movie, saying it advocated child molesting. "Huh?" you say? Well, even though the Pocahontas in the movie was portrayed as a teenager, the real Pocahontas was only about twelve, which in their minds meant John Smith was robbing the cradle! Never mind that in the Powhatan tribe at that time in history, that's the age at which most girls did get married.

Political correctness has gotten so overly sensitive that it seems like nobody can take a joke. When I went on David Letterman's show in February of 1999, I made an offhand joke about the streets of Saint Paul being laid out by drunken Irishmen. Suddenly, headlines were popping up everywhere calling me anti-Irish! They printed the comments of an irate Irishman whom I'd horribly offended. Of course, what they didn't tell you is they went out looking for an offended Irishman. They had to look pretty hard. They kept interviewing Irish people until they found one who was offended. Who knows how many people they had to talk to before they found one?

Political correctness is supposed to be linked with tolerance; I'm sure originally it was meant to apply equally to everyone. But now that it's been commandeered for political agendas, it doesn't apply to everybody anymore. Case in point: You can bash men all day and nobody will say anything. Look how many TV commercials portray men as imbeciles who can't even operate a washing machine. Next time you go to the movies, count how many times men get whacked in the groin. But don't you dare turn that same treatment on women! Christianity is okay to make fun of and misrepresent and portray as corrupt—count how many times you've seen priests casually depicted as child molesters. But Wiccans and New-Agers are off-limits; you're not allowed to joke about them or portray them as corrupt. If political correctness were actually being universally applied, there would be just as much outrage no matter who was being bashed.

But because it's become agendized, political correctness often nitpicks on small, individual offenses and misses the bigger picture. Case in point: Atlanta Braves pitcher John Rocker's disgusting anti-immigrant comments to *Sports Illustrated* in 1999. Rocker complained about New York being full of Asians, Koreans, Vietnamese, Indians, Russians, and Spanish people, and he said, "How the hell did they get into this country?" The bastions of political correctness jumped all over him for that—as well they should have. But aren't they missing the bigger picture?

John Rocker is just one man; our professional sports are loaded with racist stereotypes. Native Americans have complained for years that they don't like being made into mascots. Personally, I think the name *Redskins* is offensive. When I was a commentator, I refused to use it. I just referred to the team as *Washington*. The name is a left-over from a more racist era, and we should get rid of it. Can you imagine if somebody tried to name a team that way today? Can you imagine if they tried to start up the Philadelphia Dagos? Or the Baltimore Mackerel-Snappers?

How come professional sports as a whole can get away with this garbage, but if an individual does it, he's liable to lose his livelihood? Which is the bigger problem, one man with a misguided attitude, or an entire industry that profits from an offensive racial bias, that almost everybody just seems to go along with?

Not one media outlet took on this hypocrisy. They were all too busy denouncing Rocker as a terrible role model. I've got news for you: John Rocker got into sports because he was talented at throwing a ball, not because he was a great leader. Why do we even have this expectation that sports figures are supposed to be role models? I believe that the media missed an opportunity to bring a larger problem to light.

The Constitution only guarantees us free speech. It doesn't have the power to affect the quality of our speech. That's up to us. If we want free speech to be meaningful, we have to be willing to reflect on how we're using it. The Constitution grants us the right; the responsibility is up to us.

Amendment Number One:
Religious Freedom

*R*eligion is a matter which lies solely between a
man and his God . . . he owes account to none
other for his faith or his worship.

—Thomas Jefferson

In the middle of the fallout from the *Playboy* interview, Gary Bauer
and Geraldine Ferraro both got on national television and called me a
bigot. More than a little perplexed, I looked it up in the dictionary: Big-
ots are people who are tolerant only of their own religion. That word
doesn't apply to me: I don't care what people want to worship! I often
wonder what would happen if I sat Gary Bauer and Geraldine Ferraro
both down on national television and read them that definition.

I think the quickest way to ruin genuine faith in this country
would be to try to force everybody to worship in a way that wasn't of
their own choosing, or in a way that was contrary to their upbringing. Ultimately, I believe we all worship the same God anyway, but in
different ways. For all I know, God might appreciate the diversity.

The Founding Fathers back me up on this one. The First Amendment offers the same protection for religious freedom—even the
freedom *not* to be religious if we don't want to be—as it does for
freedom of speech and thought. The First Amendment basically says
that religion is none of the government's business. The only circum-
stance in which government is allowed to restrict religious or antireligious behavior is when it endangers somebody's physical health.
You can't, for example, sacrifice a human being to your gods. The
government has stepped in on this issue from time to time. It has
ordered a blood transfusion to save a child's life in spite of the religious objection of the parents. And it once told a bunch of Christians
who handled poisonous snakes to knock it off.

You'd never know it from the way popular culture portrays us today, but we are a profoundly religious country. Religion is woven all through our society. Religion is still going strong in America today, while in other postindustrial societies, particularly in Europe, it looks like it might be fading out.

We probably have the First Amendment to thank for the strength of religion in America. In other countries where religion has been controlled by the power hungry and forced on the unwilling, people got sick of it over the centuries. They came to see religious leaders as hypocrites and hucksters, and came to think of religious doctrine as a means for the few in power to manipulate the masses. By contrast, in America, it's very hard for people to corrupt religion to serve their own means, because the government is not allowed to get involved with religion, and we are all free to believe whatever we want.

It's extremely important for a society like ours to keep government and religion separate. But it's tough to do. Take a dollar out of your wallet and look at it: Whose name is on there? How do you think that makes an atheist feel?

Church and state are brought together in insidious ways sometimes. I recently gave a talk at Elk River High School, a public school here in Minnesota. But before I got up to give my talk, they had an ordained minister lead everybody in a prayer. Now, it happened to be a prayer in my own religion, Christianity. But imagine how that might have felt to a Muslim or a Hindu?

I'll show you another way that church and state are inseparable in our minds. How easy do you think it would be for an atheist to get elected in this country? The vast majority of atheists aren't bad people; they have principles and morals. Many atheists even respect the convictions of religious people. What's to say that an atheist wouldn't make a great leader? But in many ways, we have a bias against atheists similar to the one we have against gays and lesbians. In many cases, an openly homosexual candidate wouldn't stand a chance of getting elected, either.

We all like to think church and state are separate. But they're not as separate as we believe. Maybe there is no way to completely separate them.

In our nation's history, there have been all kinds of passionate debate over what the Founding Fathers intended by the separation of church and state. It's pretty much a done deal that we don't interpret it today the way it was interpreted when it was first written. People are usually shocked to find out that in Thomas Jefferson's day, church services were held every Sunday in the Supreme Court chambers. Jefferson himself, the author of our doctrine on the separation between church and state, attended those services regularly. Can you imagine the stink people would raise if the Supreme Court tried that today?

There is no way for us to understand the full scope of the First Amendment's original intent. But it does seem pretty clear that a major worry on the Founding Fathers' minds was that a corrupt government might start using religion to manipulate people. Religious belief can be a powerful tool in the hands of the corrupt. Just look at what the Church was doing in Europe during the Middle Ages. At the very least, the Founding Fathers intended the First Amendment to keep the government from establishing a "national church" that it could use to coerce people into doing what it wanted. That much is clear.

Was it intended to mean anything else? It's hard to know. But the fact that we have gotten much stricter over the last century or two about keeping government from interfering in religion is probably a good thing, given that our nation has become so much more spiritually diverse. With the influx of immigrants from all over the world, we've got a pretty good sampling of just about every religion in the world. In a society like that, you don't want the government playing favorites with any one religion.

The First Amendment was aimed at controlling the government's involvement with religion. But the fact that you're constitutionally guaranteed the right to practice religion in any way you wish also deters anyone else from gaining too much control over the populace. It ensures you the freedom to vote with your feet if you decide your religious leader is full of baloney. I think that's one reason why religion has endured so strongly in this country: Our freedom of worship helps to weed out the charlatans and keeps our confidence in religious institutions strong.

Even though we benefit from it, we are still trying to work out the exact definition of the separation of church and state. We've never been entirely clear where the line should be drawn, and we may never be. The First Amendment has been giving the Supreme Court headaches for centuries, because the way it's worded implies a delicate balance. There's been a whole handful of court cases where the first part of the phrase, "Congress shall make no law respecting an establishment of religion," comes into conflict with the second part, ". . . or prohibiting the free exercise thereof." By tradition, the judges have come to see that as meaning that the government can neither encourage nor discourage any particular religion. It has to hit that fine line between the two, and remain completely neutral.

Over time it's been accepted that the government can't raise tax dollars to support churches of any kind. There are other countries in which people have to fill out on their tax form what church they belong to, and part of their tax money goes to that church. Our government couldn't do that constitutionally, but it can give tax money to religious organizations for nonreligious purposes. For example, it does make federal money available to college students who want to go to religious schools. The thinking there is that if they only made it available to students going to nonreligious schools, it would look too much like it was discouraging the religious school in favor of the secular. The Supreme Court decided that this was okay, because the primary purpose of the money is education, not religion.

But there are cases where the balance gets tricky. Can you put up a nativity set on public property at Christmastime? Obviously, if you got one of those big tacky plastic nativity scenes, with garish paint and light bulbs inside all the figures, and set it up in the rotunda of the capitol, you would make it look like the government was specifically pro-Christian. But what about a small, subtle nativity scene set up in a public park, along with a menorah and a Kwanza display? If you carry the issue to its extreme, you ban government from even acknowledging that at the end of December, the vast majority of its people are celebrating some kind of religious or spiritual festival. That extreme is the side you hear a lot of arguments coming down on today: Government should treat religion as though it's invisible.

But by being so afraid to go anywhere near a religious event or topic, the government soon begins to look like it's discouraging religious practice. The issue over school prayer is a prime example of how sticky this can get. The Supreme Court has repeatedly said no to public school systems that have tried to start their school day with a reading from the Bible or a nondenominational prayer—as well they should: Public schools have no business using their authority to advocate religion. But how far do you want to take that? Do you want to say that nobody can pray if they're inside a public building, in case they might offend somebody?

Public worship is one of those tricky issues that unfortunately gets drawn up along political lines. Both the Religious Right and the far liberal Left have taken the issue of the government's role in religion to ridiculous extremes.

WHERE THE RELIGIOUS RIGHT MISSED THE CONSTITUTIONAL BOAT

In spite of the fact that the Constitution is very clear about this, there are still people among the Religious Right who are pushing to have Christianity declared the official state and national religion. They can make you some halfway decent arguments for making English the official language, so why not extend that to religion? They point to the decline of our nation's morals and they claim that

Christian discipline would raise the moral standard of this country. They argue that the Founding Fathers were Christian, so why shouldn't the nation be?

Sure, most of the Founding Fathers were Christian, but so what? They had the perfect opportunity to establish Christianity as the national religion, and they chose not to. In fact, they strictly forbade it. And back then, Christians were an even greater majority than they are today. Non-Christians were almost unheard of in the colonies. But the Founding Fathers were clear that you don't appoint a religion just because it's popular. They were far-reaching enough in their vision to realize that where you get authority, you get corruption. Religious authority alone can be vastly powerful. Couple that with the power of government, and you've created a monster. You could argue that the separation of church and state deters both institutions from corruption by cutting their power in half.

And if you get anywhere near the Religious Right, you immediately get a whiff of corruption. They're guilty of some of the most non-Christian behavior around. They themselves stand as the perfect argument against mingling church with state. The Religious Right are terrible representatives of Christian values. Jesus himself argued for peace and tolerance. Diversity didn't bother him; he was always reaching out to people that the rest of his society wouldn't go near. Christianity has always been about free will. It's all about loving God and your fellow man. And loving is the one thing you can't force anyone to do.

The Right's other big scam is going into science classes in public schools and trying to replace evolution science with what they call "creation science," as if there could be such a thing. The Right argues that by teaching evolution instead of creation, public schools are undermining kids' religious beliefs. They see evolutionism and creationism as somehow being equivalent kinds of knowledge, so that one cancels out the other. That's bull.

Evolution and creationism are two totally separate systems of knowledge. One's a scientific theory, the other is a religious doctrine. It's not like comparing Baptist doctrine to Catholic doctrine; it's like comparing the law of gravity to the Sermon on the Mount. It's beyond comparing apples and oranges, it's like comparing apples and uranium!

Any good science class will teach you what scientific theory is all about. Science can't actually prove anything true; it can only prove something false. Any scientific theory that has been around awhile is only around because it hasn't been proven false yet. That's the way science works. Evolution is a theory, just like the theory of relativity. It's hung around so long because it's an extremely effective way of explaining biological phenomena. It's been backed up a thousand different ways by scientific data. You'll never hear a decent scientist calling it "truth," because science doesn't deal in the truth, but it's one of the most valid theories you'll ever find.

Evolution gives us a lot of information about how life behaves, but the most hard-core evolutionist in the world can't tell you the "truth" about how life began. There are half a dozen theories out there on trial, but they're only theories. If data comes along that disproves any of them, we'll chuck them out. That's the main difference between science and religious doctrine.

Creationism is based solely on the Bible. Whereas science has to be open to all possibilities, creationism is totally closed to the possibility that what it has to say isn't correct. That right there takes it completely out of the realm of science. There are people out there so desperate to believe that creationism is science that they've put together a thing called "creation science," but it's not a real science, because it only looks for evidence to back itself up. And most of the "evidence" creation "scientists" come up with is shaky at best.

Evolution isn't out to disprove the biblical version of creation. It can't even touch the question of whether or not there's an all-powerful Being out there making it all happen, because that's beyond the realm of science. Science can only deal with what's observable and definable and measurable. That's why there's value in religious doctrines like creationism; in its proper place, creationism can do something that evolution, or any other scientific theory, could never touch: It can give life meaning. Science is very pragmatic; it's great at showing us relationships and causes and systems. But it can't ever tell us what it all means. Both evolutionism and the biblical version of creation are powerful, but only when properly used. I believe we need *both* kinds of knowledge.

So does that mean we should teach "evolution science" and "creation science" side by side? Not quite. We should leave evolution to the science teacher, and creation to the Sunday school teacher or the private religious school teacher. Since creationism comes from a specific religious tradition, and can't be separated from religious belief, the only place it has in public school is in the context of a comparative religions or comparative literature class.

WHERE THE LIBERAL LEFT MISSED THE CONSTITUTIONAL BOAT

In spite of the fact that there are plenty of sincerely religious people in the liberal Left, the trend that many seem to be following today is almost blatantly antireligious. I don't know whether or not they mean to be. But they have taken their position to such a ridiculous extreme that they're actually getting in the way of free religious practice. They're so adamant about rooting out any form of prayer or religious display from public property that they're encroaching on people's freedom.

I see a huge difference between barring public officials from leading prayers and barring the public itself from praying. How can you tell somebody they're not allowed to pray? How would you stop them? How is that anything but a violation of the First Amendment?

If you go tell a bunch of school kids they're not allowed to pray when they feel like it, you're directly violating the "free exercise" clause.

There's a really absurd idea on the far reaches of the liberal Left that any time anybody is overtly religious in public, they're breaching somebody else's rights to be nonreligious, or to be religious in some other way. Some people on the far liberal Left seem to think nobody should even be seen practicing religion, for fear that those outside a given faith might feel "pressured." But what happens to the kid who just wants to wear his cross to school, or his Magen David, or any other symbol of his religion, because it's important to him? Isn't that "pressuring" him *not* to practice his faith?

IS THERE A HAPPY MEDIUM?

The bottom line, in my opinion, is that both the Religious Right's attempts to get control of how we worship, and the far liberal Left's attempts to ban religious expression in public are unconstitutional. The First Amendment prohibits government from interfering in either direction. If the two most vocal positions on this issue weren't at each others' throats all the time, they could be working together to brainstorm some ways to work it so that kids who wanted to pray during school hours could, and those who didn't wouldn't feel pressured. How about a "quiet room," that could function as a nondenominational chapel? The army has chapels, and even paid chaplains, just like Congress does, because it's understood that if people are required to be somewhere and they can't get to church, the church has to come to them. We don't have to take it that far in public schools, necessarily, but the point is that if we were willing to talk it out and look for solutions instead of staking out the extremes, I bet we could reach some middle ground.

Amendment Number Two:
Our Right to Defend Ourselves

Amendment II:
A well regulated Militia, being necessary to the security of a free State, the right of the people to keep and bear Arms, shall not be infringed.

The Second Amendment, which deals with our right to bear arms, is probably about the most misunderstood and most abused part of the Constitution. It grants us the freedom to possess and use firearms— and that's about the part where most people stop reading—but it goes on to say that it grants us that right because of a responsibility.

This amendment is still another example of the Founding Fathers trying to protect us from a corrupt government. When the Constitution was written, civil militias drilled on the town common, and every male old enough to handle a gun was a member. The idea behind it was that if your general populace was armed and trained, they'd not only be ready to ward off a foreign invasion, they would also be ready to forcibly take back their own government if need be!

Those kinds of militias are long gone. Today's militias consist of all kinds of diverse groups who happen to think the government is oppressive. Not all militias are necessarily good, remember. They can be the bad guys too!

Now, in recent times, I've heard people say that our National Guard is our "well-regulated militia." And to an extent that may be true. But don't forget that even though the Guard is run by individual states, it's funded by the federal government. If the federal government became really corrupt, it could yank the Guard's funding. And don't forget that in times of war, the federal government can call up the Guard from any state and send it into battle.

Whether or not you agree on the definition of a militia, the main point that I see in the Second Amendment is that we are granted the right to bear arms along with the responsibility to bear them for the good of the people. To me, that means we are entrusted with using our firearms safely, for the protection of ourselves and others. I'm no advocate of gun control, but I do think in recent years we've made way too much noise on the "rights" side of the equation, and not enough on the "responsibilities" side.

I know that there are people out there who would debate me on this, but I believe that the Founding Fathers wrote the right to bear arms into the Constitution to protect us from the government. Firearms are our ultimate recourse against a corrupt regime. An armed populace is very difficult to rule by force; it's a powerful deterrent to tyranny.

That's why I believe that forcing people to register their firearms with the government goes against the intent of the Second Amendment: It gives government a large measure of control over the arming—or disarming—of the populace. Remember when Marcos declared himself the dictator in the Philippines? He gave everybody two weeks to turn in their arms or face the death penalty. And he knew exactly which citizens had guns, because they were all registered with the government.

Now, I'm not expecting that somebody's going to stage a military coup in the White House any time soon. And I'm certainly not suggesting that any time Congress misbehaves we should whip out our twelve-gauges and scare them into submission. A situation in which an American populace would actually need to exert armed force against its government is almost inconceivable in today's America. But in the Founding Fathers' day, it was a very real possibility. And who knows where we could be a hundred years from now, or three hundred years from now. If we give up the right to be privately armed, it will be a lot harder to get it back if the need occurs.

But in addition to the Founding Fathers' intent, which was for us to protect ourselves against the government, I think we also have a right to bear arms to protect ourselves from each other. If you make it difficult for law-abiding citizens to legally own guns, you've caused the people to be unequally armed: There will be more guns in the hands of criminals than in the hands of law-abiding citizens. But in a society where a law-abiding person is as likely to be armed as a criminal, there's a better shot at equal protection, so to speak!

A certain amount of gun control is fine. I don't want the average citizen walking around the streets carrying machine guns. It's perfectly legitimate for the government to require a permit for a weapon like that. But gun-control advocates have clouded up the Second Amendment. Clinton is particularly guilty of that. He told gun owners, "We're not going to take away your right to hunt!" But the Second Amendment was never about hunting. Back when the Constitution was written, it wasn't even mentioned, because it was a given. Everybody hunted to survive. It was written, I believe, to permit common citizens to protect themselves against governmental tyranny. But because gun control is such an emotionally volatile issue, it's easy for us to lose sight of this.

I agree that gun use should be controlled, but I don't believe the government should be the one doing the controlling. I think control is the gun owner's responsibility. These lawsuits you hear about these days against gun makers are ridiculous. What's next? Are we going to sue car makers when cars aren't used properly? Car manufacturers also make products that can be misused. As far as I know, there's no place in the United States where you can legally drive a hundred miles per hour. But most cars today come with speedometers that go over a hundred. Should we sue car manufacturers for making products that people can use to break the law? I pray that we never get to the point of suing automakers for individuals' reckless driving. But I see us headed in that direction already.

A lot of gun control is not for pragmatic reasons, it's for politics. The ban on assault weapons was a stupid piece of legislation. It banned guns for simply looking like machine guns. Deer rifles are more lethal than the average assault weapon: They use a larger cal-iber ammunition and a scope. But they're legal.

The dumbest part of the ban was on any weapon that could have a bayonet affixed to it. Since when have we had a rash of drive-by bayonetings? The government shouldn't be stepping in to ban and control things just because of their emotional content or their image. Legislation has to have a practical reason behind it, or it's meaning-less. We don't want to get into the habit of allowing the government to control things for frivolous reasons.

Now, I'm no great lover of guns. I see them as utilitarian objects, and I wish there wasn't a need for them. If we could find a way that we could magically lift every weapon of destruction out of society, I'd be the first one to go for it. But until we find a way to eliminate the need to protect ourselves, we'd better be thankful to the Founding Fathers for being smart enough to give us the Second Amendment, and be smart enough ourselves to see that it's upheld.

Amendments One, Four, and Nine: Freedom of Life-style

Conformity is the jailer of freedom and the enemy of growth.

—John F. Kennedy

Freedom works for all human beings by allowing them to creatively adapt all of their own strengths and weaknesses to the evolving situations of their lives.

—Jack D. Douglas
The Myth of the Welfare State

The Constitution is very clear on the idea of tolerance: The people are supposed to be free to choose the life-style that brings them the most happiness, as long as it's not infringing on anybody else's rights. The "life, liberty, and the pursuit of happiness" statement in the Declaration of Independence is backed up implicitly throughout the Constitution, but it's especially clear in Amendments One, Four, and Nine.

When you say "First Amendment," everybody immediately thinks of free speech and the separation of church and state. But another tradition that comes directly from the First Amendment is the idea of freedom of association: The government can't penalize you for belonging to any particular organization. You can associate with whomever you want.

Amendment Four also protects your freedom of life-style. This is the amendment that safeguards you against unreasonable search and seizure, and essentially gives you the right to be left alone by the government unless it has a documentable reason for picking on you.

The Ninth Amendment also backs up our right to choose our own life-style by telling us that even those rights not specifically spelled out in the Constitution are protected. The Ninth Amendment is sort of a catchall, it leaves the concept of personal freedom open-ended.

The Founding Fathers clearly intended that the government should stay out of the business of telling people how to live, for many of the same reasons why it has to stay out of the business of telling people what opinions to hold. Diversity of life-style is a national strength; it means we have almost limitless options in the search for happiness. It means that we can attempt to solve our problems creatively, by experimenting with alternatives. And it means that we can adapt our lives to suit our personalities, so we can be free to develop as individuals.

When we stay focused on the idea that everybody has a right to his or her own life-style, and that diversity is good, it's easy to see that tolerance applies to ethnic and cultural groups, and to religious groups. For these same reasons, tolerance extends to people whose life-style choices aren't causing any direct harm, like homosexuals.

And since the Declaration of Independence specifies that every person is equally guaranteed rights, any group in which membership is involuntary, like the disabled, the mentally ill, and the aged, should also be given tolerance.

Does tolerance mean the same thing as acceptance? If you tolerate a person or a group, does that mean you have to agree with them, or like their choices? Nope. But in the language of the Constitution, you do owe them dignity and respect.

Tolerance of diverse life-styles is a profoundly American value, one which we should all respect. But does it have limitations? You bet. There are circumstances in which it isn't meant to apply.

So who doesn't deserve tolerance? I think there is a small segment of our population who shouldn't be given tolerance; to do so would not only rob the word of its intent, but would also create a dangerous precedent for acceptance. I don't believe tolerance applies to any group that advocates harm and hatred, or to any group that argues for rights that overrun somebody else's rights. Examples: Neo-Nazis, the Ku Klux Klan, pedophiles, gay bashers, and violent crime organizations.

The government has no recourse against these groups until they break the law. And as I've said, I believe that even the opinions held by these groups are protected by free speech. But that doesn't mean that they deserve the same dignity and respect that you give to other groups. I'm not advocating violence. But I think it's very important that we exercise our freedom of speech vigorously in denouncing heinous behavior. Tolerance of evil is tolerance misdirected. Good people don't stand by and let hatred go unchallenged.

In spite of the fact that it's a core American value, tolerance has too often been lacking, lopsided, and misdirected in our country. To one extent or another, we have failed to apply it where we should (for example, when we are racist, bigoted, or homophobic) and have applied it where it doesn't belong. Tolerance may always be a problem and a challenge for us; I think that something in us, as humans, makes us fear what is different. But fortunately, it's something that we can impact by our own behavior. We can encourage tolerance in this country by teaching it to our kids and demonstrating it by our own good examples.

Amendment Four, Amendment Nine: Economic Freedom

As you read through the Constitution, one thing that will hit you again and again is the sheer number of restraints it puts on government. The Founding Fathers were very clearly advocates of minimal government. Government was to interfere as little as possible in people's lives, and only when absolutely necessary.

This is especially true of economic matters. The Founding Fathers, Jefferson in particular, believed that the best way to secure economic prosperity for the greatest number of people was to put as little restraint on their economic activities as possible. For the most part, they were right.

The most successful economy is the one where individuals have plenty of opportunities to apply their creativity and their individuality to the businesses they

> *Agriculture, manufactures, commerce, and navigation, the four pillars of our prosperity, are then most thriving when left most free to individual enterprise.*
>
> —Thomas Jefferson

create, and where they feel confident that the businesses they create are really their own. That's where Communism screws up: In a Communist society, you build a great new business or create a terrific new product, and as soon as it's a success, the government takes it away from you. It effectively kills everyone's creative impulses when they can't benefit from their own ingenuity. Even in a democratic society, too much bureaucracy, and too much regulation, can have the same effect.

Widespread prosperity brings other fringe benefits with it. It paves the way for social justice. Don't ask me exactly how this works, but if you look at countries all around the world, wherever economies are becoming stronger, civil welfare is improving too. The reverse tends to be true as well: Where there is widespread poverty and little hope of improvement, it's extremely difficult to get civil justice established.

So in general, minimal economic tampering is the way to ensure maximum prosperity. But the question that inevitably comes up after this statement is, "Prosperity for whom?" Because in the absence of government regulation, economic prosperity seems to stack up against the individual in favor of big business. And the more economically and politically powerful big business becomes, the more it usurps for itself rights that belong to individuals.

Our country first started dealing with this problem in the late 1800s, when the Industrial Revolution was going full steam. A lot of acts were proposed during that time to try to limit the powers of big business, but the legislature wouldn't pass them. Today more than ever we're struggling to keep our economic rights from being usurped by large corporations.

We've talked about the ways corporations can get the upper hand in our political system by buying political candidates. But corporations can become so vastly powerful that they can commandeer the course of scientific discovery, to make certain that there's a continuing market for their product. A perfect case in point is William Lear's helium engine, invented in the early 1960s: an efficient, nonpolluting engine whose only by-product was water. Lear's engine could have revolutionized transportation and saved us from the environmental disasters that are looming on the horizon due to our use of fossil fuels. But the automotive and gasoline industries didn't want to see a rival product siphoning off their profits, so they made sure Lear's engine never got off the ground.

We're facing a similar situation today with health maintenance organizations, which are so focused on keeping their costs down and profits up that many of them are beginning to deliver substandard care. Many of them flat out will not pay for expensive medicines or treatments, whether you need them or not. HMOs are great, as long as you don't get really sick. If you do get sick, or if, God forbid, you get old, you're out of luck.

Individuals have very little recourse against huge corporations in circumstances like these. And that's where the government must step in from time to time and put citizens first. Big business can bring tremendous benefits to society, but we need to keep corporations on a short leash, so that they don't usurp the rights of individuals.

Don't Holler for Your Rights Unless You're Willing to Holler Just As Loudly for Your Responsibilities

America has always been big on rights, but in recent decades we've become obsessed with them. Our courts are jammed with litigation over rights. We have become so fixated on arguing for our rights that often as not we forget that rights come with responsibilities. We cannot allow ourselves to become passive recipients of rights. That's not freedom; that's dependence.

Obviously, the ability of the government to safeguard your rights is only as good as its capacity to function. But in a government of, by, and for the people, its capacity to function depends on what the people put into it. If we, the people, sit back and demand unlimited rights without doing anything to support the government in its efforts, with what will the government defend our rights? In order to have an effective government, we cannot just endlessly take. That's

> **P**olitics ought to be the part-time profession of every citizen who would protect the rights and privileges of free people and who would preserve what is good and fruitful in our national heritage.
> **—Dwight D. Eisenhower**

why I get mad when people picket the capitol demanding their "welfare rights." Nowhere in the Constitution does it say you have a right to a free ride. You're supposed to "pursue" your happiness, not sit back and expect it to be handed to you!

WHEN DID YOUR RIGHT TO SCREW UP BECOME THE GOVERNMENT'S RESPONSIBILITY TO REPAIR?

There's a very dangerous assumption out there that any time anybody faces adversity, whether it's through his own fault or not, taxpayers are the ones who have to pony up. We've gotten to the point where we view government money, which is *always* taxpayers' money, as a bottomless well, an unlimited resource, that we can dip into any time there's a problem that needs fixing.

But this is a terrible misuse of government funds, and it's jeopardizing our country. When government gets into the charity business, it inevitably handles it badly. It gets itself tangled up in a knotwork of bureaucracy and procedures and accounting and regulations. It hamstrings itself. Private individuals and private organizations do a vastly better job of helping the unfortunate, because they're personally involved, in a way that government never can be.

Remember, at its very best, government is only a necessary evil. By its nature it is pragmatic and utilitarian. We can't expect it to do all kinds of things that it wasn't meant to do.

The best role government can play in charity work is to support charities that exist in the private sector. Of course, there's got to be a minimal government-run safety net, but there has to be a clear limit on cash handouts from the government. We have to train ourselves out of this habit of dipping into taxpayers' money for charity. And the more we manage to stop doing that, the more tax dollars we can let individuals keep, to donate to charities as they see fit.

There is no way to make life fair. Nobody can do it, especially not the government. It isn't the government's job to make sure you get a fair shake out of life. When we start asking government to do that, we're asking the impossible.

We act today as if democracy will perpetuate itself automatically. It doesn't. As the Founding Fathers warned us, democracy is tough to maintain. If we don't work at hanging on to it, it will slip away from us.

The Constitution guarantees our rights, but it can only fulfill that guarantee to the extent that we are willing to help preserve those rights for others. The Constitution guarantees your right to free speech, but it implies your responsibility to speak for the good of all, and to examine your facts carefully before you speak them. The Constitution guarantees your economic freedom, but it also carries the expectation of economic responsibility. It isn't up to the government to bail you out if you make poor financial decisions. The Constitution guarantees you the right to decide if and how you will worship God, but it asks implicitly that you respect that right in others. The Constitution guarantees you the right to bear arms, but it does so with the knowledge that your fellow citizens may need to call upon you to protect their freedom.

The Limits of Legislation: Where Government Ends, Society Takes Over

*L*iberty is not an absolute; indeed, granting total freedom to one individual could theoretically result in the restriction of freedom for everyone else. Social control is essential if rights are to have meaning.

—Kermit Hall
"The Bill of Rights: Liberty and Original Intent"

In recent decades we have come to see the government as the ultimate solution to all our problems. That's a terrible misuse of government. Government was never meant to be the catchall that it is becoming today. We're looking to government to do things that it can't do, like guide us morally and spiritually, and help us build self-reliance and character. Those are the jobs of religion and families and communities. The government doesn't know you; it can't possibly have a personal relationship with you. And personal relationships are the foundation of these things.

In order for a democratic society to work the way it's supposed to, we not only need an efficient, corruption-proof government run by the people, we also need a strong social fabric. It takes both reinforcing each other. Each one fills a function that the other can't. I think in recent times, as families become less stable and communities dissolve into huddled groups of strangers, we look to government to fill in the gaps for what's missing. It never will, because it can't.

THE EXTENT OF THE LAW: WHAT LEGISLATION CAN AND CAN'T DO

Legislation is not all-powerful. It can't fix everything that's wrong with society. The job of legislation should be to protect people from harm and to keep people from getting in each other's way. Legislation can help sort things out, but it can never, ever dictate meaning. That's why the old saw "You can't legislate morality" still rings true. It's been tried. It doesn't work. Morality is an issue of character. By its nature, legislation can't touch that.

We've become litigious to a fault in this country, not only because we misunderstand the nature of legislation, but because we've discovered that it can be a handy weapon. Frivolous lawsuits are a scourge on our country, as are the lawyers who make big bucks from them.

Our misunderstanding and misuse of the law is getting in the way of justice. We need to educate ourselves and our children about the true nature and intent of the law. We need to know how the legal system works, what it can and cannot do, and what our role in it must be. We need to restructure the legal system to minimize its abuse by opportunists. And we need to help our children understand that the law cannot be a substitute for the internal guidance that morality and character are supposed to provide.

YOU CAN'T LEGISLATE STUPIDITY

One of my campaign slogans when I ran for governor in 1998 was "You can't legislate stupidity!" There's a trend I've seen in recent times that consists of people trying to make laws function as an absolute safety net, so that there's no chance of anyone getting hurt. But that's impossible, because no matter how tight you make the laws, somebody will always find a way to do something stupid and get themselves hurt.

A perfect example of this occurs in Minnesota just about every spring. Everybody knows that once the temperatures have been above a certain level for a few days, the ice on our ten thousand lakes begins to get thinner from the bottom up. It may still look solid on top, but it's not nearly as thick. Every year, some yahoo who should know better tries to drive a snowmobile or a pickup truck out on that ice, and breaks through and drowns. What do you do about a situation like that? Make it illegal for people to go out on the ice? I submit to you that even if you did that, a certain number of people would still be stupid enough to do it anyway. There is no way that the law can throw a complete and impermeable safety net around us all. It just doesn't work.

WHY WE CAN'T ALWAYS SOLVE SOCIAL PROBLEMS BY THROWING NEW LAWS AT THEM

Legislation is notoriously poor at handling social problems. Most dire social problems don't have a single cause. They're a hydra. And many, like racism, have layers that are strictly within the realm of thought and opinion, which is an area that, as we've said, legislation can't touch. Legislation isn't good with complex problems like these.

LEGISLATION'S NOT ENOUGH: WE NEED SOCIAL INSTITUTIONS THAT REGULATE BEHAVIOR

The best way I can think of to tackle social problems is to work on the prevention end. The best "cure" for poverty, unemployment, racism, you name it, is to put more effort into developing higher-quality people. I believe that a huge part of the reason our moral structure is deteriorating in this country is because most of the social institutions we have that foster people's morality are becoming weaker. We can battle away at trying to deal with teen pregnancy and drug abuse and welfare dependence, but I believe our energies would be far better spent strengthening the institutions that are good at preventing these problems in the first place: neighborhoods, schools, religion, and families.

Thomas Jefferson, who created the "wall" between church and state, went to church every Sunday, even though he wasn't a man of faith, because he believed that society couldn't stay on a solid moral footing without it. Religious institutions are a great source of moral guidance. Most religions have some equivalent of the Ten Commandments; nearly all of them have clear expectations for good behavior. Best of all, they can put it in a far greater context than government ever could.

I think we're only now beginning to see what we lost when we gave up old-fashioned neighborhoods. When I was growing up, if you lived in the neighborhood, people knew you and kept an eye on you. They were there for you if you needed help, and they kept you in line if you started getting into trouble. They had expectations. But also, when you live in a close-knit neighborhood, you enjoy a satisfying sense of belonging, which I think is sadly lacking for many people today.

I think that we ought to be thinking long-term about ways we can get some of that sense of community back. It's not healthy for us to live huddled among strangers. I think that the anonymity that we have to live with today, in which so many of the people we deal with each day are strangers who couldn't care less about us, is adding to the problem. I truly believe that close-knit neighborhoods turn out better-quality people.

A terrific education is also one of the best tools there is for prevention of poverty, crime, you name it. Well-educated people are flexible; they know how to solve problems, and they know how to find information when they need it. Educated people know that they've got to get at least one job skill in order to survive. They've got a good basic tool kit of social skills. And they have been taught what will happen to them if they get involved with drugs and crime.

We're not doing as good a job of educating our children today as we were a few decades ago. We're not nearly as dedicated to our public schools. Our schools are suffering from a lack of focus. They've gotten away from the three R's and are teaching things they have no business teaching. They've gotten so gun-shy of civil liberties lawsuits they're making stupid decisions about what's best for our children. Our schools need work.

I believe that if we reinvested in our schools and refocused the goals of education, we could head off a lot of the social problems we see around us today. Government does have a role to play here: Our public schools all across the nation are underfunded. And ironically, it's costing us money. I truly believe that we would spend less on ineffective social cures in the long run if we would spend more up front on education.

And last but not least, the number one place where good people come from is the family. Ultimately, what makes a high-quality individual is someone who is willing to invest in a child, spend loads of time with that child, and put him or her first. If a parent or family member isn't willing to do that, there's very little in the way of government social programs that can pick up the pieces. There is no substitute for a strong, loving family.

If I had to point to the single major cause of our social problems today, I'd say it's because parents aren't doing their jobs. Raising a child is hard work. It takes a huge amount of time. I think too many of us leave the real work of parenting to day-care workers, television, video games, the Internet, and scariest of all, to our kids' peers. Kids can't get the grown-up skills they need from hanging out with their friends; their friends don't have them either! It takes parenting. Strong, loving families may not be the only way in the world to develop high-quality people, but they're the best bet.

Government can do little or nothing to strengthen the quality of the individuals in our society. That part is up to us. The Founding Fathers gave us an outstanding template for governing a free society, but it's up to us to provide the society. If we want democracy to work the way it was intended, we have to be ready to do our part.

5

Breaking Down the Issues: What They Look Like When We Take Out the Spin

Nothing in the world is more dangerous than sincere ignorance and conscientious stupidity.
—Martin Luther King, Jr.

In a nation like ours, social problems are everybody's problem. We're all responsible for being aware of them and keeping informed, and we're all called upon to find ways of solving them. Our government can play a role in supporting us as we deal with our problems, but it can't ever take the place of our own involvement.

There is no way to make life fair. Nobody can do that, especially not the government. It isn't the government's job to make sure you get a fair shake out of life. When we start asking government to do that, we're asking the impossible. But I think many of us wish the government could fix all our problems. And unscrupulous politicians like to exploit that wish. Especially in recent years, politicians and the media have wreaked havoc on our ability to tackle our own social problems. Politicians do it by promising feel-good quick fixes as campaign boosters. The media do it by feeding us skewed and inaccurate information.

If we cop out and accept the mass-consumption viewpoints that the spin doctors feed us, instead of thinking through the issues for ourselves, we're never going to make much headway. In this chapter, I'm going to take on a bunch of the most talked-about social issues with an eye toward stripping off the accumulated layers of political spin and media sensationalism. I'm going to hold them up to the light of the Constitution; then we'll see if we can figure out what government's role in these issues should really be. Once we have a less biased, better informed view of the issues, we can start working on plans for solving problems that have a better shot at truly making an impact.

Welfare

I'm not a big fan of government assistance. When government helps you it's a form of slavery, because it's self-reinforcing. Dependence on government engenders more dependence on government, and discourages self-reliance. It penalizes people for trying to become self-sufficient by cutting off their aid as soon as they start making money for themselves, even if what they're making isn't enough for them to get by. Government assistance appears to help people, but how much help is it really giving them? And at what cost? It's very easy for us to forget that every dollar that is given to someone who isn't working was taken from someone who is.

It's funny how college kids and young people just getting out on their own are very socialistic. They're used to getting subsidized by Mom and Dad, and now they think the government should step in and do the same thing—for them, and for anybody who isn't doing well financially.

> *L*et not him who is houseless pull down the house of another, but let him work diligently and build one for himself, thus by example assuring that his own shall be safe from violence when built.
>
> —Abraham Lincoln

They want government to take care of all the poor people in the world. But as soon as these same kids put in a few years of hard work and achieve their own self-sufficiency, their attitudes begin to change. They see their hard-earned tax dollars going to the dependent people. Then they get mad!

When I talk to college-age kids, I love to pitch them this scenario: Say you've got a job digging a hole. You're working for $10 an hour, ten hours a day, making $100 a day. You're working hard all day in the hot sun for your money. Then the government comes along and takes $40 and gives it to some guy who wasn't in the hole with you all day, but instead was kicking back in the cool of his apartment watching soap operas all day. That usually gets their attention. I tell them, "I hope I live long enough for you to come back in twenty years and tell me whether or not your thinking has changed on this."

I realize that that's a pretty simplistic way of looking at a complex problem. But sometimes you have to shake a problem down to its simplest form in order to see it for what it is. I believe that's an important element in the job I got elected to do: to bring these concepts back into simpler terms.

Welfare is often the topic of choice for political spin doctors, because it can provoke strong reactions. It can make hard-working people clutch their wallets in terror, and it can make soft-hearted people advocate silly ideas in the name of caring for the less fortunate. The conservative Right like to try to scare us by saying that America is being overrun by welfare recipients. They characterize people on welfare as being able-bodied but lazy folks who have decided to live forever off the government dole instead of earning their way in life like the rest of us. The liberal Left try to win humanitarian points by proposing larger and larger bills for social spending, as if all of our extremely complex social problems will disappear if we just throw enough money at them.

They're both wrong. Welfare recipients are a small minority in this country. There is no gigantic wave of indigent people with packs of half-wild children threatening to take over the country, as the extreme Right would have us believe. Most people who sign up for welfare are off the rolls within two years. But increasing welfare handouts, as the Left often tries to do, is never going to eliminate the problems that bring people to the rolls in the first place.

Welfare statistics are probably some of the most tweaked, manipulated, and doctored figures around; everybody has an opinion on welfare that they want to promote. But very few of these ideas seem to yield hard-core results. A case in point is the big welfare reform bill Congress passed in 1994, which was spun to look like it would get people off welfare faster. But in reality, the numbers of people leaving welfare in any given year are about the same as they've always been.

Everybody talks about welfare reform in terms of getting people off it. But the bigger question is, why are there people on welfare in the first place, in a country as prosperous as ours? The standard liberal answer is because government isn't giving out enough cash to keep them out of poverty. That's a self-destructive and counterproductive line of thinking. If people are poor in this cash-rich country, it's because they don't have the means to tap into our nation's abundant wealth. To me, that means we need to deal with the reasons why people are having trouble tapping in. Handing out money not only discourages the behaviors that keep our nation strong, it also doesn't address the underlying problems.

We need to focus most of our welfare energies on tackling the real causes of joblessness. You've heard it said that our blue-collar job base is shrinking; that the number of manufacturing jobs is dropping because of automation. If this is so, then we'd better acknowledge it and act on that knowledge. If we're smart enough to invent all these machines that put people out of work, we're smart enough to invent the means to put those same people back to work.

It makes more sense in the long run to retrain people for the existing job market than to try to manipulate the economy artificially to make work where it no longer exists. Successful people are flexible enough to adapt. We have to encourage that kind of flexibility. Government's role here is not to temper the economy to the types of jobs people want, but to make sure that people have ample and equal opportunity to get into the jobs that exist.

The vast majority of people applying for welfare are willing to work. For most of them, the problem is that, for whatever reason, they don't have the necessary job skills. About 50 percent of welfare recipients don't have a high school degree. Some of them have mental health problems. Many don't have the best social skills in the world. It's one of those situations that's tough to quantify; there can be a whole set of reasons why a person isn't very employable. Some are obvious, some aren't. Even in a great economy like today's, the people who have the toughest time finding and keeping jobs are still going without.

So if the problem is that these people aren't employable enough to make it in the job market, that tells me that we need to work on helping them become more employable. We need to make sure they have access to the education they need, both for specific job skills and for basic work ethics. We need to look at what's lacking and answer to it. There are some cases in which people aren't even able to handle job training because they don't have enough education to benefit from it. In that case, we need to make sure they get training for their training! Welfare must be organized so that it can be reflexive. It needs to be able to look at the causes of joblessness in each case, and answer to them. That's the only sensible way for a free society to handle joblessness: to fix the problems that cause it.

But another tricky aspect to welfare is, how do we make sure these folks don't starve or get evicted while they're going through job training? Welfare as it exists now isn't enough for anybody to live on. Benefits for families hardly ever exceed $400 a month. Could you live on that?

Ideally, then, the goals of welfare must be twofold: It's got to diagnose and remedy the causes of unemployment and underemployment, and it's got to help keep people going, at least minimally, while they're solving their employment problems.

Private sector charities could step in to help on that score. But additionally, why couldn't the training recipients themselves work for the welfare benefits they receive, at least part-time? Isn't it possible that they could work part of the day in some kind of job program, and attend job training the other part of the day? Or, wherever on-the-job training programs are possible, they could solve both problems at once. There's got to be half a dozen creative ways of handling this, short of all-out cash giveaways that don't actually solve the original problem.

The fact that welfare often doesn't address the causes of joblessness is a big problem. But there's an even bigger one: Who suffers the most when adults don't have decent jobs? Their children. Welfare recipients tend to be single parents. Either they're home taking care of their kids, in which case their ability to work is severely hampered, or they have to pay somebody to watch their kids, which probably eats up nearly all of a low-wage salary. There's the real dilemma: Job training and "workfare" programs are fine, but who is taking care of the workers' preschool children while they're going through these programs? No minimum-wage job is going to cover the cost of decent child care, and even if it did, no child-care worker is going to give kids the kind of parenting their mother and father could give.

It puts government in a tough situation. If childless adults don't come up with solutions to their own problems, they're the only ones who suffer. But if parents with small children can't, or won't, find a way to solve their problems, their children don't get the care they need. And kids who grow up without basic parental care are likely to become adults who, like their parents, don't have the skills to stay employed.

There's not a lot government can do in this situation, except work on programs that aid kids directly. Programs like Head Start that teach basic social skills and comprehension can do a phenomenal job with underprivileged kids. Likewise, school lunch programs can help make sure that kids eat well at least once a day. Medicaid programs can pick up the tab for their basic health care. But no government program can take the place of an involved parent.

What can government do about that? When welfare was first created, it was aimed at helping single mothers stay at home to raise their children. Well, today we have an astronomical number of single parents; to pay all of them to stay at home with their kids would break the bank.

One very practical thing government can do in this situation is go after the parent who isn't contributing to the child's upbringing. We're long overdue in this country for a nationwide crackdown on parents who don't pay child support and don't contribute to their children's upbringing.

Beyond that, it's up to the parents themselves to come up with creative solutions. What about home-based businesses with flexible hours, which would allow single parents to work around their children's schedules? What about co-oping with other single parents, so that there's always a parent there? What about getting help from family, and working an evening or graveyard shift that has you home for a substantial number of your child's waking hours?

There are dozens of other ways to solve this problem short of expecting the government to pay for child care. But it's up to us to get creative and come up with solutions. Government's job should only be to assist us with those solutions.

Ultimately, the best possible cure for poverty, joblessness, and all the other problems that cause people to seek out welfare is prevention. I think we spend far too much money and energy on mopping up the aftermath, and far too little effort on helping people avoid bad situations in the first place. Prevention is expensive too, but in the long run, it costs only a fraction of what it takes to try to repair these kinds of problems once they occur.

Sooner or later we are going to have to face the fact that a certain amount of the poverty in this country is reinforced and made worse by certain people's attitudes. Some people (and this has nothing to do with any particular race or culture) are held back from prosperity by their own distrust of authority, lack of a work ethic, and lack of any kind of vision for their own lives.

It's an ugly idea, and nobody wants to hear it; that's why politicians seldom express it. But there's an aspect to poverty that is learned, and passed on from generation to generation. And short of educational programs, it's a realm that the government can't touch.

We need to work on this as a community, through programs and volunteering in the private sector. We need to teach better parenting skills and parental responsibility. We need to find new and more effective ways to combat drug addiction. We need to raise kids from an early age with the idea that they have something to contribute to society, and that it's their responsibility to get job skills and pay their own way in life.

Let me remind you again that even on the score of poverty, America is an aberration. All across the globe and all through time, the vast majority of people have been poor. I'm not talking one-TV-set-and-Ramen-noodles-twice-a-week poor. I'm talking dirt-floor poor. I'm talking about the kind of poor where you're not sure if there will be enough food to survive. That's been the most common state for us human beings throughout history.

In America, even the poorest among us enjoy a pretty decent standard of living, comparatively, because there's so much wealth around. But let's never forget that the wealth is there because our people are free. They're able to create as much wealth as they want because they get to control the fruits of their labors to a great extent. That's what creates abundance and surplus. We have to keep that in mind, so that we don't fall into the trap of letting government take too much control of our wealth—even if it seems to be for a beneficial cause like healing poverty. Government cannot heal poverty that way. It can only wreck the economies of those who are making their own way.

Let's not ever forget that the phrase is "the *pursuit* of happiness." You're supposed to go after it. Where is it written that you have a right to have it brought to you? The government's job is to remove the barriers to the pursuit. Unless they're accompanied by job training and other measures that actually work on dropping those barriers, welfare handouts are antithetical to the pursuit of happiness.

A recent poll by *The New York Times* and CBS showed that two thirds of Americans believe that government should step in to take care of citizens who can't take care of themselves. But should the government necessarily be the first in line to step in? What about family members? Loved ones? Neighbors? Can't they do a better job of taking care of someone in need than the government can? I think the government ought to support families and communities in taking care of their own needy, rather than simply taking over for them, because the government isn't on a personal level with its citizens. It can't be. It can never do as good a job as a loved one can do. The government should only step in and assume complete control where there isn't capable family to do the job.

Welfare was created as a safety net for workers against fluctuations in the job market. It was launched after the Great Depression, when millions of hardworking, skilled people were thrown out of work. At that time the government saw that some insurance was needed against downturns in the economy. That's what welfare was originally supposed to be. But today it often functions as a catchall for the unemployable. Welfare is a poor substitute for decent job training.

When it comes right down to it, all forms of government redistribute society's wealth. That's what our government does when it collects and spends taxes. But some means of redistributing wealth are better than others. In general, in a capitalist society, I think it behooves government to concentrate on redistributing wealth before the fact, not after. When government tries to even out the wealth once it's made, it's essentially taking money away from people who made it and giving it to those who didn't. If it focused instead on evening out the opportunities to make wealth, it would do a more effective job. The opportunities for corruption are fewer that way, and the potential for good is much greater.

Besides, the ounce of prevention is always cheaper than the pound of cure. I believe that the most effective scenario for dealing with poverty, given the kind of society we are, is for the private sector to take on most of the responsibility, and for government to assist them in their efforts.

We do a pretty good job of handling welfare here in Minnesota. In fact, we do such a good job that we're in danger of losing some of our federal welfare funds. This is another case of the federal government penalizing those who do things right: If your state is handling welfare well, they cut your federal money!

Our plan in Minnesota is to channel our $173 million in federal welfare funds into two directions. Half of it will go to helping out those folks who fall through the cracks in the system. Minnesota's welfare program gives people a five-year time limit; after that they know they have to be employed because their benefits will run out. But even with five years' leeway, there are going to be people who fall through the cracks and won't be prepared when their five years are up. We'll have about $86 million on hand to help those folks back on their feet.

The other half we're going to invest in a partnership with Habitat for Humanity to provide people with affordable housing. Stable, low-cost housing is a major problem for people who are struggling with poverty and fighting to stay employed. It's tough enough for people who move voluntarily every five years or so. Can you imagine what that does to your life, to have to move involuntarily about every six months? Kids really suffer the most from this, being yanked in and out of different schools. There are kids who can't get their high school degrees because they're moving so much.

Habitat for Humanity is a much better alternative to the housing projects of the 1950s and 1960s that are now nothing but run-down slums. The people whose houses they're building get to participate. They have pride of ownership when it's all done; they've put something of themselves into it, so they're not as likely to abuse it and let it get run down. Once they sweat a little bit and pound some nails, they're much more involved. This is an example of what I'm talking about when I say government should be working in partnership with the private sector. It's a very effective alternative to the way welfare has usually been handled.

Health Care

We have to ask ourselves whether medicine is to remain a humanitarian and respected profession or a new but depersonalized science in the service of prolonging life rather than diminishing human suffering.
—Elisabeth Kübler-Ross

There's an irony inherent in the whole issue of health care: Most of our lives we don't need it, but when we finally do, we can't afford it. I think that when we look at the issue of health care, we need to find ways that we can make sure it's paid for when we do need it, rather than wasting all this money paying for health care we don't use.

I don't support nationalized health care. I think any time you get a system where there's only one provider, you get corruption. Competition creates better service and keeps prices down. I think we do need to keep an eye on HMOs, though. Many of them are going a little overboard on being cost-efficient. Plenty of horror stories have come from HMO patients who say that they were denied medical care they needed because it was too expensive.

By its very nature, medical care can't be a purely capitalist venture. If it becomes only about making money, we get to the point where we're messing with people's lives and health just to make a buck. We do need to have some kind of regulation or watchdogging system in place to keep HMOs from getting out of hand.

I believe that it's the government's job to step in when an individual can't afford his or her own health care. We have a pretty decent system here in Minnesota, called Minnesota Care. It pays the medical bills for people who can't afford them with money that it raises from a small tax on everybody else's medical bills.

But the more we as a society can do on the end of prevention, the less money any of us will have to spend on medical care. We need to make better choices regarding our health. We need to educate the public, especially kids, about the harmful effects of tobacco and excess drinking. We need to get smarter about the need for exercise. You don't have to become a triathlete just to stay healthy. A walk every evening after dinner is better than nothing. It's always easier and cheaper to stay healthy in the first place than it is to get treatment once you're ill.

Racism

Unfortunately, racism is alive and well in our country. It may have been flowered over and taken on subtler forms than it did in the days of Jim Crow laws and poll

> *In this country American means white. Everybody else has to hyphenate.*
>
> **—Toni Morrison**

taxes, but it's still with us. Somehow we've managed to pass it along to each new generation. But I'm here to tell you, we're not passing it genetically! There is no such thing as a gene for racism. Racism is 100 percent a learned behavior. So if we want to do something about racism in this country, the real question is, who's doing the teaching?

I'd be willing to bet that the number of overtly racist people in this country is pretty small. I believe we have more to fear from sub-tler forms of racism, the kinds that we may not even be conscious of. I think a certain number of politicians are very aware of the uncon-scious racism in much of America today. They must be aware of it, because they tap into it and manipulate us with it all the time.

Race has gotten politicized like many other issues because it's an emotionally charged topic. It's easy to get a rise out of people by playing the race card. But whenever we play that card when race isn't a genuine issue, we desensitize people to it.

In recent years, it's become the fashion to pretend that race is invisible. In many ways that's just as dangerous as where we were before. Remember in 1996, how Dole corrupted Dr. King's "I Have a Dream" speech to mean that we should all be blind to race? That's not what King meant! He only meant that race should not come into play in the judging of a person's character.

Race and culture do exist, and they affect the way we see things and the way we live our lives. We do each other a disservice by trying to pretend otherwise.

Racism takes odd forms in this country. Have you ever noticed that whatever a black man does, he's judged as an example of his race? I often hear blacks in public life complain about this. Nobody judges whites that way. And if you're black, then it's assumed that everything you do is going to be biased in favor of the black commu-nity. There's a weird notion out there that blacks can't be trusted as judges or jurors because they won't convict other blacks. That's bull. Black jurors convict black criminals every day.

One of the biggest fallacies you'll hear is when politicians talk about the "black vote," as if all black people vote the same. Is it not possible that black people might vote the way any other people do, based on which candidate makes the most sense? I think it's a form of racism to say that if you're black you must only care about issues that directly affect blacks. Nobody is that myopic.

You'll also hear well-meaning people say that there can't be any such thing as a "black conservative." These people assume that if you're black and conservative, you've somehow sold out to white people. I think this kind of thinking sets us back. I'm fiscally conservative and socially liberal, but I do believe that people should be allowed to decide for themselves where they fall on the political spectrum, without being made to feel guilty that they've betrayed the cause.

Having said that, I have seen that today's crop of white ultra-right-wingers occasionally try to use black conservatives for their own means. They point to the handful of black conservatives in high positions as being somehow representative of the black vote, when in reality the black vote is as diverse as the white vote.

Gay Rights

I've become known as something of a gay rights advocate. People always talk to me about how I appealed to the gay vote during my campaign. Well, I have nothing at all against gay folks, but to tell you the truth, I never specifically courted their vote. I'm for equal rights for all people. That's the founding principle of our country, isn't it? Gays and lesbians are people. Therefore, I support their rights.

I've had gay friends my whole life long, and my life has been richer for their friendship. But I don't think of them as "my gay friends." They're my friends, the same as any other friends I have. When you have friends who are gay, it makes it a lot tougher for you to be homophobic.

> No government has the right to tell its citizens when or whom to love.
>
> —Rita Mae Brown

I support the idea of a legally recognized domestic partnership for gay couples. There are honors and privileges that go along with being in a permanent committed partnership, as well as responsibilities and benefits to society, and I don't think that people should be denied the opportunity to achieve these things just because they love a person of the same sex.

It often happens today that a committed gay couple isn't permitted to function the way a committed (married) heterosexual couple would. Case in point: I had two gay friends who I knew through my wrestling career. They were together for forty-one years, until one of them died. But when one of them was ill in the hospital, his partner wasn't allowed to be by his bedside, the way a husband or wife would have been. He had to be alone. That's discrimination, and it's cruel.

Legalized gay partnerships would allow gays to become something they have never become before in the eyes of the law: family. When a man and a woman get married, they become family. They've joined their property and their fortunes together, and are legally recognized as each other's closest relative. And there's a certain raise in social status that you get when you're married. These are all benefits that are available to men and women who fall in love and decide to join together, but at the present time they are completely forbidden to gay couples. That's got to change.

But I draw the line at calling gay partnerships "marriage." Marriage is something different. My dictionary says marriage is a union between a man and a woman. I don't think we need to be diluting that definition just to make sure gays have the privilege of being in a committed union. I think a term like *domestic partnership* works fine.

There's one note of caution here, though. I think we'd better keep a clear distinction between a committed relationship, gay or straight, and a casual one. We'd better make sure that a legally recognized gay partnership is reserved for couples who are serious about creating a union, just as we reserve legal marriage for committed straight couples. It shouldn't be for people just living together for convenience's sake. There's nothing stopping anybody from living together casually if they want to, but there's no particular reason to honor it, legally or socially, as there is with a committed union.

I'm aware that not all marriages last, just as I'm sure that not all legal domestic partnerships would last. But the distinction is impor-tant. People who get married are telling the world, legally and socially, that they intend to stay together. I know that plenty of peo-ple abuse this, but just because it gets abused doesn't mean we should do away with the distinction.

I think that's the real fear behind those who say a legally recog-nized gay partnership is going to undermine marriage. If we grant the same honors and privileges to a couple that isn't interested in ris-ing to the responsibilities, we have cheapened committed unions of both kinds. But I think we need to make it clear that it's not an issue of gay versus straight unions, it's a matter of casual versus committed unions. People shouldn't be denied the opportunity to make perma-nent, legally recognized unions with their beloveds simply because they're gay.

Having said that, I sometimes wonder why we're spending so much time these days talking about legally recognizing gay partner-ships when so many other more fundamental rights are still being denied to gays. Almost any openly gay person can tell you story after story about being denied jobs, housing, or medical care. No citizen should be denied these things simply because of his or her sexual ori-entation. We're the United States of America, not the *Hetero* States of America.

How do we protect gay rights? The same way we protect everyone else's rights: by upholding the law, and prosecuting those who violate it. I don't believe we need special legislation for violence against gays. The things people do when they commit so-called hate crimes are already crimes. If somebody commits murder, it's murder. How lov-ing is *any* murder? Why does it make a difference what their motiva-tion was? I think if we just prosecute the hell out of criminals with the laws we've already got on the books, it would make a huge differ-ence to everyone's freedom and safety. There's no need to create new laws when the old ones will work just fine.

I think we've made a complete mess of the issue of gays serving in the military. Why should the government decide that just because some people are gay, they shouldn't be allowed to serve their country? All that should matter is whether they can handle the responsibilities that they're taking on and get the job done. What difference does it make what a soldier's sexual orientation is?

We really caused a lot of trouble when we decided to politicize AIDS as a disease. It's gotten in the way of public safety. The idea that people with HIV have a right not to tell their sex partners that they're infected is absurd. If it were any other contagious disease, we wouldn't think twice about expecting people to protect each other from infection. When we allow a disease to become a political issue instead of a medical issue, we put up roadblocks to dealing with that disease effectively.

There's a very vocal bunch of people on the conservative Right who keep trying to say that people choose to be gay. Well, all of my gay friends tell me that they never chose it. And there's more scientific evidence every day backing them up, showing that it's something they're born with. But still there's that vocal group that keeps saying it's a choice. I love asking the question, "So when did you make the choice to be a heterosexual?" It shuts them down pretty fast.

I don't know how much of an issue we should make out of whether homosexuality is chosen or not. It looks to me like it's not a choice at all, but even if it were, so what? Why is it anybody's business who someone chooses as a sex partner, as long as it's a consenting adult they're choosing? It's not my business. How does that hurt anyone? I know that a lot of religious doctrines have some strong things to say against homosexuality. But remember, we don't run this country according to religious doctrine. We run this country according to a set of principles that guarantees equal rights, freedom, and privacy to everybody. And that applies to gay citizens as much as it does to straight.

Women's Rights

> *If you do not regard feminism with an uplifting sense of the gloriousness of woman's industrial destiny, or in the way, in short, that it is prescribed, by the rules of the political publicist, that you should, that will be interpreted by your opponents as an attack on woman.*
>
> —Wyndham Lewis

I'm all for equal opportunities for women. Our nation is richer when women can contribute their individuality to the fabric of our society. But here again, I think we get off track when we talk about equal rights without also talking about equal responsibilities.

Our government can only protect rights, it can't always enforce responsibilities. That part is up to us. But practically speaking, you can't have one without the other. Women have done a terrific job over the past few decades of breaking down the barriers that denied them equal rights. We have more women in positions of power in our society than ever before, and our society is the better for it. I'm all for that.

But there's a vocal minority of women's rights advocates that has left behind the whole concept of equality and is just trying to score points for women any way it can. These are the women who seem to want it both ways. They want women to be protected and sheltered as they were in the olden days, but they want women to be autonomous, too—when it suits them. It doesn't work that way. If you're charting your own destiny, you've got to take responsibility for where that destiny leads you. You can't just argue for your autonomy when it benefits you.

I hear an awful lot of women arguing for equal treatment, but then the minute the going gets tough—and it does get tough for all of us, sometimes—they start hollering about harassment and abuse.

Men are lucky in that respect: Just by the way we interact with each other, we toughen each other up. Listen in on conversations in an all-guy environment. We insult each other all the time! Starting way back in grade school, guys just naturally seem to pick on each other as a way of testing their mettle. Imagine a group of girls doing that, and sooner or later, somebody would burst into tears!

Men benefit from the hassling that they get from their buddies, because they're better able to handle it when they encounter it out in the real world. I think if women truly want to be shoulder to shoulder with men, they need to figure out how to toughen themselves up better. They can't go play hurt just because things weren't made all nice and comfortable for them. That's not fair, either. How is that equal rights?

That sounds to me like we're trying to create special privileges for women. That's off track, it seems to me, from the original intent of the feminist movement. Besides, I have more respect for women than that. I've known plenty of women who were "woman enough" to take on any situation a man could take on. All through time, even when the playing field was far less level than it is today, a few powerful, determined women managed to break through and accomplish phenomenal things: Joan of Arc, Marie Curie, Indira Gandhi, Golda Meir, Margaret Thatcher, Mother Teresa of Calcutta, to name just a few. Women can be powerful when they choose to be. They don't need special treatment in order to make it in the world. What an insult to women, to assume that they do!

That's why I'm suspicious of issues like sexual harassment. We seem to have gotten so overly sensitive about harassment that it makes it look like women can't handle any kind of sexual overtures from men at all. Now, I'm all for women's rights to do their jobs without having to worry about whether they're going to be sexually assaulted. But I think we need to get a whole lot clearer on what we mean by assault and harassment, because right now the definition is arbitrary. If a guy proposes the most depraved sexual activity to a woman, and she goes along with it, there's no harassment. But in some cases, all he has to do is tell an off-color joke he heard on TV last night, and if a woman is offended, he could lose his job. How is that equality?

I don't think we ought to take things to such a ridiculous extreme that we're saying women can't handle any sexual advances from men. If women are in public, they're going to get come-ons from men. That's not going to change. It's called Nature. Any women who can't deal with that are probably better off staying at home.

Having said that, though, I do have to say that I think we need to work a lot harder at preventing domestic abuse. It's not purely a women's issue; men can be victims of domestic abuse too, and children are certainly the ones who suffer from it the most. But among adults, the vast majority of the victims of domestic abuse are women.

The whole thing is about control. We need to educate both males and females about this so that they don't grow up thinking they ought to be in control. Women and men alike suffer in abusive situations; their self-esteem drops, and they become lesser people. Worst of all, a lot of domestic abuse murders occur when the abused person finally tries to break away. It's issues like these that really deserve our focus: cases where lives and well-being are at stake. If we put this on the same level with a few inappropriate sexual remarks overheard at work, we've done a disservice to the real victims of abuse.

That's the real danger in making the definition of harassment too broad: We won't be able to take the real thing as seriously when it happens. We mustn't make telling an off-color joke weigh the same as grabbing a woman when she doesn't want to be grabbed. When there's unwanted bodily contact going on, it's a deadly serious issue, and it should be treated as such.

But for every woman who goes running to her lawyer when a man says something with a sexual connotation to her, I know plenty of women who can handle the situation just fine on their own. A self-confident person of either sex knows how to handle a verbal situation they don't like. That's not an issue of gender; it's an issue of maturity. And for women who work in situations where they might get physically molested, there's nothing quite like a black belt in tae kwon do, karate, or jujitsu for deterring unwanted sexual advances. I'm not saying that every woman has to have a black belt just to be in the work force. But there are dozens of options, other than simply playing victim, which I think would strengthen the women's cause in the long run.

Just as I don't think it's fair for women to demand special privileges under the banner of equal rights, I also don't think it's fair the way some women have turned the tables on men in recent decades. There's an undercurrent of antimale sentiment in a lot of our culture today. Have you ever noticed that women can get away with making blatantly sexist jokes about men, but if a man tells a similar joke about women, he is in a world of hurt!

How is that equality? It is *equality* we want for women, isn't it, not replacing female subordination with male subordination? In that case, we'd all better learn to play fair. If women want respect, they'd better show respect. As long as there's this stupid "war between the sexes" mentality, equality between the two sexes is going to be undermined. Why do we need to have a war?

I think we need to educate our young men and young women in terms of what's appropriate sexual behavior in public situations. We should raise both sexes to respect the fact that no means no. Likewise, we need to be teaching our kids respect for people of the opposite sex. We are equal in terms of our personhood and our natural rights, but that doesn't mean we're the same. There are some very real differences between men and women, and I don't think we ought to pretend those differences don't exist just because it's politically fashionable these days to do so. I think we ought to respect the differences between us, understanding that both sexes have valuable, irreplaceable contributions to make to our society.

Abortion: The Ultimate No-Win Issue

I'm not pro-abortion. I don't think I could ever participate in an abortion, and I would never encourage anybody to solve their problems by getting one. But does that mean I think abortion should be illegal? Nope.

The emphasis must be not on the right to abortion but on the right to privacy and reproductive control.

—Ruth Bader Ginsburg

One of the best arguments I've ever heard for the legalization of abortion came from my mom. She was a nurse, and she remembers back in the days before abortion was legal, seeing the women who were rushed into the emergency room hemorrhaging uncontrollably from a do-it-yourself abortion that had gone wrong. More than a few women died from back-alley abortions, and many more became sterile.

There are some things that legislation can't control. Just as with drug use, abortions don't stop just because they're made illegal. They simply go underground, where they become far more dangerous.

Let me give you another reason why abortions should be legal: Imagine for a moment that you're a young woman with three small children. You find out you're pregnant again, and you're thrilled. But then something goes wrong with the pregnancy. The doctors tell you that you've developed a rare complication and the fetus's life is threatening your own. If you try to carry this baby to term, you have a 95 percent chance of dying before nine months is out.

Suppose you decide you'd rather risk dying yourself than be responsible for terminating your baby's life. You're ready to put the situation into God's hands, until one night your husband comes to you and pleads with you to reconsider. Suppose he says he can't take care of three small children alone; he needs you, they need you.

What do you do? Is the new child going to take that much importance over the kids that exist already? Do you even have a right to jeopardize your own life when you've got four other people who depend on you?

Now, let me ask you, whose decision should this be? The government's? Or should it be made by the woman and her family, along with the support of her doctors and her clergy? How could the government possibly presume to tell her whether or not she should risk her life to bring this child to term? This is an extreme example, of course. But the point is that of all the viewpoints in making a decision like this, government's is the least helpful.

It's not so much that I think abortion should be legal as it is that I don't think it can be made illegal without abusing the Constitution. Unless the government barged in at the precise moment the woman was there in the operating room with her feet in the stirrups, how would the government know she was getting an abortion? How could they even know she was pregnant without infringing upon her rights?

Ultimately, no matter how I feel about it personally, I have to support keeping it legal, because I don't think it's an issue that can or should be solved by politicians. The government has to stay out of this one.

Immigration

Immigration, like abortion, is another political hot button of the radical Right. They love to create images of our beloved Norman Rockwell America being overrun with smelly, surly, dark-skinned people who don't speak English and who will all be on welfare, but will still somehow manage to steal all our jobs.

> *Our flag is red, white and blue, but our nation is a rainbow . . .*
>
> —Jesse Jackson

I suspect that what anti-immigration people don't like is not so much immigration itself but who is immigrating. I smell racist over-tones in a lot of anti-immigrant rhetoric. I have to wonder, if the bulk of immigrants to this country were pink-skinned, blond people with college degrees, would there be this much protest against it? You never hear any protests about Scandanavian models or Canadians crossing our northern border. But the anti-immigrant crowd is very vocal when it comes from our borders on the south.

We're a nation of immigrants. We always have been. It's built into the very fiber of our country. America is meant to be a haven for those who crave a new way of life. We would lose a huge part of our identity if we gave that up. Immigration, to a large extent, is what has provided our country with such an incredible amount of diversity. We have ideas, languages, music, food, and inventions from all over the world. We're a richer nation because of immigration.

Of course it does make sense for America to uphold a smart immigration policy. I see no problem with a cap on the annual num-ber of people admitted for citizenship. I see no problem, either, with a citizenship course and test to make certain that all new American citizens understand our system of government and the principles of our society. I just wish we did as good a job teaching Americans born here about our nation's principles as we do with immigrants to our country. It's ironic that we require more knowledge of new citizens than of natives. It ought to be standard for everybody.

Now, even though I'm all for a sensible policy of legal immigra-tion, I draw the line at illegal immigrants. Anybody who comes into this country illegally should be sent back. I think the case of that Cuban boy in Florida, Elian Gonzalez, is very clear. It was right that he was sent back home with his father. Nobody has been able to show that the father is unfit. I don't like it when the government steps in and takes authority away from parents. That sets a bad precedent. We don't want to go there. Besides, I think the only reason Elian's situa-tion got to be big news is because he became a political opportunity. It put Florida in the spotlight. Somebody scored votes for it.

If we really wanted to help out that kid, we could lift the embargo on Cuba. How come we haven't done that, after all these years? We trade with China, why not with Cuba?

The Environment

The extreme Right has done a terrific job of spinning environmental concern into an "extreme Left wacko" agenda. They've worked hard to make environmentalism synonymous with tree huggers and people who throw buckets of blood on fur coats. Politicians tread carefully through environmental issues, for fear of getting one of those unfavorable labels stuck on them.

But the rare politician who does take on environmental issues doesn't necessarily have the environment's best interests at heart. Remember that many of today's politicians are beholden to whoever pays their campaign bills. Often the money for their campaigns has come from a large corporation. If by chance environmental legislation comes along that affects that company's bottom line, who do you think the politician is likely to side with?

> *I* am I plus my surroundings and if I do not preserve the latter, I do not preserve myself.
> —José Ortega y Gasset

Now, granted, there are corporations out there that are working hard to be environment-friendly and promote recycling. But for each of them, there are other businesses that are only after the bottom line, who don't mind dumping illegally if it's the cheapest alternative.

How do we get big businesses to behave? To an extent, it can be done by grassroots action. If enough of us report environmental abuses to our representatives in Congress, it will get their attention. But before we can expect a whole lot of response from our politicians, we have to get back to campaign reform and get big corporations out of the campaign finance business. Otherwise, there is always the potential for a conflict of interest.

For the most part, I think our policy toward the environment should strive for a happy medium. We should be sensible about the way we treat our environment, of course. But until somebody proves to me that we're not at the top of the food chain, I'm going to believe that we take priority.

There are some things we ought to be doing, both for the environment and for our own best interests. I think we should encourage and subsidize the use of ethanol, alcohol from corn, as a gasoline alternative. Why not? We subsidize the use of foreign oil by keeping a military presence in the Persian Gulf.

I think we'd better find ways to overcome our dependency on foreign oil in particular, and fossil fuels in general. We probably could have grown beyond our dependence on fossil fuels a long time ago, if it weren't for the automotive industries. They've stopped at nothing to push us into cars, and limit our transportation options. It's yet another case of the power brokers of government getting in the way of what's best for us.

Crime

*P*rohibition will work great injury to the cause of temperance. It is a species of intemperance within itself, for it goes beyond the bounds of reason in that it attempts to control a man's appetite by legislation, and makes a crime out of things that are not crimes. A Prohibition law strikes a blow at the very principles upon which our government was founded.
—**Abraham Lincoln**

A little-known fact about being governor is that I get about one death threat a week. I don't even hear about all of the threats, but generally if the threat is taken seriously, my security has to inform me. They want me to be on my toes. They want me to be a little more reluctant to shake hands with the public, which is something I generally love to do. It's sad.

The threats take every form: phone calls to my receptionists, E-mails. We usually catch them on the E-mails because E-mail leaves tracks. We caught one guy who threatened to violate the first lady and chop my kids into pieces. He sent the E-mail from a computer at the University of Minnesota, Duluth. We traced it to him and busted him for it.

It turned out he was just an eighteen-year-old kid. He ended up writing me a full letter of apology, but he wouldn't assume total responsibility, because he said he was angry that he had gotten on one of my mailing lists and asked to be taken off, and he wasn't taken off as quickly as he'd wanted. That's typical today. Nobody is responsible for their own actions. It's always somebody else's fault.

The kid was working at a Toys "R" Us when my people went in, whipped out their badges, and took him. They asked me if I wanted him charged here in Minneapolis or there in Duluth. I said, "Charge him in Duluth." We chose Duluth, because it's a smaller community and things like that don't happen there much. We figured they'd be a little tougher on him.

At least when people threaten me, they're lashing out at a public figure who has the ability to affect their lives. But when they try to threaten my daughter, a sixteen-year-old special ed kid who is completely innocent, it totally blows my mind. It's a side of human nature that makes no sense to me. I don't understand the level of violent, disgusting, criminal behavior in our society today. I don't understand the form it takes. I doubt that anyone in our society fully understands it. Yet, rest assured, any politician up for election will be out to convince you that he or she has the answers.

Politicians love to crow about how tough they're going to get on crime. What does that mean, anyway? What can a politician do about crime, unless he's willing to pack his own heat out on the streets and kick some butt? When was the last time you saw a senator or a president do that?

I'd be willing to bet that once these supposedly crime-tough politicians get into office, more than half of them forget all about doing anything about crime. Probably most of the other half pass a bunch of stupid laws that only duplicate laws that are already on the books, or they go to the pork barrel to fund more meaningless crime studies.

There's only one way politicians can really affect crime, and that's to advocate that we make better use of the laws we've already got on the books. We have all the legislation we need. We have too much, in fact. We could probably throw away half the criminal laws on the books and still get tough on crime, if we'd just get serious about enforcing those laws.

I think we do a disservice to our society when we try to make prison into something it isn't. I really don't think American prisons are ever going to be much of a crime deterrent. Criminals aren't scared of prison in this country. The Constitution forbids us from really making it into something to fear, because of the "cruel and unusual punishment" clause. We're fooling ourselves if we think criminals are going to toe the line just because we threaten them with prison.

Prison should be viewed as a pragmatic necessity. It should be for getting violent offenders under control; locking them up where they can't do more harm. Anytime we get off track from this concept of prison, we end up costing taxpayers more money with no real benefit to society.

I don't think the way to get tough on crime is to lock away nonviolent offenders. I believe that prison is meant for the violent. There are probably dozens of alternatives to prison for nonviolent criminals. I'm partial to community service, personally, because when criminals work off their debt to society that way, it amounts to something society can actually benefit from. And in many cases, it can provide an eye-opening learning experience for the criminals themselves, if they're amenable to it.

It's weird how we're totally intolerant of certain crimes like illegal drug use, which seldom hurt anybody but the addict, yet we're very tolerant of crimes like drunk driving, which are often fatal to the drivers' victims. There's no excuse for it anymore. It's a misdemeanor, when it ought to be a felony. A car out of control at 70 miles per hour is as lethal as any gun.

We've gotten better about drunk driving, but we have a long way to go. It was looked upon as a joke, more or less, until MADD came along. We in Minnesota are still behind the times; we've got twelve-time offenders. That shouldn't happen. Once drunk drivers get caught, their licenses should be yanked, or they should be given very restricted licenses that only allow them to drive to and from work.

Of course, I suspect that people who drive while using cell phones also cause many accidents. I was in an accident once because of it. While I was stopped at a light, a guy hit the car behind me and pushed it into my car. The guy in the third car said his brakes failed, but I saw the cell phone in his hand. We need to discourage cell phone use while driving. How hard would it be for people just to pull over when they need to make a call?

I think we ought to adopt more of the European attitude toward driving: It's a privilege, not a right. We're far too dependent on automobiles anyway. We need to work on getting more mass transit, so that we don't force people into cars and limit their choices.

I don't believe that a free society like ours ought to have a death penalty. I'm not comfortable with the idea of granting the government the power to put its citizens to death. The margin for error is too great. I used to be pro–death penalty, until I became governor, and I realized that I could actually hold in my own hands the responsibility for decreeing somebody's death. What would that feel like, if I allowed somebody to be put to death, and then evidence surfaced, a year or ten years later, that proved the dead person innocent? That margin for error is enough to convince me that we shouldn't be putting people to death. Death is kind of irreversible. Besides, in a civilized society, should the power of the government really be used to execute people?

But there are a few things we need to get straight in our legal system before we can do away with the death penalty. Life in prison has to mean life. I doubt that maintaining a prisoner for life is really going to be that much more expensive, in the long run, than all the endless appeals that an inmate on death row goes through. Besides, who's to say that a prison lifer couldn't earn his keep? There must be jobs that prisoners can do to defray their expenses.

Nobody's ever been able to explain to me why we waste prison cells on drug addicts. Drug addiction is a consensual crime, it's a "crime against oneself." Why are we locking up addicts? To protect them from themselves? How can we justify letting violent criminals go because of overcrowding, when there are so many people behind bars whose only crime is that they're addicted to something? Drug addiction is a health problem; it should be treated medically, not criminally. If we treated it that way, it would provide a tremendous amount of relief to our prison systems. Not only that, but many of the users could be paying taxes while they were in outpatient treatment instead of being a burden to the rest of us taxpayers.

I keep hearing case after case of somebody doing ten years for drug possession sitting in a cell next to somebody doing two years for a violent crime. Marijuana can get you more time than assault. We've got to change that. Prisons should be reserved for violent criminals. Putting anybody else in there is a misdirection, and a complete waste, of government resources.

I'm against legislation that puts the state or federal government in the position of caring for somebody for life for trivial reasons. That's why I'm opposed to the Three Strikes law, as it's now written. We should be prosecuting felons severely the first time around. If somebody has done a violent crime and served his time, you don't then put him away forever for stealing cookies. Mandatory sentences are awful. They take power away from judges. Judges should be allowed a certain amount of discretion. They should be able to treat each case individually.

Three Strikes would work fine if it put people away for three violent felonies. But it's a stupid waste of taxpayers' money otherwise. Plus, it causes a backup in our court system, because nobody who gets caught a third time wants to plead guilty and face certain life in prison. Legislators love tough-sounding programs like Three Strikes; unfortunately, like a lot of their pet legislation, it makes them look good at campaign time, but it causes us more problems afterwards. And many times, they don't even bother to fully fund their own legislation.

I think we need to work on decriminalizing drug abuse in this country. The decision to use drugs in the first place is pure stupidity, and we can't make stupid decisions against the law. First of all, it's impossible, and second, a free society has no business doing that.

The war on drugs is political. The government thinks it needs to have a "common enemy" to rally the public and keep the public on its side. But they're fighting this war on the wrong side. They're trying to curb the drug trade by fighting on the side of supply, when they should be fighting on the side of demand. As long as there is a demand for it, somebody's going to find a way to supply it.

While I was working on the Pardon Board, there was a guy who came before us who had twenty-nine drug possessions on his prison record—even though he had been in a maximum security prison, twenty-four hours a day! If this guy could get drugs whenever he wanted, anybody could. And for the twenty-nine times he got caught, the actual number of times he possessed drugs was probably in the hundreds.

When something becomes illegal, prices go up, and it tempts more people into the business. It's gotten ridiculous: We're now sending people and resources into Colombia to fight the drug war there. We've got no business going into somebody else's country! Barry McCaffrey, the drug czar, says drugs are illegal because they're dangerous. Well, so is alcohol. So are cars. So are cigarettes. So is sky-diving. So are hundreds of other things. The government can't make all dangerous things illegal. It doesn't work. You'd think we would have learned our lesson with Prohibition, but apparently we didn't.

I'm going to give you an example of the way that legislation against certain activities can have the opposite of the desired effect, not only by turning people who do the activity into lawbreakers, but also by increasing other kinds of crimes as well. The first lady and I visited Amsterdam a few years ago. The Netherlands has a unique way of dealing with three things that are mostly illegal in this country: Prostitution, marijuana, and pornography. All three are legal there, but are carefully regulated. Amsterdam has its own red-light district, where all of these kinds of activities are concentrated. You don't see them anywhere else in the city. But people who want to partake can go there.

While we were walking along one evening, we saw a bus of senior citizens pull up and unload. They all went off on a walking tour of the red-light district, in the dark! There are parts of most of our major cities that are the equivalent of that part of Amsterdam, but you wouldn't want to go walking there at night! I wouldn't dare take a busload of senior citizens down to certain parts of cities, even in the daytime. But in Amsterdam, because these activities weren't illegal, they weren't a haven for crime. That neighborhood had no more crime than the average suburban neighborhood. I believe that in some cases, making something illegal actually encourages crime, because people are going to partake whether it's legal or not.

Now, even in the Netherlands, the harder drugs are illegal, and rightly so. I wouldn't advocate making things like heroin and cocaine legal. But at the same time, it doesn't make sense for us to criminally prosecute people just for using them. Addicts should be able to check into a hospital and get help for their addiction without worrying that they'll be carted off to jail. Hospitals should be allowed to help wean addicts from their addictions, as may be medically appropriate. Making addicts into criminals doesn't do anything positive.

But marijuana is a different issue. I see no reason for marijuana to be illegal, and especially not for it to carry the bizarre stigma that the government has placed on it. Besides, we're wasting a huge amount of time, money, and resources on trying to control marijuana, and so far what we've been doing is ridiculously ineffective. You may have heard it said that alcohol and tobacco buy their freedom. They generate revenue for the government with the taxes we pay when we purchase them. Marijuana is the opposite: The government spends a huge amount of our money trying to fight it, for no gain. It would make a lot more sense for us to legalize it and tax it.

It's hard to get a reasonable discussion going on what to do about consensual crime. Just bringing it up is enough to get people riled. When I was campaigning for governor, I explained to people why I thought that making drug use and prostitution illegal wasn't doing much good. I tried to explain that there are some things that legislation just can't do a good job of controlling. I was trying to get people to think, to brainstorm, to get creative, and maybe to generate some new ideas on how we could control these problems. But the media somehow decided that I was advocating legalizing drugs and prostitution, and they got all excited over that, so my message never got through. Whenever the subject came up, I always ended up having to spend the time quashing the rumor that I wanted to make them legal.

But when you look at the statistics on drug use in this country, it's pretty easy to see that our nation's war on drugs has failed. I may be one of the only political figures around with the guts to say this, but those few of us who are willing to say it are finally beginning to gain some supporters. There's got to be a better way to control drug use. When it comes right down to it, is it really the use of drugs that's causing the problems? Or is it the violence and theft associated with the use of drugs?

I believe the war on drugs is a failure for the same reasons Prohibition was a failure. My mom told me about that. She lived through it. She saw that as soon as the government made alcohol consumption illegal, criminals cornered the market on liquor. Getting alcohol went from a safe, legal, affordable activity, to one that often involved bloodshed and obscene amounts of money. And it gave rise to half a dozen other crimes as well. It caused a huge groundswell in organized crime. It made a lot of criminals rich. Today, illegal drug use is doing the exact same thing.

Just imagine if we could find some way for addicts to get their drugs cheaply, safely, and legally. The bottom would drop out of the illegal drug market. I'd be willing to bet if we did that, we'd see a huge drop in organized and violent crime.

Legislation is a terrible way to try to control drug use. Drug use is another one of those issues that falls under the heading of "You Can't Legislate Stupidity." If people are dumb enough to get hooked on drugs—and don't try to tell me they don't know that the drugs are addictive, everybody knows that—then they're not likely to be smart enough to follow the law just on principle.

But as useless as it is to try to make dumb activities illegal, at least prohibition laws try to regulate conduct. There's a movement out there right now that is potentially much more harmful, because it's subtly moving legislation out of the realm of action and into the realm of thought, where it has no business whatsoever. I'm talking about the movement toward hate crime legislation.

Hate crime legislation is political fluff. It's politicians saying, "We've gotta show the public that we're not gonna tolerate this." It's feel-good legislation. It's not going to solve anything. Worst of all, it sets a dangerous precedent. We're now beginning to prosecute people not just for what they do, but for what they think.

No one should be prosecuted for what they think or say, unless it results in illegal conduct—then you prosecute them for the action. We start a dangerous trend when we try to prosecute people for what they're thinking. Remember, Jefferson warned that government should be concerned only with actions. It had no authority to touch thoughts or speech, no matter how heinous.

Do you remember the recent story about the fellow in Texas who was dragged to his death? His killers were tried for committing a hate crime. But he's no more dead than he would be if they had done it for some other reason. Is it really worse that they did what they did out of hatred than if they had done it just for fun? How can we place a value on people's motivations?

We have no business penalizing people for their thoughts. We're placing far too much judgment on people's thought and speech today. It's a slippery path, and I don't think we're going to like where that path is taking us.

WHY ARE OUR KIDS KILLING EACH OTHER?

When the Columbine shooting happened, the media came up to me for a statement. Of all the things they could have asked me, their question was, "How do you feel about the state of Colorado taking a conceal-and-carry bill off the floor in response to the Columbine shooting?" I told them over and over again, "I have no comment on that. That's Colorado's business."

But throughout that entire day, every chance they got they'd rush up to me and try to get me to say something. At the end of the day, I said, "Look, had there been a licensed conceal-and-carry in that building, chances are, lives would have been saved."

What you had in Columbine was two sick kids who went in and executed people. Nobody was going to be able to reason with these kids. They had to be taken out, and if people don't believe that, they're living in a dream world. But do you know what came out in the paper? "Governor Says People Should Be Armed in School." All I said was if there had been someone legitimately armed, they might have gotten the drop on these killers, and maybe not as many kids would have died.

That was my one criticism of the SWAT team. When they arrived and heard shots being fired on the inside, they should have gone in. The SEAL in me says that if you know shots are being fired, you have no time to make a plan. The time for negotiating is over.

What you had at Columbine was an act of terrorism. Terrorists are cowards. They don't attack well-armed people. Have you ever heard of terrorists attacking a military installation? There was that one rare attack in Lebanon, but even that was with a truck bomb, when everybody was asleep. But generally, they'll do it in the most cowardly, sneaky way they can think of. It's never man to man with terrorists. And that's why those two twisted kids went after their school.

That's also why since Columbine I've been asking, what do we value more, our money or our children? If you go to any bank and try to steal money, there's a guard on duty who will shoot you. Do we value our money more than our kids? It's sad that things have gotten to a state where we even have to consider this, but I don't think it's unreasonable to talk about having armed guards at our schools.

I think it would be a great idea to have a single well-trained guy posted at every school, who could pose as a janitor. Only the principal and maybe the vice-principal would know what he was really there for. He'd wear an ankle holster; he'd be packing heat, but every day he'd be there pushing the broom, just doing what janitors do. But he'd be there, already in place, if anything went down. That way you'd have at least one person there who could shoot back. Do you think those two kids would have been shooting if they thought somebody was going to shoot back? No way.

The saddest development in American crime these days is the seemingly epidemic number of kids who suddenly show up at their schools one day and open fire. Every time I hear on the news about another one of these episodes, I feel completely bewildered. What could possibly be causing these kids to snap?

I wish I had some answers. Whatever it is, it's a recent development, because you never heard of this kind of thing happening when I was growing up. When I was in school, we had no need for metal detectors and armed guards. Kids didn't bring guns to school. When we did fight, it was with fists, to settle a dispute. You never heard of kids opening up full bore with the kind of deadly rage you hear about now.

You've probably read the same statistics that I have. In America today, crime is down a bit all across the boards—except in the realm of juvenile offenders. In that demographic, it's getting increasingly more bloody and more lethal. What the hell is going on with our kids today? Whatever it is, we'd better figure it out fast, before more of our sons and daughters end up dead.

I have to think it has something to do with the fact that the kids who do this aren't getting the attention and supervision they need. It's hard for me to say whether or not most parents are doing a worse job of raising their kids these days, because I meet terrific kids all the time. I sometimes think it's just that a minority of bad kids are grabbing all the headlines. But the bad kids that make the headlines are getting more and more violent, and there's no way that could be happening if their parents were paying attention. How could a parent who spends a lot of time with his or her children not know that the kids are building pipe bombs in the basement?

It could be that lack of involvement is a major factor in creating the rage that leads kids to do these things. They don't have a solid sense of belonging, they aren't being taught the basic skills we all need to cope with the kind of teasing, rejection, and general BS that everybody goes through during school, and they aren't being taught how to handle their anger and their impulses. That's my best guess.

That, coupled with the violently stimulating crap they see in movies, on TV, and in video games. I don't blame Hollywood for kids' violence; I blame the parents who allow their kids to watch violent stuff. I think it's hypocritical of us to talk about cleaning up Hollywood. Parents can decide whether or not their kids watch the stuff Hollywood puts out. If we're so worried about what our kids are consuming these days, why isn't anybody hollering about cleaning up the evening news? It's some of the most sordid, violent stuff around! But there, too, parents have the power. They decide whether what's coming into their households through the TV set is really fit to watch.

We live in a culture today that encourages irresponsible behavior in many ways. The mechanisms that used to keep ordinary kids from going bad, and that kept bad kids from doing harm, are weaker than they were a generation ago. I believe a tiny minority of people are just born bad. There have always been twisted kids, throughout history. But I think today's culture doesn't provide the right kinds of mechanisms for catching these kids and diagnosing them before they get out of hand. In the past, involved parents, family members, and neighbors would probably have seen things going wrong, and would have stepped in. We've lost a major layer of crime prevention in our society.

I'm big on prevention where crime is concerned, for the same reasons I believe that prevention is the best way to control poverty and drug use. It's a lot easier, safer, and cheaper to keep it from happening in the first place than it is to pick up the pieces after the damage is done.

I think we need to work a whole lot harder on addressing the factors that lead to criminal behavior. Study after study has shown a strong link between an unstable home life and crime. Any time a kid grows up without a strong parental bond, he or she is much more likely to get in trouble. After all, what have they got to lose? I'm sure that's why gangs are appealing to some kids: At least they get a sense of belonging from being in them.

We all need to belong. If we're not getting that at home from an early age, there's very little standing in the way of antisocial behavior.

I have a hunch that if we really want to do something to prevent crime, the best thing we can do is find out how we can strengthen families. The strongest families in the world are never going to be a 100 percent deterrent against crime. But I believe they are our best defense.

Education

The liberally educated person is one who is able to resist the easy and preferred answers, not because he is obstinate but because he knows others worthy of consideration.
—Allan Bloom

Few things are more important to a democratic society than a solid education for all of its citizens. When you think about the power every citizen of this country has whenever they go into the voting booth or into the juror's box, you begin to realize how important it is that they know what they're doing in there.

How many presidential candidates have told you that they're going to be the "education president"? Al Gore is the most recent voice in this particular chorus; he's started yodeling about how important education is to him. It's a very effective vote-getting technique. Most of us have kids, and we love the idea that we could put somebody in the White House who will make it easier for our kids to get a decent education.

But in the long run, few elected officials seem to do much to affect the quality of the education our kids are getting. My guess is it's because education reform yields long-term results, and those aren't the kind that matter when reelection time is right around the corner. Short-term, quick fixes are what make incumbents look good. But much of the reform our education system needs isn't going to manifest itself that quickly. Our education system is in need

of deep, profound, long-term change. It may not be politically expedient, but it's desperately needed.

We need to do a long-term, top-to-bottom overhaul of our public school curricula. We have to make sure that what we're teaching is
going to be relevant to students' lives. Also, there are a few vital skills
that we aren't teaching yet, which we desperately need to add to the
school curricula.

We don't do a good enough job teaching our kids sound thinking
and reasoning skills. In a democratic republic, this ought to be a
basic cornerstone of public education. Kids may or may not pick up
some of these skills in English and science classes. They may or may
not have opportunities to get into debate clubs and forensics teams. I
think we need to take a more direct approach to teaching good
thinking habits.

Thinking is largely a learned behavior; it's a skill. It can be taught.
There are specific, teachable principles to follow in constructing a
valid argument and a sound opinion. I think we ought to start kids
off at an early age learning the basic skills required in thinking for
themselves, and we need to reinforce that training in all twelve
grades. When you consider how much of our society today is working against free thought, when you realize how much media of all
kinds contribute to the dumbing-down of our kids, you begin to see
how vital this kind of training is.

I think public schools need to take on teaching money manage-
ment skills. This ought to be mandatory for every student. Kids need
to be taught the basic principles of a free market economy and their
role in it. They need to learn how to balance a checkbook, how to
avoid debt—especially crippling credit card debt—and how to save
and invest for the long term. They need to be taught that financial
well-being is their responsibility. And they need to be taught, specifically, that job skills are an absolute necessity if they are going to avoid
poverty.

Ideally, kids should be learning these kinds of life skills at home from their parents. But these days, since so many kids aren't getting the parenting they need at home, maybe our schools need to function as a fail-safe. At best, this will reinforce what kids are learning at home. At least, they'll get it from one source, if not from the other.

We need to strengthen and retool civics classes to help kids develop a working understanding of our system of government and their role in it. They need to be taught, and have the lesson reinforced at every grade level, the principles of the Constitution and the structure of our government. They need to be taught specifically about those duties that are their responsibility: voting, jury duty, and public service. We need to make sure that all kids are getting this information. We don't want to leave it to chance.

It's clear to me that we'd better start educating kids about parenting. They need to know the facts of life. I'm all for abstinence; we should definitely be teaching it. But for those kids who are going to go ahead and have sex anyway, they'd better know about condoms. After all, there's the ideal world and then there's the real world.

And I think it's about time we introduced a basic morals and values curriculum into our public schools. You know me well enough by now to know that I'm not talking about a specific religious doctrine or code of ethics. But there's a basic set of morals that all civilized societies have in common. They're what make it possible for people to get along and live in peace. And these are the kinds of behaviors we should be teaching.

As with the financial stuff, it would be ideal if public schools didn't have to take this on. But because it's so crucial to our kids' development, and because fewer and fewer kids are getting this kind of training at home anymore, we need to make sure that they're at least getting the basics of civil behavior.

We all need to make an effort to salvage our public schools. Just as with any other aspect of our society, our schools are only as good as our commitment to them. The reason we're seeing a deterioration in our public schools today is because we've gotten lazy about our commitment to them.

I don't like the kind of talk that encourages people to abandon our public schools in favor of a private education. Public schools are one of the greatest institutions of a free democratic society, and we ought to fight to keep them strong. If they've got problems, which they do, then we need to fix what's wrong with them, not abandon them.

That's why I've taken such a strong stand against private school vouchers. I think they increase our bias against public schools. Besides, nobody has figured out a way yet to apply vouchers fairly. If your income rises above a certain cutoff point, you can't get them. Plenty of people are going to fall into that gap between qualifying for private school vouchers and actually being able to afford private school.

But if we start encouraging people to opt out of public schools because the schools have problems, then we remove more and more of the incentive to fix what's wrong with them. So those of us who get stuck sending our kids there have to put up with a substandard school system.

I believe that instead of rejecting public schools in favor of private ones, we ought to fight to make public schools better. That's why, in spite of the fact that I'm strongly against increasing government spending of almost any kind, I'm advocating spending increases for schools. We need to get more teachers into our public classrooms, and we need to be able to pay good teachers well enough that they will want to stick around.

I've advocated an 11 percent education spending increase here in Minnesota. The bulk of that money is going to be spent on hiring more teachers. We've got specific goals for decreasing class size over time. I'd like to see more states do this. Decreased class size is a phenomenally good investment. It means every kid gets more individual attention, which, as my lieutenant governor Mae Schunk will tell you, is the key to effective learning.

I'm all for leveling out educational opportunities so that everybody who wants to take a shot at college can do so. But I draw the line at having the government simply hand out money for college. College should never, ever be a free ride. There are at least a dozen alternatives to having the government simply pick up the tab. There's work-study, assistantships, private scholarships, and if all else fails, there are government-funded student loans.

It's not going to kill kids to earn their way through college. Remember, most college students are in their twenties. If they've got the energy to party all night, they've got the energy to hold down at least a part-time job while they're going to school. I know plenty of people who busted their butts to get through school, working two and three jobs, and studying half the night away. Can you imagine what a slap in the face that must feel like to those kids who are working their way through school, to be sitting in class beside somebody who's coasting along on the government's bankroll? What kind of message does that send?

I don't think we ought to encourage people to accept handouts when they can achieve what they're after for themselves. Besides, if they're smart enough to figure out how to get into college in the first place, they're smart enough to figure out how to pay for it. Ultimately, we value more those things that we've had to work hard and sacrifice for. I believe that we're better off as a society when we place a high value on education.

What Are Family Values Anyway?

When *George* magazine came to interview the first lady, one of the questions they asked her was how she felt about Monica Lewinsky. She thought it was

As the family goes, so goes the nation and so goes the whole world in which we live.

—Pope John Paul II

weird that they even asked. She said, "Why does anyone *care* what I think about Monica Lewinsky?"

I think it's bizarre that Monica Lewinsky became such a fixation for the American people. How did anything Monica did affect any of us? I don't like the fact that the President lied to us. But when you think about what he lied about, it wasn't about foreign policy. It was nothing but a tragedy between him and Hillary. It's none of our business. It offended me that he did it in our house, the people's house. And it offended me even more that he still went on TV and crowed about family values. But we made far more of it than we should have.

I find it humorous when politicians talk about family values. Many of them wouldn't know a family value if it bit them in the ass. And even for those who do have a clue about what it means, think about it this way: Of all the couples you know who have been married more than ten years, how many of them could truly stand up to the kind of scrutiny the press and the public give public figures these days? Because in most cases, within the strongest marriages, both partners have done things that are wrong. But they love each other enough to learn from it, forgive it, and move on.

When you make a long-term commitment to somebody, stuff is going to happen to you. Life is hard. It's not fair that we judge people on things they did a long time ago, and learned from, and came out the better for. It's pointless, and it's destructive.

At heart, family values are about commitment. I think the *real* family values come through when times are tough, when people do screw up—which we all do from time to time. It's the value of commitment that keeps families together, and keeps them willing to turn themselves around and get back on the right path.

All through the 1980s and 1990s, when "family values" was the hottest sound bite of the day, it seemed like every political candidate was scrambling to convince the voters that he or she was pro-family. Remember that? Politicians of the day had probably seen some statistic somewhere that told them the vast majority of the people in the voting booths had children, so they assumed that all they had to do to convince everybody of their wholesome, well-rounded character was to invoke the phrase *family values.*

But while all those politicians were running around crowing about how they lived and breathed family values the rest of us were standing back going, "huh?"

It was a mindless, empty phrase, but it didn't have to be. If politicians had bothered to think it through, they could have made it mean something. We've been talking about the fact that a democratic republic requires a high-quality, self-reliant populace. And we've said that government can't do much to directly affect the quality of its people. So where do high-quality people come from?

You got it. From families.

Everybody in our society, whether they have a family or not, should be pro-family for the same reasons they should be pro-education or pro-health: We all benefit from living in a community where people are self-sufficient, well-rounded, and emotionally healthy. And the best way to make sure people develop these qualities is to give them the chance to grow up in solid, loving families.

Now, this is something very important for us to get straight. If I say that I'm pro-family, that doesn't mean I think that everybody should run out, get married, and have kids. There's absolutely nothing wrong with being childless, whether you're single, married, gay, straight, or whatever. I have more respect for people who acknowledge that they don't want kids than I do for those who get married and have kids just to go along with what they think society sees as respectable.

But if you're going to create a family, then for God's sake, see it through. Be there for your kids, show them that marriages can last and work and stay strong. Make sure that you put their needs first. That's what family values are: If you're gonna have a family, your responsibility to the family you create must be your number one value.

I think we owe it to kids to do whatever we can to give them the ideal situation to grow up in. The best possible place for a kid to be raised is in a stable, loving, financially secure, two-parent household, where one parent is female and the other is male, and where the two parents are married to each other, and have figured out a way to stay married.

Now don't go ballistic on me yet—I said that's the ideal. Where we can create that environment for kids, that's what we should aim for. Anybody who's planning to make a family should be thinking in those terms. But does that mean that people who are in less than ideal circumstances (say, when a spouse dies, or turns out to be a jerk) can't do a great job raising a child? Of course they can. It's going to be a lot harder, and it isn't ideal, but it can be done. But you don't choose that from the beginning; you don't plan a less than optimal existence for your child.

So does that mean that single people or gay couples shouldn't become parents? I think to answer that, you have to look at the reason why you want to become a parent, just as any married person should. If what you want is a sweet, cuddly little thing that will adore you and keep you from being lonely, who is there to fulfill *your* needs and not the other way around, then you should get a hamster, not a child.

But if your goal is to be a parent, if you have a deep, driving desire to care for and raise a child, and you're willing to sacrifice your own convenience and happiness to do it when necessary, then I have a question for you: Instead of making a brand-new human being and bringing it into a less than ideal situation, why not adopt? There are so many kids out there in need of loving homes—older kids, and kids with health problems, who nobody else wants. If you've got all this extra love to go around, why not give it to a kid who desperately needs it? Then you're not robbing the kid of anything; you're taking the kid out of a bad situation and giving him or her a comparatively *great* situation.

I believe that the only reason you hear talk these days about redefining families is that, in this era of entitlement, the old definition of a family has become inconvenient for many people. Many people in our society today believe that they have a right to live however they want, and the fact that they have children shouldn't get in their way.

But all you have to do is look at juvenile crime statistics, and you'll see a huge correlation between crime and single-parent homes. The vast majority of families below the poverty line are also single-parent families. When parents aren't married, or can't figure out a way to stay married, kids generally don't have a model for stability and commitment. And when parents are busy divorcing and dating and remarrying, and bringing new kids into the family, expecting everybody to just get along for the sake of *their* happiness, it's no wonder so many kids from divorced homes have trouble adjusting. It might be a great situation for the parent, but it's chaos for the kid. Still think we ought to redefine the word *family*? Just remember, it ain't the kids asking us to do that!

Kids' needs must come before adults' needs, because kids can't take care of their own needs yet. We can. And I believe that one of the most frequently overlooked needs that children have is the need for a high-quality, ongoing relationship with parents who have time for them every day. Kids need for their parents to be around and available. Children don't understand the concept of "quality time"; that's another idea invented by parents who didn't want the inconvenience of rearranging their lives to fulfill their kids' needs. What children need is quantity time. They need you to be there. A lot. When *they* need you, not when you have time to squeeze them in.

People are forgetting, in this era of personal liberty, that some choices are irreversible, and some come with responsibilities. If you voluntarily bring a child into this world, your choice has been made. That choice is going to limit some of your options, because you're obligated to care for that child to the best of your ability. You've given up some of your freedom for the privilege of being a parent. Having children means radically altering the course of your life for at least the next twenty years. If you're not willing to do that, don't have kids.

Raising preschool kids is a full-time job. I know; my kids were little once. They needed to have someone with them all the time. That's just the nature of children; they learn independence gradually, over time. They have to be taught the skills they need for functioning in society. And who better to teach those skills than the parents? How much sense does it make to farm out that responsibility to a stranger?

But I don't believe that just because you have kids, you're owed government support so you can take care of them. If you're going to have kids, you have to take the responsibility to plan ahead for their care. Hold off having kids, if you have to, until one of you makes enough for the other to stay home full- or part-time. It's only five years per child, until they start school. It's not a lifetime.

I often hear people say, "But doesn't happiness matter? I can only be a good parent if I'm happy." That's more bull. Being a responsible adult means you do what you have to do whether you're enjoying it or not. Mature adults aren't obsessed with whether they're happy every minute. They're focused on doing the right thing, because they know it will turn out for the best in the long run. True happiness isn't about whether or not you're feeling cheery at any given moment. It's about the deep, long-term satisfaction of knowing you've lived an honorable life.

A democratic society had better be pro-family if it knows what's good for it. A free society requires a populace that is capable of handling the responsibilities of freedom. Can a high-quality person come from less than ideal family circumstances? Sure. It's possible. But I wouldn't bet on those odds. Strong families are the best bet for developing solid, responsible people.

But what's government's role in keeping America's families strong? Pretty minimal, unfortunately. Family life is a private matter;

it's basically none of the government's business. That's what makes the "family values" politician such a joke. What can politics do, really, to strengthen families? Not much. We can pass legislation that helps families financially and doesn't penalize them for taking time from their careers to be with their kids. Beyond that, there isn't much government can do. This is another case where it's up to us. We have all the power in this situation, by the choices we make.

6

Building Your
Ideological Tool Kit

*T**he revelation of Thought takes men out of servitude into
freedom.*
—**Ralph Waldo Emerson**

I've never had a bad experience yet at a school. Even though the kids
may not always agree with me on everything I do, they respect me
because they know I tell them the truth. They know that it may not
be what they want to hear, but they know I'll tell them what I really
believe.

It's just the same with raising your own kids. If you lie to them—
even once—they're never going to trust you again. I think you're far
better off being completely honest with them, even though honesty
can be painful at times. In the long run, you *must* be honest with
children, because it's so important for them to trust you.

I think that's what's behind the generation gap we're facing today.
Children see a generation of adults who they know are dishonest.
Notice how there are no hippies left today. Few adults of my age are
willing to come clean to their kids and say, "Yes, I was a hippie. I was
rebellious. I protested. And yes, *I did drugs.*"

I grew up during that time, and I remember that in the late sixties
and early seventies there were more hippies in my generation than

there were straight kids. But almost nobody will own up to having been a hippie. Terry's sister is one of the few exceptions I know. She's told her kids, "Look, there isn't anything you can do that I haven't done. So don't try to come home and tell me that you haven't been drinking, or that you're not high. I know exactly what you'll look like, how you'll talk, and how you'll defend yourselves. So don't even bother to try." And every time they've tried something, she's been standing at the door waiting for them!

But we have a generation of adults today who are in denial. I believe it's because of the war on drugs. When the cold war ended, and the Communists weren't a threat anymore, drugs became our new common enemy. And now nobody wants to own up to having experimented with drugs. I'm not saying we should brag about it, and there's no need to tell our kids every detail. But parents should at least be honest with their children, because then they know they can come to you if they're faced with tough choices, and they can trust that you'll give them an honest perspective.

In the spring of 2000, my son Tyrel went up to Canada to work as Sean Penn's assistant on a movie. Often when Sean couldn't get to sleep at night, Ty sat up with him until three or four o'clock in the morning. They talked philosophy. Now, Tyrel has chosen not to try drugs, because he doesn't want anything to hamper his creativity. But one night when they were sitting up together, Sean Penn asked him, "Ty, have you ever done drugs?" And Sean said, "You know what? Don't even try 'em. Because they'll suck you in. And pretty soon, you'll forget what's important in life. You're not missing anything."

Sean told Ty, "All that stuff you hear about how it makes you more creative—it's all bullshit. It's all a lie. It takes everything out of you, and it gives nothing back." And it meant a lot coming from Sean, because Ty admires him. I've always been open with my kids about things I did when I was their age, even the stuff that wasn't all that easy to admit to. And I believe they respect me for that. But for

Ty to have it reinforced by a mentor of his own choosing—outside his own family—really brought the lesson home.

I don't think it's any different with kids and parents. Kids want to be able to admire their parents, and nothing will destroy their esteem for you quicker than if they find out you're lying to them. I remember what we went through with Ty when he found out there was no Santa Claus. He came home from second grade one day and said, "Mom! Everybody at school says there's no Santa! Can you believe that? What's the matter with them?" And Terry said, "Um, Ty. Actually, there is no Santa." And Ty got this horrified look on his face. "You lied?" And he refused to talk to her for a couple of days. Because he'd defended Santa to his classmates!

I truly believe that the reason I'm sitting in the governor's office today is because I'm committed to being forthright and honest. You may not always like what I have to say, but you know that whenever I give my opinion on something, it's what I really think, not what the pollsters have told me to say I think. I believe most people recognize that we have a severe sincerity deficit among our public officials these days. The people can see that poll-chasing is not the same thing as genuine leadership, and that it isn't taking us where we need to go. They're hungry for honesty, even when it isn't pretty.

A lot of politicians today circumnavigate the need for thinking through a given issue by simply following whatever the polls, their parties, or their campaign contributors tell them to do. That's taking the easy way out. As a public servant, my job isn't necessarily to follow popular opinion (although I always take the public's opinions into account) but to put my best efforts into understanding the issue at hand and deciding on a course of action that benefits the greatest number of people. That's the bottom line of what my job is all about.

I form my opinions by observation, the same way I live my life. I don't decide what opinions make me look best or suit my interests, and then go looking for facts to back them up. I look for facts first, then I draw my conclusions from what those facts tell me. I consult the experts in a given field—that's why I hired the most qualified people I could get as my commissioners. I'll listen to what just about anybody has to say, but I don't take on their opinion as my own unless I've done my homework and seen that they've got a point.

I learned a valuable lesson from the Navy SEALs that I've applied throughout my life. The SEALs taught me never to assume anything. That's one of the most important rules to apply as you're sifting through the issues of the day: Don't assume that what you're hearing is true. But on the other end of the spectrum, you don't want to assume that it's not true, either. That's just as foolish. It's hip these days to be cynical. But blanket cynicism is just the flip side of naiveté. It's naiveté with a bad attitude.

The best thing you can do in order to spinproof yourself is to listen for the basic assumptions in the information you hear, and go looking for evidence for and against them. Until you have that information, and have had a chance to draw a solid conclusion from it, there's nothing in the world wrong with saying, "I don't know." I think I'm just about the only political figure these days who says that. It always gets a shocked response. Elected officials aren't supposed to say "I don't know!" But we don't know everything. We can't possibly have the answers to everything on the tips of our tongues. Rest assured, there are plenty of times that politicians don't know the answer to a question; they're just not willing to admit it. Professional politicians are masters of the slick response. They even pay people to help them gracefully cover up their ignorance.

I grew up in that great era of the sixties and seventies when the rallying cry was "Question Authority!" It's a great slogan, and a smart policy. It's not telling you to reject authority altogether; it's not saying that authority is necessarily wrong. It's just reminding you not to accept what you hear blindly. That's healthy. We need to do much more of that today, especially given the corruption in our media and our politics.

These days we're all too ready to believe anybody who sets himself up as an authority, as long as he's cynical. But cynicism is a poor substitute for thinking things through. Ultimately, in a democratic society, there's no getting around the need for the public to be able to think for themselves. And if we want to fix what's wrong with our political system and our irresponsible press, we're all going to have to work a lot harder at making up our own minds.

In this chapter, I'm going to take a closer look at the most common fallacies you hear from public figures and the media today, so that we can recognize them and arm ourselves against them. My purpose here is to educate; I'm going to help you tune up your BS meter, so that you can quickly identify this stuff when you hear it. We all need to train ourselves to listen through the spin. We need to recognize when we're being told to think a certain way, so that we can counteract it with our own independent, sound thinking.

If We Want to Create a Culture of Honesty, We Have to Start with Ourselves

It's no good trying to create a more honest society unless we're willing to start with ourselves. We need to take a long hard look at the attitudes and agendas that are driving us. We need to make sure that our own motives are sound.

> *T*ruth is the glue that holds government together.
>
> —Gerald R. Ford

And so that we don't waste time on insignificant matters, we also need to rethink the demands we make on public figures to disclose certain information. We really have gone in for trivial pursuits these days, when a politician's sex life can become more important to us than where he or she stands on the issues. Not all that is true needs to be publicly disclosed. If it only concerns the public figure and his or her family, if it happened in the past, if it affects no one in the present, and especially if bringing it out will cause harm in the future, it doesn't need to be told. We need to develop a clearer understanding of which truths we are required to share with others, and which are none of the public's business. And we need to learn to put issues into their proper perspective.

Here again is a realm that legislation can't touch. The quality of our decision making is entirely up to us, the private citizens. Sound information, common sense, and courageous thinking are the best defenses against lies, spin, and propaganda. We need to teach ourselves, and our kids, to look for possible hidden agendas carried by the people who set themselves up as authorities. We need to teach ourselves to examine our own minds, to challenge our own assumptions, to see if they stand up against common sense. And we need to learn to distinguish what levels of information are appropriate to a given situation in everyday life.

If we're going to become a more honest people, we need to take a long, hard look at the biases and agendas that are driving us. We can't fix what we don't know is broken; we must first become aware of the kinks in our own thinking, so that we can straighten them out.

We also need to become aware of the ways we form our opinions. Many of us form them unconsciously; we're not in the habit of checking to see where our opinions come from. We need to make sure that the tools we're using to build our opinions are the right ones for the job. And finally, it would help us to become aware of the common ways that information is distorted, so that we're better able to recognize unreliable information when we come across it.

Tricks and Traps the Spin Doctors Use to Make Up Your Mind

There's a stock bag of tricks used by people who want to manipulate your opinion, including politicians, the media, and PR people of all types. Often these tricks are pulled intentionally, but at other times they're simply the result of poor thinking habits or ignorance. We can fight back with knowledge: The more we become aware of the way facts are manipulated behind the scenes, the better we'll be able to decide for ourselves what we're going to believe.

Knowing nothing about a subject is frequently healthier than knowing what is not so.

—Darrell Huff
How to Lie with Statistics

Politicians, the media, special interest groups, and spin doctors of all kinds are manipulating your point of view whenever:

1. They try to tell you something is true or right because it's popular. Back in the 1940s and 1950s, Chesterfield cigarettes launched a series of ads featuring glamorous movie stars who said they smoked cigarettes for the good of their voices. Imagine trying to pull that one off today! Cigarettes were wildly popular in that era, because they were seen as a symbol of sophistication and glamour. Even then, I'd be willing to bet, there were reports going around that cigarettes were harmful, but millions of people chose to believe what the famous movie stars told them.

A similar mentality is operating in politics today. I believe that a good many of today's politicians have actually convinced themselves that "right" and "popular" are the same. Why else would they be so obsessed with the polls? What else are polls but demographic popularity contests? When you get tempted to follow the crowd, just remember that old bumper sticker from the 1970s telling you to eat shit because "a million flies can't be wrong."

2. They overlook alternative viewpoints and actions in favor of the quick, easy, and politically expedient. Sometimes the best solutions to a problem aren't going to be the prettiest ones. Some solutions, like welfare reform and education reform, and even tax reform, are going to cost money in the short run, but will save us vast amounts of money in the long run. We've become very nearsighted in our political thinking, and we can't afford to be that way much longer.

Politicians often capitalize on our obsession with the quick fix and the short haul. They throw their lot in with the most attractive solution, and ignore the others. Then they try to rally us to their cause by denouncing all other viewpoints.

We need to train ourselves not to automatically buy into "feel good" solutions to complex problems. We shouldn't assume that because a particular course of action for a given problem has been portrayed negatively, it doesn't have worth. Remember, there are tons of people out there who have ulterior motives in the way they present certain ideas or potential legislation.

3. They try to make you think of the issues in extreme terms. You can't "win" in a political contest unless you have an opponent. It's a common trick of politicians to set every issue up as a contest between two sides. Often, in order to make themselves look good, they'll paint the other side in the most extreme terms possible, so that it looks like their side is the more moderate choice. All this does is misrepresent the issue and limit your options.

The assumption is that if you're not hard-core on one side of an issue, you must be hard-core on the other. This is the thinking that's behind all wedge issues. Case in point: I don't know how many times I've been approached by somebody who thinks that I'm advocating the wholesale legalization of drugs. I think making all drugs legal tomorrow would be a horrible idea, but as I've said again and again, we have to come up with some other alternatives, because the way we've approached drugs in the past simply doesn't work. There are probably an infinite number of options between an all-out criminalization of drugs and an all-out legalization of drugs. But somehow all this gets boiled down to two extreme, skewed choices.

We can't let ourselves get roped into limiting our options. If you're not a liberal, that doesn't have to mean you're a conservative. If you're pro-family it doesn't mean you're antigay, or antisingle, or antianybody. If you're a populist, that doesn't mean you must be pro-union. If you're pro-choice, that doesn't mean you can't be anti-abortion. Don't let anybody convince you that you have to be on one extreme or the other. Free thinkers have more choices than that.

4. They leave out important information and emphasize only information that promotes their viewpoint. Opinion pollsters are notorious for this. They often tend to simply trash all results that are unfavorable and keep going until they get something favorable. But presidential candidates aren't above using this trick. One of the most recent cases of this occurred during the primaries in February 2000, when George W. Bush held up a piece of campaign literature and accused John McCain of mudslinging. McCain denied that the literature was his, because at that point he had been trying to avoid that tactic. Well, that was just what Bush was trying to get him to say, because the literature did indeed come from McCain's campaign, and Bush wanted to get McCain on record denying that it was his. But Bush left out one important little detail: *There was no mudslinging in that particular document!*

Your best defense against this kind of trick is not to assume that you have all the information. It's always healthy to look for a second opinion. If it's an issue that really matters to you, there's nothing wrong with doing a little detective work of your own. With the Internet, you have instant access to a wide variety of information on just about any topic.

5. They attack the person rather than their argument. This is the weapon of choice for today's media, but it's prevalent in just about every facet of public and professional life. It's painfully easy to make a bad label stick these days. I've talked to teachers who are terrified somebody's going to charge them with molestation. All that it takes is for somebody to make the charge: It's a modern-day witch-hunt. They could be completely innocent, and even prove it in court, but once they've had the word "molester" put in front of their names, many find they're unable to get rid of it. The same holds true of charging someone in the business world with sexual harassment: Everyone remembers the charge, not the dismissal of the charge.

Name-calling is a popular tactic because it works. I'm reminded of the politician of a century ago who announced that his opponent was known to have matriculated at college, that his brother was a practicing *Homo sapiens,* and that his sister was a thespian. That politician won the election.

I've had a ridiculous number of obnoxious labels used to describe me. Luckily, none have stuck so far. I've been called a bigot, a musclehead, an idiot, even a "bullet-headed, shovel-faced mutha." And I've heard endless variations on my former moniker, Jesse the Body. It's a lot easier to throw unkind names around than to actually debate the issues, isn't it?

Whenever the media describe me, they love to throw in adjectives that subtly editorialize. I'm the "prickly" or "combative" governor. They like to imply that I'm hard to get along with. If you ask just about anyone on my staff, they'll tell you exactly the opposite story. But an easygoing governor doesn't make for a good story. Nobody wants to read a headline that says, "Governor Ventura Is Easy to Get Along With." A congenial governor doesn't fit with the image of the tyrant they want me to be so that they can make their complaints against me look more legitimate.

The minute I hear a public figure ridiculing somebody instead of arguing the facts, I'm suspicious. We should bear in mind that when people stoop to name-calling, it's either because they can't be bothered to fight fair or because they don't have a solid argument behind them.

6. They caricature the opposition to make themselves look good by comparison. This is a close companion to the name-calling, personal-attack school of debate. The way this one works is to take your opponent's point of view and misrepresent it until it's easy to knock down. They call this the "straw man" tactic in the language of debate.

A number of newspapers used this very tactic by taking a portion of my November 1999 interview with *Playboy* and blowing it all out of proportion. In discussing the way the Religious Right kept trying to grab up political power in order to force their agenda on the public, I made the now infamous comment that religion is for weak-minded people who need strength in numbers. Now granted, I should have clarified that I didn't mean *all* religious people are weak-minded. But I think to an extent that should have been somewhat obvious. People who know anything about me at all know that I'm religious myself. I consider myself a Christian, although it's not something I go around talking about a lot because I don't think it's anybody's business. But my wife, Terry, is more overtly religious than I am. So guess what the media gleaned from that comment, and turned into a banner-sized headline: "Ventura Says Terry Is Weak-Minded!" It's easy to garner ill will against a man who would say something like that about his wife.

Again, our best defense is to stay informed. If something seems hard to believe, you're probably right to trust that instinct. Chances are, if you go looking for more information, your suspicions will be borne out.

7. They generalize from incomplete information. The media are masters of the generalization. Reporters often pass along information without finding out what it means. I feel especially sorry for pilots, because they seem to get picked on a lot. Just about every time a private plane crashes, the media are always quick to point out that "the pilot had not filed a flight plan." As if that had something to do with the crash! Private pilots aren't required to file a flight plan. They generally do it just for an extra bit of protection, so that somebody officially knows where they're going and when. But it's not required. No airplane yet has fallen out of the sky because it didn't have a flight plan.

The other one you'll hear a lot in small plane crashes is that the aircraft was "experimental." They make it sound like the plane was somehow unsafe because it didn't come off an assembly line. They usually mention this long before any investigation could give the vaguest ideas of what caused the crash.

If your source of news is in the habit of making generalized assumptions in lieu of actual facts, I'd suggest to you that it's time to look elsewhere for your news. The problem is, it's so prevalent these days, it's hard to find a news source that consistently does its homework. But when you hear a reporter drawing a conclusion from a given story, just stop and ask yourself if that conclusion is really warranted. Sometimes what sounds like a conclusion is nothing more than an editorial opinion dressed up in story clothes. Also remember that the average reporter doesn't usually have any special expertise about the subject, but only reports what others have said. And, as often as not, because the reporter doesn't fully understand the subject, the report is oversimplified, generalized, and oftentimes just plain wrong.

8. They peddle their points of view by appealing to emotion. You see this kind of thing over and over again in an election year. Special interest groups love to say of a given piece of legislation that it "hurts working families." It's very effective, because it provokes an immediate emotional reaction: If I let this legislation get passed, I'll become unemployed and my kids will starve! That's all they have to do in a lot of cases: Drag out the "bad for working families" slogan, and it's almost guaranteed to kill any legislation—even legislation that would ultimately *benefit* working families.

We need to stay focused on the facts in a case like this. Sure, we should give our emotional reaction at least some consideration. But it's no substitute for examining the facts. Don't let them play your emotions like a cheap fiddle.

9. They oversimplify. It's a lot easier to get people behind you when you can articulate a single, clear, easily understandable reason for a given social problem, and a single, simple solution. This is the logic behind every sound bite. But it reduces complex issues to non-sense, and often masks the true nature of a problem. It leads us to assume there is only one cause when there might be many, and to assume that the solution is singular.

Nobody wants a politician to tell them that there's nothing he or she can do about a given problem, but sometimes that's just the way it is. We need to train ourselves to resist the urge to assume that a complex problem can have a simple solution. Here again, there's no substitute for doing our homework.

10. They manipulate statistics. But the out-and-out lie from a politician is probably a bit rarer than another kind of lie: doctored statistics. Polls are manipulated and loaded and skewed all the time, so that they'll yield whatever "facts" the politician wants to promote. Then any time they're challenged on a particular policy they can point to their highly manipulated statistics.

When somebody gives you an "average," be suspicious as hell, especially if they don't tell you what kind of average it is. There are many different types of averages, and the results they yield vary widely. You may have heard the old saying, "Nearly everybody is below average." Averages are meaningless unless they're backed up with an explanation of what type of averages they are, and how the source arrived at that number.

There are all kinds of ways to express a number, depending on the impression you want to give. For example, a local real estate company might advertise that they have eighty years of experience in the business. Sounds impressive, right? But if you investigate further, it'll turn out that they've only been open four years, and their twenty realtors were all brand new to the business when they started. Or worse, they've got eighty employees, and the company's only been open a year! Everybody in the company is a bare-bones beginner, and yet, with those numbers, they can make it sound like the most experienced real estate firm around!

Darrell Huff, author of *How to Lie with Statistics,* writes that there are five questions we should ask of any statistic we hear. First, who says so? We should ask ourselves whether the source could be biased, consciously or unconsciously. Is it possible that they didn't tell us about the unfavorable data, and only reported what supports their position?

Second, how do the sources know that what they're saying is true? If they conducted a survey, was their sample big enough to be reliable? Was their sample really representative of the group they claim to represent?

Third, what's missing? If they don't even tell you how how they arrived at their conclusion, that's a reason for suspicion.

Fourth, is one thing being reported as another? Oftentimes, polls are meaningless because what people say they do and what they actually do are different.

And finally, does their conclusion make sense? We tend to get lulled into a false sense of security by statistics and percentages. We'll accept a conclusion that's got legitimate-looking numbers attached to it, even though the conclusion itself is ridiculous. Don't get roped in. Question the statistics you hear. Question the conclusions they draw. Question the source.

We know that dishonesty and insincerity are rampant in our political system. We know that many of our political leaders have made their careers out of yanking our chains. But what can we do about it? I believe that the quickest, most powerful means of getting more honesty into politics is the power of our own vote. If you don't think you can trust a given candidate, vote for someone else! But what if none of the major contenders, none of the candidates who have a genuine shot at winning, inspires your trust? Then I submit to you the idea that you should cast your vote for honesty anyway. There are plenty of excellent candidates out there who get dropped from the public eye way too early in the race. That doesn't mean you can't vote for them anyway. Voting isn't the same thing as gambling.

The goal in casting a vote isn't supposed to be to try to vote for the winner. Your vote is a statement about the policies and attitudes you want to see in government.

I truly believe that the best way for us to combat all of these tricks is to become experts at thinking for ourselves. Every citizen needs to understand the basics of sound thinking, and needs to apply them by staying informed. The more you're armed with good information, the less any of these tricks are going to work on you.

Spinproofing 101: What a Sound Argument Looks Like

The citizens of our country need to be better at sound thinking than any other people, because they are our ultimate authority. It's vital that we know how to put together a solid argument on a given issue. Now, when I say "argument," I'm assuming you know I'm not talking about a fight. My dictionary says an argument is " a course of reasoning aimed at discovering truth or falsehood" and "a set of evidence or explanations supporting a conclusion." Since not all points of view are equivalent, examining the strengths and weaknesses of arguments is a way to figure out which viewpoints are better.

A good argument isn't just taking your same biases and restating them in consumer-friendly packaging. That's what spin doctors do. Good arguments are put together from an actual search for facts. They're not a showcase for your opinions; they're a statement of the reasons behind them.

If you're going to put together a solid argument, you can't just start out with whatever point of view first occurs to you, and then try to build an argument around that. You have to start from a reliable position.

When you're gathering information on a given subject, don't forget to consider the source. Try to get your information from sources that are knowledgeable and unbiased. When you think you see real-life examples that back up your position, ask yourself if they really are representative. Be wary of numbers and percentages that don't come with any background information to put them in perspective. Remember how easy it is for people to lie with statistics.

If you're really serious about forming a sound opinion, I challenge you to go looking for opposing viewpoints and counterexamples. Better that you go looking to challenge your opinions yourself than that you leave it to your opponents. A sound argument is one that can stand up to challenges.

Advanced Spinproofing: Stay Informed

It doesn't matter how good our opinion-forming skills are if we don't start with reliable information. I believe that we all have to take responsibility for the infor-

> *I was brought up to believe that the only thing worth doing was to add to the sum of accurate information in the world.*
>
> —Margaret Mead

mation we consume. We need to become smarter news consumers; we have to train ourselves to go for the nutritious stuff, not the "candy" news that's all around us these days.

I think if we started placing a higher priority on staying informed, we'd work harder to carve out niches in our busy schedules to at least scan the top stories. Even if we don't have the luxury of a few free minutes, there's bathroom time, commute time, time on hold. We make time for what's important.

Ideally, we ought to be getting our information from several different reliable sources. We should never let any one news source become our sole authority. If anybody tells you they're the only source of information you need, chances are they've got ulterior motives, so run like hell!

Spinproofing in Action: Doing Your Part

But of course, staying informed is only the beginning. As a wise Eastern philosopher once put it, "To know and not to do is not truly yet to know." We all have a responsibility to participate in keeping our country strong. We are the people our Founding Fathers meant when they wrote about a government by, for, and of the people. We have to put our knowledge into action.

When we have an opinion, we need to make ourselves heard. I know that's not easy in today's climate. All you have to do these days is be seen in public holding an opinion, and you've made yourself a target. But we can't knuckle under to that. We have to have the courage to speak our minds anyway.

Of course, the most direct form of putting our political opinions into action is with our vote. Low voter turnout is a vicious circle: The smaller the number of people who vote, the less government represents the public. When people begin to feel that government doesn't represent them, they start to feel that their vote doesn't make a difference. And the less people feel that their vote makes a difference, the less likely they are to vote.

We have to turn that around. When I was elected governor, people came out of hibernation in record numbers to cast their vote. Many of these folks hadn't voted in years, or had never voted before at all. I believe that that election was an indicator of something big on the horizon. Now is a great time to get back into the voting booth. There's a growing wave of momentum behind the reform movement. If you're coming back to the polls for the first time in years, you're in great company.

Another way you can serve your country and put your knowledge to work is through volunteering. If you've got a candidate you want to get behind, go to his or her local campaign headquarters and help out. There's real power in actually getting in there and participating firsthand in a grassroots campaign. It's exciting. It feels fantastic. Don't miss out on the opportunity to be part of that at least once.

And while you're at it, I'd like you to consider holding a public office of your own at some point in your life. You don't necessarily have to run for president—I wouldn't wish that job on anyone! But you could serve in a local office in your city or town. It's an outstanding opportunity to make a difference.

7

Getting Our Nation
Back on Track

*I*nsanity is doing the same thing the same way and expecting
a different result.

—Tavis Smiley

In February of 2000, thousands of Minnesota Republicans (and for all
I know, Republicans all across the country) received an urgent letter
in the mail signed by the national party chairman. The letter bore a
photograph of me and the words, "Are You Strong Enough to Take on
Jesse Ventura?" It turned out to be nothing more than a fund-raising
letter for the Republican party. They were using my name and likeness
to get people to send them more money.

The letter came to my attention from two different directions.
One was through my friend George Pillsbury, a Republican who is
working closely with me to lay the groundwork for a unicameral legislature. I have no idea why they thought the letter would appeal to
him. But even if George hadn't brought it to my attention, I still
would have found out about it because, for some reason, they sent
one to Mr. Jim Janos at my address in Maple Grove. Jim Janos is me!

Not only had they used my name and likeness to raise money,
and not only had they not bothered to do their research to figure out
who *not* to send the thing to, they also made reference to my mem-

bership in the Reform party, which I had publicly quit a week earlier. The letter had obviously been printed up before I quit the party, but they hadn't bothered to reprint it to reflect the change. Apparently, it didn't worry them at all to be disseminating false information.

Fortunately, I may have legal recourse. I trademarked my name back in my wrestling days, and in 1994 I established that I own exclusive rights to use my name, voice, and likeness in a federal court lawsuit. Not too many other politicians have that kind of protection, though. Maybe I should take it as a compliment that the Republican party sees me as such a threat, even though I've said repeatedly that I have no aspirations to go to Washington.

This kind of stunt has become commonplace in today's political world. It's business as usual. When the institutions that were founded in order to serve the people are playing stupid games like this, it's an indicator that something is fundamentally wrong.

Partisan politics often plays out like a giant chess game. You make a move, your "opponent" in another party makes a countermove. They assume that a move you make is a move against them. A case in point: Early in March 2000, the Minnesota senate decided not to confirm my appointment of Reform party member Steve Minn as Commissioner of Commerce and Public Service. The senate has the power to confirm or reject commissions that I appoint. They denied his appointment, not because he was unqualified, but because they said he was too abrasive. They didn't like him. Since when did the appointing of commissioners become a popularity contest? If that were the criteria for public service, do you think they would ever have let me in?

But the senate's rejection of Steve's appointment didn't just come out of the blue. Our last Commissioner of Commerce, David Jennings, resigned from his job to take a position in the private sector. As I was looking to fill his vacancy, I realized that the Department of Commerce and the Department of Public Service, which sit right across from each other, could easily fit together in the same building. I figured that this was a perfect opportunity to streamline government a little bit and save the taxpayers some money. So I moved them into a single building and appointed Steve Minn to head them both.

But the state senate got all upset because I didn't consult them before doing this. I think they actually took it as a slight. I hadn't consulted them, because at the time, they weren't in session. They're part-time legislators, and wouldn't have been back for another six months. They only get paid when they're in session. In order for me to consult with them, I would have had to call a special session and put them all back on the payroll, just for this one decision. How cost-efficient would that have been?

I made an executive decision. I took what I thought was the most efficient course of action. But I have no doubt that it was because I didn't include them in the decision that the senate retaliated by rejecting Steve Minn. I also suspect that their retaliation may have something to do with the fact that Steve Minn is a Reform party member.

It's a classic example of politicians talking about streamlining and efficiency, then not taking advantage of the opportunity when it stares them in the face. They would rather use the issue as an opportunity to make another partisan chess move than as a chance to serve the people. They talk the talk but they don't want to walk the walk.

Much of what's wrong in our government today can be blamed simply on the nature of all governments. This is what happens to the best of them over time. Governments are corrupt by default. It's only by the conscious effort of the people that they are kept in line.

But in order to get our government back on track and find a way to keep it there, we may have to get a little bit experimental. We may have to learn to color outside the lines in some cases. This is a great opportunity for us as a nation to put our diversity to good use, and to be open and creative about discussing solutions. As I've said, we're still very much in the process of inventing democracy as we go along.

In this chapter I'm going to suggest some basic courses of action I believe we should be taking, along with some new policies we should consider trying, in order to get our government back on track.

Government Reform: We've Gotta Clean Up Our Act

I doubt that it's intentional, but in many ways our government seems to have developed a backwards attitude: Today's government often penalizes those citizens who behave well and rewards those who misbe-

> Society in every state is a blessing, but Government, even in its best state, is but a necessary evil; in its worst state, an intolerable one.
>
> —Thomas Paine

have. A case in point: property taxes. If you keep your house in great shape and make improvements to it, you have to pay higher taxes. But if you have the ugliest house on the block, all peeling paint, sagging porches, and plywood over the windows, you get to pay a lower tax rate. Another example is the way the government insists on taking money away from you whenever you try to save it. The government actually penalizes you for saving money by hitting you with estate taxes and interest income taxes and gift taxes.

And it's not just a bias the government has against responsible individuals. I've told you about the ways the federal government penalizes state governments for being efficient. If you handle federal money well, you lose it! It's not that the federal government is out there trying to be a tyrant. It's just that public servants' minds are elsewhere. Nobody's seeing the big picture.

We need to get government to look at things differently. It's very shortsighted for the government to stick its hand out every time it gets a whiff of money. It would be a lot smarter in the long run for the government to make policy that will encourage the kinds of behaviors it wants to see—not for the government's sake, but for the citizens' sake. Government policy should always be guided by what is ultimately best for the people.

This seems like common sense, doesn't it? But it's amazing how much of government is run by entirely different criteria. A prime example is the way that elected officials generally appoint their administrations these days. Rather than looking for the most qualified people to do the jobs, newly elected officials generally fill those positions with the people who supported their campaigns. They dole out offices in their administration as political favors. And they make sure to put their party's people into positions. Their criteria is not who's going to do the best job, but who's going to support them and promote them and help keep them in place when it comes time for the next election. As a result, the quality of our government suffers.

I took an unusual approach to appointing my administration. I simply appointed the best and most qualified person to every position. I figured the best way to work it was to give the job to the person who could do it best, then get out of their way and let them do it! I figured, if they excel at their jobs, then I'll shine.

Professional headunters volunteered to go through the applications for commissioners. These are the same guys who are out there recruiting for top corporations. They sent me the top three applicants for each position. I was totally blind to political affiliation. I never even asked what party they belonged to until after I had hired them. Interestingly enough, what I ended up with was a pretty even mix of Democrats, Republicans, and independents.

And they are a phenomenal bunch of people. I have Ph.D.'s on my staff. I have Jerry Carlson as my head of Trade and Economic Development. Jerry was the head of Ecolab, the international cleaning and sanitizing products company, for thirty years. He had retired on what I'm sure was a comfortable pension. When I won the election, he came to me, all excited, and said, "I'm not ready to retire yet!" He's doing the same job for Minnesota that he did for Ecolab, but for a whole lot less money. He's only able to do it, though, because he doesn't need the paycheck.

So far, it's proved to be a very effective strategy. Even Skip Humphrey, my Democratic opponent, once came up to me and said, "You have the best administration in the United States of America." But isn't this how it's supposed to be done? How is it in the public interest to do it any other way?

But you can see that a major reason why it's tough to get good people into public service is because the pay is lousy. When you consider what they have to sacrifice financially to do the job, you wonder why anyone would have an incentive to do it. None of my commissioners makes six figures, even though they could probably be making a quarter million a year in the private sector. That drastic a pay cut is enough to keep plenty of great people out of public service. Why should they get paid less than they're worth?

But the real sticker isn't the money. It's the scrutiny they have to endure from the media. Rest assured, if you go into politics, you're going to get pounced on. The media will do whatever it takes to dig up dirt and create a scandal. The loss of privacy can be even more painful than the loss of income. Why should anyone have to go through that just to do public service? I fight against this all the time by defending my people publicly whenever the media abuse them. As governor, I'm like the captain of a ship, and the captain is honor bound to defend his crew. But I've got to admit it's like swimming against the tide. The media are relentless these days.

We're missing out on a lot of terrific leadership because public service has become such a painful, impractical proposition. It's not much of a recruiting pitch: Less money, more abuse.

But for those who do sacrifice the private sector pay and take on the media gauntlet, that's only half of it, because they have to wade through an awful lot of bureaucracy. So much of business as usual in politics seems to be done in the most impractical way possible. When I first took office, I was surprised to find out that Arne Carlson, the

with everybody else. And they're a lot more autonomous than
ody in Congress. They have a lot more leeway to exert their indi-
al leadership.

I worry that we may have to struggle against Washington in the
ar future to preserve states' rights. I see indications that the federal
overnment is on a campaign to leach away powers from the states. I
on't like the idea that issues like life-style choices, which were once
left up to the states' discretion, might become mandated by the federal government. We'll become a lesser nation if that happens. One of
our strengths as a nation today is that our states vary somewhat in
their modes of thinking, and they can experiment with different
solutions to the same problem. That gives us freedom of choice. If we
don't like the attitudes prevalent in one state, we can move to
another. I don't think we should allow this diversity to slip away from
us. We've got to be on our guard against the federal government's
tendency to suck the power out of the states.

Making Elections Work
the Way They're Supposed To

My father used to say, "You wanna know why they're all crooks in
government? Because they spend a million dollars to make a hundred thousand dollars a year." He had a point. There's power and
prestige to be had in high public offices. And in our current electoral
system, power and influence are bought. I read a statistic somewhere
that said George W. Bush has been spending about $3 million a week
on his campaign. He spends more in a day than I spent on my entire
gubernatorial campaign. Granted, mine was a state campaign, and
his is national. But even so, what Bush is paying to become president
is obscene. Where does it end?

The cost of campaigning severely limits the field of candidates.
Who has that kind of money? Only a tiny handful of Americans can

governor before me, never even held meetin,
Carlson's was a typical administration in tha
gave the orders, and everybody below him car,
was little or no communication between departn.

One of the first things I did was to go out and
heads of different departments. Then I got them al.
introductory session. Now I make a policy of brin,
department heads together in one room once a month
gets to look at the big picture together.

Since then we've been working hard at taking down
cades between departments. The way it's been in the |
department typically doesn't even know what the other depai
are doing. We're helping them learn to communicate with
other. In some cases, they were inadvertently duplicating each o,
I found out that there are four or five departments that deal w
alcoholism. We need to cut it down to one. In the private sector tha
would be common sense. In government, it's radical thinking.

I think it's strange that with all the resources at government's dis-
posal, there isn't more communication going on between offices and
departments. They have the means. Why aren't they using them?
When I was in Washington in February, people told me they were
impressed with the amount of contact they had with my office there.
All governors have an office in Washington; mine has three full-time
staffers. People in Congress tell me that they've never before had so
much contact with that office. They like it.

I sometimes hear people today claiming that the federal government is a lost cause; that it's too far gone to even attempt to reform it.
I get tempted to believe that sometimes. It may be that the best we
can do on the federal level is to try to keep a rein on the corruption.
But I believe there's still hope at the state level. Governors have more
opportunities to stay in touch with the people than politicians in
Washington do. They live in the communities they govern. They're
right there on the scene, living with the legislation they work on right

manage it. Perot was an exception to the bipartisan rule; he proved that a candidate outside the two traditional parties could break through at the presidential level. But he only managed it because he had millions of his own dollars to spend. That's a high cost of entry into the presidential arena.

And if you think the threshold is high at the presidential level, just try running for Congress, where you get no public financing at all. Third-party candidates are constantly getting spent to death by the two major parties. It has nothing to do with the quality of the candidates of the third parties. If they can't afford to get their candidates out there in the public eye alongside the major parties' contenders, no one's going to know another choice exists.

Why do campaigns cost so much? It's not just the expense of all the travel. You've also got to spend money to get name recognition. That's very important. If they don't know who you are, they're not going to vote for you. I was lucky in that respect. I already had a lot of name recognition because of my wrestling, radio, and film careers. But ultimately, very little of that money is spent directly on getting a set of ideas across to the public. Only a fraction of the time, money, and energy in a large campaign actually goes to making the candidate's vision available to the voters. It happens in every election: Voters go to the polls having little or no idea where the people they're voting for stand on the issues. So what is it we're voting for, if we don't know what our candidates plan to do with the jobs we're giving them?

I suspect most Americans would agree with me that we need a major overhaul of our campaign system, and I believe that as we work through campaign reform, we need to keep as our goal the idea that what matters most in any campaign is the candidates' stand on the issues. Not who's telegenic and slick in front of the cameras. Not who's winning the debates. Not who's grabbing up the black, gay, Hispanic, or female vote. But who's got a genuine plan for governing.

And above all, we need to arrange it so that it's not a matter of the winner being the candidate who's got the most bucks. We need to find a way to level the playing field, so that a wealthy candidate doesn't spend all the others into the dust. I'm not generally a social- ist, but on this issue I think we need to even things out. The media could provide an equal block of free air time to each candidate. How you'd make that work, I'm not sure. But I think we need to be talk- ing about it.

A more equal campaign system would mean that government, or donated funds, or some combination of public and private funds, would be distributed equally among all qualified candidates. We'd probably get challenged in court if we tried to do that. Somebody would say it violated the First Amendment. I would argue against that, though. We already have limits on campaign donations, and those laws have passed the constitutional test. The principle is the same, it's just a matter of degree.

Not only are elections obscenely expensive, there's too damn many of them! Why do we have to have elections every two years? The system works fine for senators, who serve a six-year term. But representatives in Congress serve only two years. It often works out that rookie representatives spend the first year learning the ropes, then spend the second year, an election year, campaigning again! If they don't win the election the second time around, it's all for noth- ing. It limits what they can do, and it forces them to focus on the quick fixes that will sound good in campaign literature, not on sound, long-term solutions.

Why not do away with the two-year electoral cycle in favor of a four-year cycle—for everybody? I believe that all elected offices should have four-year terms, and all should be voted on in the same year. That way, we get a three-year respite from all campaigning. Three whole years in which our elected officials have nothing to do except concentrate on the jobs we hired them to do.

A four-year election cycle wouldn't mean a complete turnover of government every four years. Remember that most incumbents get reelected every time they run. But that's another problem in itself.

Putting the term-limits issue aside, a four-year election system would save us a huge amount of money. We'll never know how well it could work until we give it a try. Nothing in government is written in stone; if we try it and it doesn't work, we can always go back to the system we have now.

We need to make elections and voting as simple as possible. Career politicians prefer them to be complicated and inconvenient, because when fewer people vote, they have a better shot at getting reelected. They count on being reelected by their small, loyal core of supporters. High voter turnout is bad news for incumbents. That's why they hate Minnesota's policy of same-day voter registration: It brings new blood into the polls, and that new blood isn't likely to vote for them.

You see how backwards that is? Anybody who understands the way our government is supposed to work knows that the more citizens who vote and take part in their government, the better government represents them. An elected official has no business hampering the electoral system.

In my election in November of 1998, we led the nation in voter turnout. Sixty percent of voters came out to the polls that day. That's high for a state election, especially in a nonpresidential election year. It's a step in the right direction, but to me, that says that four Minnesotans out of every ten didn't vote! Is that really fair representation?

I don't claim to have the key to increasing voter turnout, but I suspect that voter education is a good start. If more people understood the power and the value of their vote, if more people were able to take a genuine, if not enthusiastic, interest in the issues at hand, I think we'd see a lot more people at the polls.

Busting Up Bipartisan Gridlock

One of the worst results of the party system as it stands today is the homogenizing effect it has on party members. I truly

He serves his party best who serves his country best.

—Rutherford B. Hayes

believe that the vast majority of people come into their party with a vision of changing things for the better, but the party won't allow them to pursue that vision. They have to follow the party platform religiously, or they get into trouble. They can't vote their conscience, because if their conscience leads them too far off the party-approved path, they get put back in line. They can only gain power by bowing to party leaders. The result is that you get a party that consists of half a dozen major players and a whole bunch of minor players. It ruins individualism. It kills diversity of opinion. It limits our choices.

We need to reform our party caucus system so that it won't be so hostile to individuality among its members. Of course it's important for party members to be in a certain amount of agreement on the party platform, but the only legitimate reason for a member to go along with any given part of the platform is because they sincerely believe in it, not because they have to give it lip service in order to get ahead.

Pioneering Smarter Legislation

We have an enormous excess of laws within our legal system, both at the state and the federal level. I understand that legislators believe that it's their job to make laws, but as it is now, our system allows laws to just keep piling up on the books, whether they're pulling their weight or not.

It's very shortsighted of us to let our legislative system get cluttered up that way. It's understood that every citizen is responsible for knowing the laws. But in order for us to actually do that, we would all have to plow through hundreds of musty law books. We'd have no time left to do anything else. There's a whole overgrown industry, the legal profession, that thrives on cluttered, incomprehensible legislation that the average person couldn't possibly make sense of.

We need to start placing a sunset provision on the laws we pass, so that after a certain number of years, we would be required to go back and reexamine each law to see if it really is doing what it was supposed to do. I have an idea that I'd like to put into effect here in Minnesota, which would declare every fourth year a law-review year. No laws would be passed that year. Instead, all recent legislation would be gone over and tested for its relevance. Legislators' jobs shouldn't simply be to crank out more laws; they should also be entrusted with the responsibility of making sure those laws make sense.

Unicameral Legislation: Streamlining Government at the State Level

I doubt that much of the American public is aware of this, but within the two parties, a small minority controls all of the other party members. You've got a handful on one side and a handful on the other who are the real power brokers. They're the ones who come to me to do the real negotiating. They're the real mediators between governor and legislature. They have the real influence over what will happen on a bill. The rest are just cannon fodder.

Here in Minnesota, to show you how bad it can get, 10 percent of the legislators sit on 86 percent of the conference committees. You figure those odds out, and tell me who's really wielding the political power.

That's what the two-party system, the caucuses, and the conference committees create. And that's why I'm in favor of unicameral legislature. Unicameral legislature is very citizen friendly, very open. Bicameral legislature makes all kinds of opportunities for bipartisan manipulation. When you do away with conference committees, every legislator becomes more equal; their vote means more, and it's cast in the light of day for all to see. There are far fewer opportunities for political power brokers to usurp the voices of other legislators and of the people they represent.

I've been studying the idea of unicameral legislation for some time now, and I've come to the conclusion that it really is the hottest ticket around for true government reform. Switching state governments from bicameral to unicameral legislation not only trims an entire redundant layer away from government, it also fixes half a dozen other problems.

I'm all for bicameral legislation at the federal level. It's absolutely required. You need to have both houses to even out the differences in population from state to state. If you had only one house with two senators from each state, Rhode Islanders would have a huge amount of representation, and Californians would have hardly any. Or, if you had only the House of Representatives, with everybody represented according to population, you'd have the opposite problem: Congress would be overrun with Californians and Texans, with only a tiny sprinkling of Delawareans and Rhode Islanders. At the federal level the bicameral legislature makes sense. Not only that, it's constitutionally mandated.

But it makes no sense at all on a state level. All bicameral legislation does for states is make a redundant layer of government. It's wasteful, and it's expensive.

Unicameral legislation is much more citizen friendly. It makes officials stand on their own votes, because they no longer have the mediating influence of the other house. They know they'll be held accountable, so they have an incentive to do their homework. Unicameral legislation, as we're constructing it here in Minnesota, puts an end to the conference committee, one of the most corrupt government institutions around. Today, most of the critical decisions in legislation are made by conference committees behind closed doors. Membership in these committees is exclusive. You have to butter the right palms to get in. In a unicameral legislature there are no conference committees. It's all done out in the open. That's one less way for anyone to gain an unfair advantage.

Unicameral legislation makes public servants more accessible to the people because it frees them up from a lot of bureaucratic red tape. The time house members would have spent shuttling legislation back and forth between the two houses can be spent making themselves accessible to the people. In addition, a switch to unicameral legislation frees up money from the salaries of those vacating the second house. We can then use that money to increase the pay for those in the remaining house. Better pay is likely to attract better legislators and may help wean them off special interest funds.

Unicameral legislation should be a mainstay of any state government's reform platform. It's one of those great solutions that hits a number of problem spots all at once. So far, only Nebraska has gone with a unicameral system; they've had theirs for years, and it's served them well. I'm going to try to get the issue on the Minnesota ballot for the November 2000 election. If the people decide they want to try it, we'll be ready.

Tax Reform

Pick out any given American walking down the street, tap him or her on the shoulder, and ask what he or she thinks of the IRS. I can almost guarantee the reaction you'd get. A huge majority of us believe that the IRS has become corrupt, greedy, and way too powerful. Our tax system as it currently exists is a nightmare. It's stuffed with loopholes and unfair advantages. With the income tax system we have now, the IRS has almost unlimited power. They can take as much of your money as they want, and unless you're self-employed, they take it before you even get your check.

Our forefathers would be appalled to hear that today the government gets your money before you do. The IRS is even allowed to act in direct contradiction to the Constitution. Do you know what an audit does? It assumes you're guilty. You have to prove yourself innocent. That's the exact opposite of the way our justice system works. I've been audited twice, and I'm here to tell you that even if they find you completely blameless, you're out a hell of a lot of money and time. The money you paid to an accountant to help you plow through it all can never be recovered. The IRS is the epitome of bloated, corrupt, wasteful government, and if we're serious about government reform, the IRS deserves to take the biggest hit.

Whatever we decide to do about tax reform, it's got to be a sweeping, complete revolution. It has to be a vastly more simplified system, with clear limitations on the amount of money the government can take. Otherwise, the government will continue to find ways of snapping up more than its share by taxing us three or four times for the same dollar, and plenty of people will find loopholes to escape their responsibilities again.

I'm not crazy about the idea of a flat tax, for two reasons. The first reason is that even a flat tax is still an income tax. I think the Sixteenth Amendment, the one granting government the power to collect taxes on income, should be repealed. To make that happen, we would have to get the votes of 290 members of the House, 67 members of the Senate, and three quarters of all the legislators. It would be extremely tough to do, but I think it would be worth trying. The other reason I'm against a flat tax is the fact that we've already got one: It's called Social Security. And look at what a mess that's in.

I'd like to see us do away with income tax entirely and go for a national sales tax. The federal government could collect the money it needs by placing a tax on the goods and services we buy. Then states could add their own taxes on top of that.

A fair national sales tax wouldn't touch the necessities of life like food and clothing. It would make sure that people were able to provide themselves with the basics before it collected any tax from them. Taxes would only be collected on optional purchases. That would make us, the taxpayers, much more powerful. We could decide how much tax we're going to pay by controlling our level of consumption. We would have the option of hanging on to our money and living off the basics, or of spending as much as we felt like spending. We wouldn't be penalized for saving or investing. We wouldn't have to hand the government money just because we're looking out for our own financial welfare.

Just imagine, you'd be able to clear seven years' worth of useless documents out of your attic. You'd never have to face another audit. You'd never have to waste your time and money preparing complicated forms. The IRS as we know it would become obsolete. With a national sales tax, we wouldn't have to do away with the IRS completely; we could just scale it down drastically and reverse its function. Instead of being a watchdog over us, the taxpayers, the IRS could keep an eye on the government. It could be reprogrammed to protect the people from government corruption. Wouldn't it be great to have the IRS swoop in and audit a government agency for buying $200 toilet seats, instead of having it harass private citizens?

People who oppose the national sales tax worry that it would cause a boom in the black market, that a lot of the economy would go underground to avoid paying the tax. But I think the opposite is true. With a sales tax, we'd be able to collect taxes on illegal industries that an income tax couldn't touch. Every illegal business has to buy things occasionally, and whenever they did, we'd get the taxes. And we would impose strict penalties on anybody who didn't pay the tax.

Another objection I've heard raised to the national sales tax is that it would upset our free market economy by raising the effective cost of consumer goods by 20 to 25 percent. But there again, I believe the opposite is true, because it puts the government in a direct line with the economy. The better the economy is doing, the more money government collects. It would force the government to work hard to keep the economy strong. I like plans that get the government to focus on *our* best interests. That's the way it should be.

Our property tax code is almost as much of a mess as our income tax code. Here in Minnesota, Commissioner of Revenue Matt Smith has been conducting town meetings all over the state to find out what people feel are the worst trouble spots in the tax system. From what he's hearing, more than anything else, people want to see their property taxes reformed. We have to be extra careful with this one, though; we've got to make sure that we find another source of money to cover what was once covered by property taxes, because property taxes pay for schools.

I think it's high time we switched to a different source of funding for schools, because when the bulk of education money comes from property taxes, schools get funded unevenly. Where property tax collections are high, as they are in wealthy neighborhoods, the schools have a lot of money. Where property tax collections are low, some schools don't get the money they need to operate properly. It's not fair to the kids: Children in poor neighborhoods need a good education as much as kids in wealthy neighborhoods do. If we switched from property taxes to a more level source of funding, we could even things out among school districts, and shorten the gap between the haves and the have nots.

A cut in property taxes would also probably be the best way we could give struggling farmers a shot in the arm. Their property taxes are extremely high. Many farmers are so deeply impoverished that an income tax cut wouldn't even help them, but a property tax cut would give them relief right where they need it most.

Property tax is a tough issue to tackle. The legislature doesn't want to deal with it. Despite what the people say they want, legislators are more interested in an across-the-board income tax cut because that's what they think will make a difference in the next election. The last four governors before me all tried to reform property taxes, but they couldn't do it. I may not be able to, either. But I'll try.

Tort Reform: Civilizing Our Civil Courts

While we were wrapping up our work on a bonding bill for Minnesota, former attorney general Warren Spannis and former vice-president Walter Mondale came to see me to ask if I would add money to the bill for the University of Minnesota's law school. I looked at them squarely and said, "You're asking me to support putting more lawyers into the world?"

We are indeed a country with too many lawyers. Anybody can file a lawsuit over anything. I get hit with a frivolous lawsuit almost every week. They take up a lot of my time and money. But even though I win them, I still have to pay my lawyer.

It's not just me. Our courts are clogged with frivolous lawsuits. No matter how ridiculous a lawsuit may seem, the courts have to treat it seriously. People don't even need to hire a lawyer to file a lawsuit. They can fill out the forms and file one all by themselves. The cost to them is minimal, so they have no incentive to make sure they have a good case. People can even use frivolous lawsuits as a means of harassing the people they don't like. That shouldn't be allowed to happen.

I really like the English court system, where the loser has to pay the other side's attorney. If we tried to implement that here, people would probably argue that only wealthy people could afford to file lawsuits. But there's got to be ways to make it work. How does England work that out, for instance? One way we could get around the problem is to give the judge discretion to waive the fees, if the losing plaintiff or defendant really had a good faith basis for his claim.

We should also put a cap on the amount of awards that can be given. Some of them are so ridiculously huge, they remind me of major league sports figures' salaries. They can get up into the tens of millions—and for what?

Tort reform will be hard to get through because so many politicians are also lawyers. It's a conflict of interest for them. Why would they voluntarily cut themselves out of more business? I've never understood why lawyers are allowed to become politicians. The work of government is largely legislation. When lawyers are the ones doing this, it means they get to make the laws that they'll work under. They're not going to cut off their noses to spite their faces.

So we're going to have to fight tooth and nail over this one, just like we do over all the other aspects of government that handicap citizens and benefit politicians. But it's a fight we've got to take on. Consider the alternative: If we don't take back our government and turn it around, career politicians will have won.

The Case for Minimal Government

No government ever voluntarily reduces itself in size. Government programs, once launched, never disappear. Actually, a government bureau is the nearest thing to eternal life we'll ever see on this earth!

—Ronald Reagan

The twentieth century saw a massive, worldwide shift toward gigantic government. That's bad news for everybody, because historically, the bigger and more complex a government grows, the more wasteful and inefficient it becomes. It's especially bad for us. Gigantic, overgrown bureaucracies are particularly hazardous in a free society like ours. They invariably begin to control aspects of our lives that they have no business controlling. They lose touch with their citizens and become insular. They stop representing us.

That's what we're facing today: a government that has outgrown us. If our Founding Fathers could see the size our federal government has grown to today, they would be shocked. They believed, as I do, that the federal government should be as utilitarian as possible, that it has no business doing anything more than providing the bare necessities.

I'm an advocate of minimal government for much the same reasons as the Founding Fathers: First, because I agree that it's government's nature to become corrupt. The bigger the government, the bigger the corruption. And second, I have a great deal of faith in people. I think that left to our own, we can take care of ourselves pretty well. We don't need the government to take care of us. I believe that government's job should be to assist us when we need assistance, but at all other times, to stay out of our way.

In terms of reforming government, I think we need to do a complete shakedown. I understand that sweeping change needs to be incremental and gradual; it makes no sense to rush in and change things hastily. But we do need to be rigorous and thorough. We need to scour every bureau, every program, and every department for wastefulness. Just as important, we need to reform government's basic attitude; we've got to retrain it to think in terms of efficiency, not growth. I believe that the government that serves us best is one that can keep its own growth in check—and one that never forgets who it exists to serve.

8

The Challenge of the Future

*R**eal generosity towards the future lies in giving all to the present.***

— **Albert Camus**

One day in late 1999, the first lady and I made an appearance at a rural high school. As we walked in the door, the school band struck up a tune. When I heard what the band was playing, I did a double-take. I had to listen for a couple of seconds to be sure I was really hearing what I thought I was hearing. I looked over at Terry, and I could see from the smile spreading across her face that she recognized it too. The band was playing Black Sabbath's "Iron Man."

We couldn't believe it! In our day, Black Sabbath was considered extreme, radical, pushing the envelope. We had gone to see Black Sabbath on our honeymoon. And now here it was on a high school band's sheet music, right alongside Gershwin. It made us feel so old.

If that doesn't tell you how fast things can change, what would? I believe that as the Information Revolution takes hold, we are going to be experiencing change on a scale that's never been seen before. You think change came fast in the twentieth century? Because the transfer of information today is almost instantaneous—and because it's linked to an increasing number of other information sources all across the globe—change of all kinds is going to be happening at a far more rapid pace than ever before. We are truly on the brink of a new era: the Information Age.

The Information Revolution

*T*ransport of the mails, transport of the human voice, transport of flickering pictures—in this century as in others, our highest accomplishments still have the single aim of bringing men together.
—Antoine de Saint-Exupéry

We have no idea how lucky we are to be living during this time in history. We're on the cutting edge of a revolution that's going to transform humankind. In the course of all human history, we've had only two other revolutions that rank even close to the magnitude of this one. The first one began several thousand years ago, when human beings first started figuring out how to grow their own food. Agriculture made it possible for us to stop being nomadic; it allowed cities and large populations to grow, and it made it possible for people to begin to specialize in various trades. The second gigantic-scale innovation, the Industrial Revolution, was just building up to full steam a century and a half ago, and look how far it has already taken us. Compare the technological progress we made just within the twentieth century to all the other centuries of humankind. It was the beginning of the industrial era that made all of modern technology possible.

And now we've entered what I believe will be the greatest leap for humankind yet: the Information Revolution. It's mind-boggling what this development promises to do for us. It's linking all of humanity together in a way that's never happened before. It's giving us the opportunity to truly become a global people. And it's putting every kind of information at our fingertips with astonishing speed.

As we Americans head into the new millennium, we need to remain aware of the magnitude of this change. We owe it to ourselves to jump onto the Internet with both feet. It's our new frontier. It's still new enough that it's yielding all kinds of fertile ground to the pioneers who are willing to invest themselves in it. It would be prudent of us to get in there and make it as widely available to as many people as we possibly can. I truly believe that the best policy government can adopt for dealing with the Internet is to keep regulations and restrictions to a minimum, to foster access and competition, and then to get the hell out of the way.

As impressive as it is, the Internet is still in its infancy. Our legislative policies toward the Internet should reflect the fact that it truly is uncharted territory. We should be keeping the frontier open for as long as we can.

When I was at the annual governors' conference in Washington this year, we discussed the question of whether or not states should be taxing Internet sales and access. Any time somebody's making money, the federal government is sure to stand up and take notice. Frankly, I don't believe this issue is any of the federal government's business. The federal government doesn't have the right to tell states whether or not to tax something. As I told everyone at the conference, I believe that it should be left up to the individual states to decide if they want to tax Internet purchases.

I understand the concern many of the governors expressed, that states are losing important sales tax revenue to Internet sales. For many of them, sales tax is the way they pay for education and social programs. But I suspect that a tax on Internet purchases would put a severe damper on an industry that's still getting its feet wet. Best to leave it up to individual states to decide whether or not they're going to tax Internet sales.

I've been doing what I can to guide Minnesota as deeply into the

Information Age as possible. In 1999 I helped put together the Telecommunications Strategic Plan for Minnesota, with the goal of opening up communications to the people. The plan will grant subsidies to telephone and cable companies, and offer aid to communities that don't have high-speed Internet access. The emphasis is on competition, because that's what's best for businesses and consumers in the long run. It's almost becoming a cliché these days for people to be unhappy with their cable companies, because there's generally only one cable company in each area. That makes for terrible customer service, because they know they've got you—if you want cable, you have no other options. This is the kind of situation we need to prevent. We want to expand communication opportunities for everyone and keep competition strong, so that there's an incentive to keep business standards high.

Another concern that often comes up in discussions about the Internet is the issue of safety. With so many of us venturing onto the information superhighway, it ought to be general knowledge by now that, like any new frontier, the Internet has its dangers. There are predators out there taking advantage of the fact that most people are still new at navigating the Web. Many people have unwittingly handed over credit card numbers and other personal information to Internet crooks. We need to work harder at educating the public about the fact that there are plenty of people out there who know how to manipulate the system. We need to be teaching everyone how to prevent electronic con men from ripping them off.

Parents are particularly worried about their kids going online and being exposed to the huge flood of pornography that exists on the Web, or worse, becoming the target of a stalker. Obviously, we need to make sure that our children can use the Internet safely, but I think we'd be better off accomplishing that with education than with regulation. Rather than imposing a whole bunch of new rules on Internet "speech" (to put it in First Amendment terms) it would be better, I think, for parents to monitor their childrens' activities on the

Web. There are plenty of great software programs available today that block out any material that isn't family friendly. If the Internet isn't what we want it to be, better that we change our Web-crawling habits, rather than expect government to restrict the Internet in order to protect us.

I believe we also need to be careful how we use the Internet as a source of connection between people. E-mail can be a terrific way to stay in touch; it may even be a great way for people to meet. But it's a poor substitute for face-to-face contact. I doubt that a purely "cyber" relationship could ever be as satisfying to our psyches as having somebody there in the flesh, a physical presence in our lives. We've got to make sure we don't begin thinking of cyberspace as a substitute for communities. Our communities are suffering from neglect enough as it is.

In light of the big picture, the long-term goal we ought to be striving for is to make sure that every citizen has an equal opportunity to tap into the Information Revolution and use it profitably. It's a core belief of our nation that every person should have an equal shot at prosperity, and that should apply to the Internet as it does to any other venue. It's a very lofty ideal, one that we may never achieve 100 percent. But that's the star we should be steering by.

Humanity's Going Global

The Information Revolution is connecting humankind in ways we never have been connected before, and that can't help but change us on a social and cultural level. The real question is whether or not it's going to change us for the better. Ultimately, that's up to us. I don't believe that technology is inherently good or bad. It's all in how we use it. It's all in how we respond to the challenges it puts before us.

I feel the same way about television. You often hear people talk about the way television is corrupting our youth and rotting our brains. But the bottom line is that it's not the technology of TV that's doing it, it's the choice we make to watch the garbage that's on instead of the nutritious stuff. Nobody told you you had to watch *Married with Children* instead of the Discovery Channel! It's the same way with the Internet. You have the freedom to choose between a porn site and any one of dozens of on-line university libraries.

Depending on how we choose to use it, the technology that's now allowing us to participate in a global network of instant information could potentially transform us into a more unified, more knowledgeable people. It carries the potential to promote understanding across cultures. It's definitely going to force a change in the way we interact with those who are different from us. You hear a lot of talk these days about the future blending us all into a single homogenized world culture. Now, I'm all for governments getting along and for tolerance of cultural differences, but I don't think humanity is headed for a single culture or a single language. It goes against our nature to conform that much. Diversity is essential to what we are; it's our strength. I think the world would be a far less interesting place if we allowed ourselves to become homogenized.

Personally, I like the challenge of reaching across cultural boundaries. Diversity doesn't scare me. I see it as a chance to learn and expand myself. Besides, whenever I've traveled in various foreign countries, I've always found that no matter how much cultural difference there is between me and the people I meet, we always have more things in common, just by the fact that we're human, than we have differences.

I believe that the one-world government everyone's chattering about probably isn't going to happen, either, for the same reasons. People are incorrigible individualists; they're never going to be happy with a single system of government. I think enough people realize that they're better off with choices. If they really can't stand the government in one country, they can emigrate to another. Just look at the people from around the world who line up to get into the United

States of America. And if enough people get fed up with their government, they can change it—witness the fall of Communism in Europe.

Can you imagine the potential for corruption that would exist within a single global government? We have enough trouble trying to rein in the corruption in our own federal government! The temptations to abuse power on a global scale would be sure to attract the worst of humankind, and historically they have. It would be a nightmare. I'm all for nations cooperating with each other, being peaceful and friendly, and keeping trade free and borders open, but I don't ever want to see a single worldwide government.

Light-Rail: Getting a Jump Start on the Transportation Needs of the Future

I'm convinced that one of the best things we can do to prepare for the transportation needs of the future is to invest in light-rail systems. Eventually, we are going to be forced to find alternatives to combustion-engine vehicles; it makes sense that we should start working on those alternatives now.

The federal government is offering funding to states who want to put in light-rail systems, and from what I can see, Minneapolis is desperately in need of one. Arne Carlson, the governor before me, laid the groundwork for light-rail in Minneapolis; I'm just following up on what I think is a great idea.

But as with every other issue I'm working on, I've got some vocal opponents to light-rail. Some people are convinced that if we put in a light-rail system, nobody will use it. But if you look at cities where it's been put in, in the majority of cases, the opposite has happened. When I visited Colorado recently, Governor Owens said they had the same naysayers when they were putting in their light-rail, but now that it's up and running, the turnout has been phenomenal. Ridership is way above what they expected—and now they don't have enough parking spaces at the stations to accommodate all the riders!

It's remarkable to see what they're doing. We're so behind here in Minnesota where transportation is concerned it's embarrassing, and yet I've got people trying to keep us from moving forward. It's already passed, it's already been approved, we've got the federal funding in place to put the system in, but they're still trying to get it shut down. I think we got a deal: The federal government had $500 million earmarked for any state that would kick in $100 million of its own money. If you think about that in business terms, who would turn down an offer like that?

And it's not as though we'd get that money back in a tax cut if we didn't spend it. If Minnesota doesn't use that money, it will be given to another state. I'm sure Colorado hopes that we do pass on it, because they'd probably like to have that money to put in another couple of lines! And we'll still sit here with nothing. I asked Governor Owens if he thought this was a liberal or conservative issue. He said, "Neither, it's an economic issue. It's keeping up with the global economy. Transportation is so important."

The Challenge Ahead

The future holds a special challenge for us as Americans. We have a unique role to play as the planet's last true superpower. We're a model to the rest of the world for the power of democracy. Ever since the signing of the Declaration of Independence, the world has been watching us to see how it's done. That's why it's so important for us to get our government back to what it should be.

> **S**ometimes people call me an idealist. Well, that is the way I know I am an American.... America is the only idealistic nation in the world.
> —Woodrow Wilson

The greatest challenge we will face in the next decade is getting citizens involved in government again. How great a light for democracy the United States can be in the coming decades depends on how successful we are at bringing the people back into government.

Right now we're seeing the beginnings of a great movement toward reform. The citizens of this country have finally had it with unresponsive government. People want someone to tell them the truth, not the same old song and dance; not the same old poll-driven politicians talking out of both sides of their mouths, telling them everything they want to hear. We need to see real people getting elected again. If we can just get to the point where our citizens' faith in their elected officials is restored, I believe we'll see citizen involvement soar.

We need to focus on a policy of free trade with other nations. The Communications Revolution is guaranteed to boost international trade to a new level. We'd be shooting ourselves in the foot if we left ourselves out of the global trend toward international free trade. Free trade was a big issue in my fallout with the Reform party. A number of folks within the party believe in sheltering our economy from the international market. That kind of protectionism is an outdated idea. It was only a limited success even in its own time. It simply doesn't work today.

Should the United States Open Trade with China? Why the Business Deal of the Century May Also Be the Century's Greatest Coup for Human Rights

While I was in Washington this spring, the U.S. Trade Representative to China, Ambassador Charlene Barchevsky, who is active in the World Trade Organization, called me in for a private meeting. I had written an op-ed piece supporting world trade and bringing China on board, which is also one of President Clinton's great concerns.

The President even remarked that my article was the best thing he'd read all week, because it was in full support of what he wanted to do.

Ambassador Barchevsky encouraged me to take an active role in worldwide trade, especially where China is concerned. She said, "They'll listen to you." She asked me if I'd be willing to testify in Congress about why we should bring China into the World Trade Organization.

I told the ambassador, jokingly, "Well, okay, if I do this, I want something in return." She said, "Name it." I said, "I want to be ambassador to Fiji!" I think it would be great to get posted to a little South Sea island where all you have to do is count waves and take water temperatures, and you can report back, "Yep. Same as last month." I wouldn't mind taking that job, after all this! (Only joking, of course.)

It was only later that the real significance of what she was asking me sunk in. I lay awake in bed most of one night trying to grasp the scope of what I'd been asked to do. I realized that this could be the single most important economic issue of the coming century.

China is home to one fifth of the human population. As a businessperson, would you want to cut yourself out of that much of your potential customer base? That's 20 percent of the market. We can't afford to be left out of that market—or any other market. The United States could outcompete anyone if it wanted to, and yet we're already falling behind technologically in some areas. We're already racing to play catch up. As I always say, it's far better to be on the field than in the stands. Trade with China could give the United States' economy a gigantic shot in the arm.

In opening up trade with China, we'd be giving nothing and getting everything. What they sell to us will probably change very little. But what will change dramatically is our access to them. Up until now, they haven't allowed us into their market. Now we'll have access to over a billion new customers. And if we don't move on this opportunity, the rest of the world will. We could end up being the only country not trading with China.

It's a no-brainer in my opinion. It doesn't mean that anything more will come to us from China, but we'll be selling a huge amount of stuff to them. It will drop tariff rates from 30 percent down to 10 percent. In most cases it will be particularly beneficial to our farmers, because China is out of farmland.

I recently met with about twenty Chinese students at the University of Minnesota (Minnesota has the highest population of Chinese students in the United States). I'd never been in a room with so many Ph.D. students. They told me that China's farmland is maxed out. Eighty percent of their population farms. They can't grow any more food than they're already growing, but they don't grow enough to feed their people. The students laughed when I said, "So farmland in China is like lakeshore property in Minnesota?" But it's a good analogy. There's only so much of it.

They're suffering from a shortage of food while our farmers are suffering because they produce more than we need. We've got grain literally rotting in silos, and you know what happens economically when you get a situation like that. Whenever you've got a surplus of a commodity, prices go in the tank.

But if U.S. farmers could sell our surplus to China, prices would rise and the profit would be enormous. It's the same as if you were in the publishing industry, and you had an opportunity to sell your books to Barnes & Noble. They're one of the biggest booksellers around. Would you turn down a market that huge?

And yet, we've got Senators like Paul Wellstone who oppose free trade, and then go out and lead marches for the farm problem. What he wants for our farmers instead of economic opoortunity is a bigger government subsidy. Here we have an opportunity to get our farmers *off* government subsidies by opening up the markets, and giving them new marketplaces.

Senator Paul Wellstone is a believer in big government, in government involvement in everyone's life. And as long as government subsidies are going on and the government controls everything, that makes him important. Wellstone wants to keep farmers dependent upon government. He marches for all these farm-aid causes, yet he works to keep them in what amounts to a mild form of slavery. If you're dependent upon government, you're not a free person. Opening our farm markets up to China would mean a huge boost in sales and a rise in prices, which would go far in getting farmers off government subsidies and on their own feet again. But if that happened, they wouldn't need Senator Wellstone, would they?

On principle, anybody who finds themselves on the same side of an argument as Senator Paul Wellstone and Pat Buchanan should look at that fact and say, "Somehow my thinking's wrong on this; I'd better take another look!"

Economic isolationism is a complete failure. Yet the public isn't generally given opportunities to see that it is. It's a shame that the truth about NAFTA isn't more widely known. There hasn't been a giant sucking sound, as Ross Perot described it, of jobs draining away from the United States. We're at the lowest unemployment rate in history. How do you explain that? If Mexico is really sucking all those jobs away, why is our unemployment the lowest it's ever been?

If you're an exporting nation, your wages are higher, and you have more jobs available. Because in order to export you have to create. Certain jobs did go to Mexico, but many of them were jobs that people here in the United States won't do. NAFTA's been a terrific success, but the media generally hasn't reported it because Perot's "giant sucking sound" makes a more interesting sound bite.

If you need any more convincing, just look at what isolationism has done for us in Cuba. We cut off trade with Cuba for the sole purpose of getting Castro out of office. Has it worked? After this next election, Castro will have been in power during ten American presidencies. Almost forty-five years. It haven't worked; it still doesn't work. Enough is enough! Rest assured, Fidel Castro isn't missing a meal because of our embargo.

People who oppose trade with China are always quick to mention the human rights abuses going on there. I understand that unspeakable human atrocities have happened in China, and you'll never hear me excusing them. I sympathize with people's concerns about China's human rights abuses, and I feel the same urge as they do to do something about it. We've all heard the stories coming out of China. The government does inhuman things to its people to keep them in line. That's a by-product, it seems, of Communism.

But if you want to talk about human rights, what about the human right to have enough food in front of you? To be able to eat every day? So wouldn't we be doing a humanitarian thing in selling them our excess food? It seems to me, if we sold our surplus to China, it's win/win. We get good money for a product we have an overabundance of; they get enough food to feed everyone.

It's weird that the first thing we do when we want to punish a country for not doing things the way we think it should is cut off its food. Our farmers, then, are used as government pawns, as political weaponry to effect policy. Yet it seldom works, because the first thing that happens is that some other country steps in and replaces us. I'm tired of them using our food as a weapon. To me it makes a lot more sense to be feeding the world, and getting at least something for it, than to have food rot in silos.

Trade barriers aren't going to do anything to change the human rights situation in China. I think the opposite approach is called for: The best catalyst for change that China could possibly have is to get a taste of the good things democracy can create. By engaging us, and by becoming more associated with our view on human rights, I think they'll be bringing a flood of new ideas into their country. They're going to be watching us and saying, "Hey—that's pretty good, why aren't we doing that?"

I think opening our markets to China will be the ultimate downfall of China's Communism. Because when China gets a taste of what capitalism can allow them to do, its people won't stand for it anymore. And I think the exposure the Chinese government would get in the World Trade Organization would open them up even more to international criticism. Whenever they do something atrocious, they'll have not 1, but 134 fingers pointing at them.

I believe, too, that in some cases there's a certain amount of ignorance on our part that gives us a skewed perspective on some of China's social problems. I'm not advocating the kinds of atrocities that are going on there in the name of population control, but I don't think we Americans have a good sense of the magnitude of China's population crisis. Faced with that dire a problem, who knows what desperate measures we might be tempted to resort to ourselves? Fundamentalists love to quote the scripture, where it says, "Go forth and multiply." But I don't think that scripture applies to the Chinese—they've already done it! Free trade will bring new opportunities for the people of the United States to talk to the people of China. We'll be able to come to a much better understanding of what life is like for them.

If we don't trade with them, somebody else will. If we don't take advantage of the opportunity, we'll simply lose it to someone else. If we don't make this move, America will be cutting off its own nose to spite its face. I've met with agricultural leaders, businesspeople—everybody is on board with this, except the human rights people and the unions. I don't understand the union position, either, because if you export more goods, you create more jobs. It would be good for the unions.

And I'm convinced that China's global influence is only going to increase as we get further into the new century. China is going to be the most computerized nation in the world, because they have the most people. And computers are outstanding tools for bringing people together on an international scale. We're working right now on technology that allows us to talk directly to our computers, and have the computer translate our words into any language we want. Can you imagine the barriers between people that are about to come down? One day we'll all be able to talk, person to person, with anyone in any nation, without having to go through the media or the leaders. And we'll be able to realize that every person around the world has virtually the same feelings as we do—we all laugh, we all cry, we all experience happiness and sorrow.

Of course, with any change as gigantic and sweeping as this one, it makes sense to pace things accordingly. Many of the Chinese students at the University of Minnesota were worried that China might not be ready for a flood of new trade opportunities with the United States. They thought the timing might be better in five years. They're afraid of what could happen if a bunch of their people suddenly started a mass migration to the cities. It would be a disaster, because there are so many of them. So of course, we have to handle this change sensibly and carefully.

Economically and socially, it makes sense for us to be as open with other nations as we can. It's the direction of the future. It's the way most of the rest of the modern world is operating. We can't afford to leave ourselves out of that. We can't afford to build a wall around our nation.

9

Election 2000

*T**he ballot is stronger*
than the bullet.
—Abraham Lincoln

When I was on my way out of Washington to come home from the annual governors' meeting in March, I was met by crowds of people cheering and calling out to me, "The wrong governor's running!" I've had people offer to come and work for me once I get to the White House. Even the media project me as a national leader, although I don't consider myself one.

I'm honored that people would want me as their president, but the truth is, I don't want that job. The more exposure I get to the business of politics, the less appealing it looks to me. For one thing, the fund-raising I'd have to do really disgusts me. It's not my style to go to people with my hand out, asking for money. I can't help thinking of that as "political panhandling."

Running for president is a dirty, ugly job. Especially in recent years, campaigning for the presidency just seems to automatically taint anybody who goes through it. They'll do anything to win. They'll say anything. They'll pull whatever dirty trick they have to to bring their opponent down.

The brave souls who decide to take a shot at the White House don't have time to concentrate on the issues. They've got to focus all their attention on getting past each of the hurdles that await them along the campaign trail. The way the system works now, the first ballot, the primary, is the biggest hurdle. They first have to get past their own party. If they can get the nod from their party, it frees them up a great deal, and it gives them a fresh infusion of cash. But then they have to focus their remaining energies on wooing the public and bringing down their opponent in the opposite party.

Despite the fact that it's politics as usual among the candidates, some exciting developments have been taking place with the voters. More people are beginning to come back to the polls. The majority of nonvoters have traditionally been middle- and low-income people. In Minnesota at least, we're now seeing a resurgence of lower-income people in the system.

I think a large majority of Americans are growing restless with the way politics has been treating them. They know that the two traditional parties don't have their best interests at heart. The two parties are portrayed in the media as being the majority, but the facts paint a far different picture. Here in Minnesota, for example, 15 to 20 percent of the people consider themselves Democrats, and 15 to 20 percent consider themselves Republicans. That leaves a huge majority of us—60 to 70 percent—stuck in the middle, without representation!

Yet the media continually try to say that the two parties represent the majority of the thinking. I mentioned that very thing once when I appeared on *Meet the Press* with Tim Russert and two other governors, one a Democrat and one a Republican. Neither one denied it. But nobody seemed to want to talk about it.

The time is ripe for something to change. Any candidate, any party, that can tap into that disenfranchised middle majority is going to be welcomed with open arms.

Honesty

The key to this election is honesty. The American people are sick to death of candidates who will tell them anything to get their vote. The American people aren't dumb; they know insincerity when they hear it. Whoever the public thinks is being honest with them is going to get the greatest number of votes.

Politicians today are terrified of telling the public things that it doesn't want to hear. They've come to believe that unpopular opinions are death to a political career. But if that were true, I'd have been history long ago. I stand as living proof that you can speak your mind, even when some of your views are unpopular, or even downright shocking, and if you truly stand behind your convictions, you'll survive.

A case in point: the controversial *Playboy* interview that I did in 1999. In the most frenzied part of the fallout from that interview, my approval rating dropped by 18 percent, and people were saying I'd finally gotten my foot permanently lodged in my mouth. But I stood behind what I said. I clarified and elaborated on some of my points when I needed to, but I didn't back down from any of them. Within a few months, my approval rating rebounded to about the same level it was before the interview. And when the second half of the interview was printed a few months later, we heard hardly a peep from the media.

It was kind of a trial by fire. I think the public finally learned once and for all that I'm not interested in being the world's most politically correct governor. I can say anything now without fear. I'm living proof that honesty isn't a career-killer. I truly believe that even though the public may react negatively when they hear something they don't like, they would still rather listen to sincerity.

The Jesus Factor

The weirdest phenomenon that has happened in this election so far is the way religion has come into play among the candidates. Early in the campaign, there was suddenly this mad scramble among all the major candidates except McCain and Bradley, the two outsiders on opposite sides of the political fence, to play the religion card. It's scary when you remember that we are a nation that believes in the separation of church and state. Why should a candidate's religion enter into the picture at all?

I have to commend McCain and Bradley for not hopping onto the religion bandwagon. It says good things about both of them that they weren't about to be picked up by any wind that happened to blow through the campaign. I'd be willing to bet a pretty good number of people switched their allegiance to McCain because he was the only major contender who wasn't trying to co-opt Jesus for his own political purposes. Most of the other candidates, as soon as word got out that religion was a major factor, were knocking themselves out to convince voters how religious they were. Bush talked about how his life had been transformed when he found religion, and told us that Jesus was the philosopher who most inspired him. Even Gore tried to convince us that he makes every decision in his life, political and otherwise, by asking himself, "What would Jesus do?"

Religion is a greater factor in this election than it has been in any other that I can remember. This time the line between church and state has become really blurred. I believe that this is exactly the kind of scenario the Founding Fathers were trying to warn us about, because what's at stake is not religious faith in general, but a single faith in particular. The theme of this election has become "Elect the best Christian." I'd like to see the candidates explain that to the millions of Americans who are Muslims, Jews, Hindus, or any other religion.

How did Jesus get dragged into this campaign? I'll give you a hint: It's not the quiet, gentle, mainstream Christians who are behind this movement. It's the ones who are the most extreme, and the most politically vocal. This election ought to terrify us all because it shows how deeply entrenched in our political system the Religious Right has become.

That's what's scary about Election 2000. Geraldo Rivera had Jerry Falwell on his show to dissect the primaries—why? What does Falwell have to do with a presidential race? The way this election has been going has laid bare the evidence that the Religious Right is extremely powerful in politics today. Trust me, it wasn't for the average American's benefit that all the candidates suddenly got religion. The Religious Right has bashed a hole in the wall between church and state large enough to drive one of those big blue church buses through. We should be terrified.

He Who Slings Mud

This election has taken the art of smearing one's opponent to new depths. By now everyone's familiar with the way it's done. You start out your campaign making some kind of idealistic statement about how you refuse to be drawn into the muck. You're not going to stoop to name-calling and smear campaigns. You'll leave that to your opponent. But then, as the campaign progresses you feel compelled to rebut something your opponent said about you, he rebuts your rebuttal, and it all starts to get ugly. It happens every time. It happens to the best of them, whether they intend it or not.

Bush and McCain are both guilty of it. Shortly before the Michigan primary, Bush paid a visit to Bob Jones University, which is a rabidly fundamentalist, so-called Christian school. That visit speaks volumes. It tells us that Bush knows what side his political bread gets buttered on. It can't be making the Catholics of this country happy to know that Bush is friendly with people who have called them Satanists, and who have claimed that the Pope is the anti-Christ.

But McCain proved he was no saint either with the way he reacted to the whole deal. When the news broke of Bush's visit to Bob

Jones, somebody in McCain's camp jumped on the phones, calling a bunch of Michigan voters with a recorded message telling them what Bush had done. McCain denied that he had authorized those calls, but later he admitted that he had.

Gore isn't getting out of this one looking pristine either. He blatantly went on the warpath against Bradley, grossly misrepresenting his viewpoints to make him look further left than he actually is. If you were hoping to vote for the candidate who behaved himself and didn't resort to dirty tricks, I'm afraid you're out of luck this time around. All the major players have mud on their hands.

George W. Bush: Centrist Talk, Far Right Walk

George W. Bush flew into Minnesota for a fund-raiser, and while he was here he called to thank me for a statement I'd made to the national media. I'd told the media that Bush was somebody I could enjoy going fishing and drinking beer with. I like the man. He's an easygoing, personable guy.

But just because I'd hang out with him in a bass boat doesn't mean I'd go with him in the voting booth. If we elected George W. Bush, I have

> However beautiful the strategy, you should occasionally look at the results.
>
> —Winston Churchill

no doubts that we'd be casting our votes for business as usual. I have nothing against the man personally, but as a politician, he is a classic example of the modern-day say-anything public figure. He goes in for platitudes the same way his father did; he's got his catchphrases about "enlisting the soldiers of the army of compassion" to "usher in the responsibility era." He learned well the mantra of the nineties: Why go to all the trouble to actually do something if you can just *say* you do it and accomplish the same thing?

That's why he's taken to calling himself a reformist at every turn.

He knows reform is a word that gets votes in this election, and he's very focused on saying the "right" words. But interestingly enough, that strategy is really starting to work against him. The public has indicated time and again that he comes across as insincere to them. That's his big mistake: He's trying to please everyone instead of standing tall and saying what he honestly believes—whatever that is. He won't take a position, because he's afraid to make enemies. But that would have shown the American people that he had the courage of his convictions. And that's what people are really interested in voting for this time.

Bush's strategy has been to make friends with the Religious Right, which controls the party, so that he has their support squarely behind him. In reality, if you go by his voting record, Bush is not all that far to the right of center, but he's painting himself that way for their benefit. He's doing essentially what my gubernatorial opponent Norm Coleman tried to do: He's gotten in good with the far Right, now he's got to carefully tiptoe his way back to center. He's got a fine line to toe: He's got to make himself look like a centrist to the public, but still be able to pull off the Religious Right act for his party's power brokers. That's where Pat Buchanan may throw a monkey wrench into things; Buchanan could dice up the far Religious Right vote against Bush.

For a so-called reformer, George W. Bush sure has played the more dysfunctional elements of the electoral system in his favor. He knew how to work the system well enough to know that initially he had to spend his own money currying favor with his party. Once the primaries gave him their nod, he was done with the out-of-pocket expenses, because the soft money kicked in. How likely would the special interest groups be to endorse him if they didn't have expectations that he would return the favor?

I also don't buy Bush as a "people's president." I don't know how well Bush can truly represent the concerns of the average working American. He's a son of wealth and privilege; he hasn't spent one day of his life in the world that most Americans live in. Bush talks a lot about equality, and I want to believe him. But the way he's lived his life tells me that he's comfortable with white, male, upper-class privilege, just as much as the way he's campaigning tells me that the political system suits him just the way it is.

Al Gore: The Beige Tiger

Al Gore was making a speech at the governors' meeting this year, saying something about bipartisanism, when I corrected him. I said, "Mr. Vice-President, on behalf of independent governor of Maine Angus King and myself, I'd like to teach you a new word: tripartisan!" He laughed and said, "So noted!"

Gore's a nice guy; he's got a gentle, earnest manner about him. And he's smart enough to keep the economy, a perennial election-maker, as a major focus in his campaign. A lot of people think this makes him a shoo-in for president. But in many ways, even at this late stage in the game, he's an unknown quantity. It's hard to get a handle on what he really stands for. It's not completely his fault. He's been in the shadow of the President for eight years. His job as vice-president is largely to support his boss, so we can't fault him for that.

I get the impression that once he's out in his own light, we'll see that Gore is a bit more liberal than Clinton. Clinton is in many ways a centrist. But Gore didn't need to reposition himself on the political continuum to get the nod from his party. The main thing Gore had to do to get an edge over Bill Bradley was to paint Bradley as being even further left than he is, even though Bradley's voting record shows that he's not as far left as all that. Gore did a thorough job of making himself look closer to center by comparison.

Bradley didn't get a fair shake out of this election. I could never have supported him myself; even though he wasn't as far left as Gore wanted us to believe, he was too far left for me. But I do feel sorry for him, because between Gore and the media, his stand on the issues was grossly misrepresented.

Gore successfully moved his opponent's image on the political continuum so that he didn't have to bother to move his own. But he did have to reinvent himself slightly, to show that he had a bit more fire than Bradley. Bradley doesn't put a flame in people, and I think Gore recognized that that was a serious credential for the job. That's why the gentle Gore we'd known for eight years suddenly came out of the box with both fists flying.

Eight years in the public spotlight is a tough edge to beat. Gore has more name recognition than any candidate would dare hope for. And I think his image benefits in some ways from Clinton's personal misbehavior. It makes him look squeaky clean by comparison, kind of the way Dan Quayle made President Bush look smart. I have nothing against Gore personally, he's a fine contender. But I wish the rest of the candidates in his party hadn't given up so soon. As fine a candidate as Gore is, our political system always does better when the people are given choices. I don't feel that Democrats were given much of a choice this time around.

John McCain: Solid Thinker

John McCain called to touch base with me one day last fall. I told him I admired his outspokenness and his stand on reform. I've always wondered what he was doing in one of the two traditional parties. He doesn't seem to fit. I was still with the Reform party when he called me, so I asked him, "Why don't you join us? You're for tax reform and campaign reform. You belong with us." He said, "No, I'm a Republican through and through." Too bad they don't seem to have the same loyalty toward him as he has toward them.

The fact that John McCain was a major player for a time in this election gives me hope. The man's got a lot of points in his favor. For one thing, he's no chickenhawk. Do you know what a chickenhawk

> *What counts is not necessarily the size of the dog in the fight—it's the size of the fight in the dog.*
> —Dwight D. Eisenhower

is? It's someone who talks tough as long as there's no real danger to himself, but when it comes time for action, he's chicken. John McCain has proven himself. He flew for the Navy; he served his country as a genuine hero. We know he can keep it together under pressure, because he spent years in a Vietnamese prison camp and kept his wits about him. If he survived that, he could surely handle a stint of internment at 1600 Pennsylvania Avenue.

He would have made an outstanding Reform party candidate, at least in terms of what the party was six years ago. He's a little to the right of them on social issues, but he's got a true reformist attitude. He's not just calling himself a reformer because it gets votes, the way Bush is. He's got a genuine plan for campaign reform and for restructuring Social Security. He's against campaign contributions from special interest groups, although he's got the guts and the integrity to admit that even he has benefited from their support.

McCain's campaign sounded a good bit like mine. He followed a lot of the same strategies, and he said basically what I would have said if I were running. He and I are alike in many ways. He's aggressively devoted to honesty. McCain spoke nicely of me on one occasion; he said, "We have a lot in common. We both speak our minds."

In fact, John McCain told me he named his bus, the *Straight Talk Express*, in honor of me. The public really responded to his candor. Even when his campaign was officially on hold, he was still getting 32 percent of the popular vote. I was only getting 28 percent the night before my election.

From here on out, it all depends on how much of his platform the party adopts. If they slam the door on him, and don't represent any of his ideas, there's a sliver of hope that he could go independent. He keeps saying that he doesn't want to leave his party. But he has to say that now because he doesn't want to alienate them while there's a chance they'll still support him. But I can understand, too, why it's tough for him to think about leaving his party. It's very hard for people to sever their party ties. It's like cutting an umbilical cord. Without your party, you have to get yourself elected totally on your own.

John McCain struck a chord when he talked about campaign reform. The public responded enthusiastically. But the Republicans are never going to do anything about reforming the campaign system, because it's the party's lifeblood, as much as it is for the Democrats. I don't think that's ever going to happen without the rise of a third party. As long as just two parties are in power, it's not going to change.

McCain did a smart thing in going after that middle majority that doesn't feel they're represented by the two traditional parties. He appealed to the people in that wide gap in the middle who don't feel at home with Gore's left leanings or Bush's far-right rumblings. What ultimately brought him down, I believe, was the fact that he belonged to the Republican party. Many of the folks in that middle majority have come to deeply distrust the two traditional parties and anyone associated with them. They may have liked what they heard from McCain, but they knew who held the other end of his chain.

With all the bold things he has to say about government reform, it's an irony that he's got all this loyalty to the Republican party, one of the main institutions behind the political corruption we're dealing with today. It's amazing that he managed to break through with all those outspoken ideas and still kept his party affiliation intact. But as long as he was trying to maintain the support he got from his party, he knew he could only stray so far from the official party agenda. Being a member of one of the two major parties makes you very powerful, but that power doesn't come without a price. Rest assured, as long as he keeps his party affiliation, John McCain is owned, as much as any other Republican or Democrat.

I predicted pretty early on in the game that McCain wasn't going to get his party's nomination, even if he had glowed in the primaries. His party is controlled by the far Right; he's too close to the center to suit the real power brokers in the Republican party. It's happened plenty of times before: The party will blatantly disregard the will of the people and get behind a candidate who supports its ideology. It happened here in Minnesota just a few years ago. Republican Governor Arne Carlson was extremely popular, yet he couldn't get his own party's endorsement.

I'm still holding out hope that McCain will break away as an independent. It would be a smart move for him to make; he'd be very powerful. If he ran as an independent, and was able to appeal successfully to all those disenfranchised voters who haven't been voting because they don't feel that anyone represents them, he'd have a solid shot at the White House. And if he ran as an independent and picked somebody like me as his running mate, he'd have it in the bag. At the governors' conference in Washington, I tossed around the notion of an independent McCain/Ventura ticket—just for fun, just to see their reaction. They were terrified.

An independent McCain/Ventura campaign would be virtually unstoppable. We'd get the veteran vote, the youth vote, the reform vote, and of course, the vote from that all-important silent majority in the center of the political continuum. Now, truth be told, if he called to ask me, I'd take the call. I have so much respect for the man that I'd entertain the possibility. But as I've said repeatedly, I don't want that job. I don't want to go to Washington. Minnesota is my home. I'm sure John McCain would do a fine job without my help.

Profiles to Discourage

Pat Buchanan and Ross Perot bear mention, not because they were ever serious contenders in this race, but because their presence in the election

> *There's small choice in rotten apples.*
> —William Shakespeare

tells us something important about the state of our political system. I'm glad they're involved; I'm not one to discourage anybody from getting out there and running. The more choices the public has the better. But I think in both cases their presence in the race is symptomatic of something wrong with the process.

PAT BUCHANAN

Pat Buchanan is a perennial candidate in presidential elections. This year marks his third or fourth attempt. I've got to give him credit, at least, for standing for something. Certainly he has a vision for the way he believes America should be, but it's not a vision he shares with the majority of Americans.

Buchanan's choice to defect to the Reform party was one of the most incongruous political moves I've ever seen. The Reform party's platform has virtually nothing in common, that I can see, with Buchanan's thinking. It's a fundamentally centrist party, and Buchanan is about as far from being a centrist as a person can get. I can only think of three reasons why he would make such a move. The first explanation is that he was facing a very crowded race within his own party, and he knew he couldn't count on support from the mainstream rank-and-file Republicans. Maybe he thought his best chance would be to do something to make himself stand out from the crowd.

The second scenario sounds a bit wackier, but in today's political climate, you never know. I sometimes wonder if Buchanan was sent to destroy the party. It could be that Buchanan was the sacrificial lamb. His presence in a party is divisive, and the Reform party was already threatening to rip apart at the seams. In the last several elections, the Reform party has been a thorn in the Republican party's side. It could be that somebody in the Republican party was looking for the Reform party's strategic weakness, and decided that Buchanan would be just the right person to aggravate it.

The third possibility is the most plausible: money. There is about $12 million in federal money available to the Reform party's nominee. If Pat can get his hands on that money, he can keep himself in the spotlight for quite a while. And, when the election is over, it's back to the lucrative lecture circuit for him.

Buchanan didn't like it when I called him a "retread" from another party, but that's what he is. The week after I announced I was leaving the Reform party, Buchanan came to Minnesota. I think he was planning on trying to draw me into a public debate over my decision to leave the party. But I wasn't going to give him the satisfaction.

He accused me of waving a white flag, of running away from a fight—a fight that he said would have been beneficial for Minnesota. It's pretty pathetic, I think, for a guy like him to criticize me about walking away from a fight. Buchanan's a classic chickenhawk: He never served in any military capacity; he's never "stood a post," in the words of Jack Nicholson. He doesn't know what it means to put his life on the line to defend his country. I do. I know more about fights than he could possibly know. I know enough to pick the fights that are worthy of my time, and walk away from the rest.

Buchanan's now trying to distance himself from the fact that he got David Duke's endorsement, because he knows that politically, David Duke is poison. But it doesn't matter whether or not he accepts Duke's endorsement. The point is that a guy like David Duke thinks that Pat Buchanan is somebody to get behind politically. Buchanan appeals to Duke's sense of the way things ought to be. And that ought to send a clear message all by itself.

The fact that Buchanan has enough power to affect the national political scene in any way tells us that it's not the will of the people that's driving partisan politics these days. I've been told that Buchanan's followers are a very loyal bunch. But I suspect that if you put them all together, there wouldn't be enough of them to populate a small county, let alone a nation of fifty states. Buchanan is able to make as much national noise as he does only because power is distributed unevenly within the political system. A small minority, whose ideologies don't even vaguely resemble those of mainstream America, has the money and influence to keep him in the spotlight, election after election.

ROSS PEROT

Against all better judgment, it looks like Ross Perot is lining up to make a third run for the White House on the Reform party ticket. Shortly after I left the party, the committee tossed out party chairman Jack Gargan, who supported me, and put in Pat Choate, Perot's running mate in 1996. He's building himself back up as the party's one and only legitimate leader.

The fact that he's even considering doing this a third time has convinced me beyond a doubt that his party isn't really what it was pretending to be. Back in the early nineties, the Reform party had a terrific platform, plenty of national coverage, and a shot at eventually growing into something that would give the two traditional parties a real run for their money. But in the end, the whole thing turned out to be hardly more than a vehicle for Ross Perot's ego.

Even when it was clear that the party was going to stagnate if Perot didn't step aside and let some fresh blood in, he still wouldn't let it go. There have been plenty of great candidates who have come into the party, who I would have been proud to get behind, but Perot consistently made sure they never got a chance to run. He would rather kill the party than let somebody else into its spotlight.

And in spite of what the media tried to get you to believe, I never wanted that spotlight. I wasn't looking to become the leader of the party. I have my job to do here in Minnesota; I don't have time to lead the party. The so-called war between me and Perot is just more media fiction. The media created a split between me and Perot. I'm not out to take away his power. I just don't agree with him on a lot of the ways he's trying to run things.

Fortunately, I believe that even if Perot's Reform party is a bust, the third-party movement is strong enough to survive without it. It's now got a legitimate toehold in American politics, and I suspect it's going to snowball from here. We have Perot to thank for helping us get it started; it's just too bad that he and his party weren't able to evolve enough to stick with it for the long haul.

How It Will All Shake Down

So, the bottom line for this election is that we've got the Democrats behind Gore, the Republicans backing Bush, and what was once the most promising national third party groaning under the weight of Ross Perot's ego and trying to figure out what it stands for. The Democrats didn't give their people a whole lot of viable options. In spite of the stir McCain caused, and the legitimate issues he raised, the Republicans decided to go with somebody they knew would keep the party tiller pointed hard to starboard. And the Reform party proved that it's less about reform, more about one man's ego. And while the parties are wrapped up in all this internal squabbling, the majority of Americans are still hungering for some genuine representation. Where do we go from here?

Actually, I like this discord that's sprung up within the major parties. It's healthy. It's shaking things up; it's letting new voices come through. It's busting up the death grip the small minority of party members holds on the reins of their party. Good things may come of this.

I'd like to see moderate Republicans come forward with their own party—a new, centrist party. I'd join them if they did. It would be the shorthand way to break free of the extreme Right's stranglehold on their politics. A new, well-organized centrist party would have the potential to be very powerful, and extremely popular. They would have the chance to tap into that vast, unrepresented majority of people who don't belong to either of the traditional parties.

But the bottom line is that with the shake-up within the two parties, and with the third-party movement gaining some momentum, change is in the wind. Change is good.

10

Reform's New Direction

*T*hings must be done by parties, not by persons using parties
as tools.

—Benjamin Disraeli

February 11, 2000, was one of those raw midwinter days in Saint Paul,
with the temperature hovering around 13 degrees. Mae Schunk and
I stood shivering outside on the steps of the governor's residence,
which was mobbed with reporters. I'd wanted to get as much media
coverage for our announcement as I could, so I had hedged my bet a
little.

I made sure that the media would be there in force. I knew that
they wouldn't be interested in covering a purely political announcement, no matter how important it might be to the general public. So,
starting the week before, whenever I encountered the media, I had
told them, "Listen, I'm gonna be making a public announcement at
the residence next week, and you're going to want to be there. I can't
tell you the exact details right now, but for all I know, I might very
well be announcing for president."

That got them there. The street at the governor's residence was
jammed with media trucks. CNN and several of the other major net-

works carried the announcement live. Some of them were mad at me afterward, because I'd beaten them at their own game.

At one P.M. all the cameras rolled, and Mae Schunk and I announced that we were leaving the National Reform party. I explained to the crowd, "Based on what I have seen in prior years and especially in recent months, I have come to believe that the National Reform party is hopelessly dysfunctional. In Minnesota, we cannot maintain our socially moderate identity while a right-winger heads our national ticket." I told them, "The national party has become unworthy of my support and the support of the American people."

It wasn't a decision I made frivolously. I thought about it long and hard. I consulted with the people whose opinions I respect. I talked to Donald Trump about it, because he had recently joined the party and had even been considering a presidential run on the party's ticket, until he realized how closed the party's leadership was to anybody new.

I like to think that I'm not a quitter, but there comes a time when quitting is the right thing to do. When you've faced a tough decision and you know you've made the right choice, a tremendous sensation of relief washes over you. You feel 10 pounds lighter. We were so happy that day. We knew we'd done the right thing.

At the governors' meeting in Washington later that month, President Clinton walked up and shook my hand, and told me that what I did took courage. He said quitting the party showed I had the courage of my convictions, because a move like that could have easily taken me out of the media spotlight.

The media are used to coming to me for commentary on Reform party issues, and now that they won't be doing that anymore, I stand to lose a lot of my national exposure. Today, when the media come to me for a statement on the goings-on within the national party, I say, "Go ask *them* what's going on. I no longer belong."

Surprisingly, quitting the Reform party seems like it's strengthened my standing as a national figure. Last year at the governors' convention, I had been seated in the middle of the room, in among every-body else. This year, I got a seat at Hillary Clinton's table! When I shook the President's hand that night, I told him, "If I'd have known that by quitting the Reform party I'd have gotten to sit with the First Lady, I would have quit a year ago!" I was sitting so close to the President this year that I even got to touch glasses with him during a toast!

What Happened to Our National Reform Party?

Three separate incidents over the course of the last four years con-vinced me that the party wasn't what it was represented to be. The first inkling that something wasn't right within the party came to me in 1996, when it failed to back former Colorado Governor Dick Lamb as its candidate. He was a natural choice; he should have been the next rising star of the Reform party, and he came along just as Perot's star was definitely showing signs of wear. Lamb would have made a great candidate. But Perot cut Lamb's legs out from under him. Perot wanted to remain the only star of the Reform party. The fact that the party didn't evolve in 1996 when it needed to was what started it down the road to ruin.

But in retrospect, I see now that the party was doomed from the start. The Reform party failed because it was formed the wrong way. It was built around Ross Perot; every facet of its construction was designed to keep him in power. Parties that are built on anything other than solid ideologies can't survive for long. Parties must be grown from the ground up, like plants, not from the top down like corporations. Parties build their steam little by little, from grassroots movements and from small local elections.

The National Reform party started off as a tremendous idea, but then degenerated. Perot wouldn't allow it to grow beyond him. Whenever the party showed signs of growing in a direction that didn't include Perot in the middle, he strangled all of the growth out of it. He didn't want other reformers in high places, because that would mean they'd have power that he wouldn't directly control.

That's what I learned during my campaign in 1998. And that was the second time I realized that the Reform party was saying one thing and doing another. The party was happy to back me with words, but they weren't interested in forking over any cash to help me with my campaign.

Any legitimate party would have been pleased to have one of its own members in an office as high as governor. I was the first Reform party member to make it to an elected office that high. But the Perot loyalists took every opportunity to focus all of the attention back on Perot.

My popularity was seen as a threat by the Perot loyalists. After the *Playboy* interview came out, party chairman Russ Verney, who was put in place by Perot, sent out impassioned letters and even went on television demanding that I resign from the party because I was, in his words, "unfit" to be a member. Yet when I later chose to quit for political reasons, Verney went on record saying, "Ventura had a chance to be a leader or a leaver and he chose to leave." I think he was just mad because he couldn't force me out.

So the first bit of evidence that the party was going downhill came to me in 1996, when Perot slaughtered Dick Lamb's campaign. The second was during my own campaign, which the party refused to support.

The third, and most convincing, was Buchanan.

With the arrival of Pat Buchanan, I knew beyond a doubt that it was time for me to fold and come back to Minnesota. When Buchanan came in, the party lost all sense of direction. It ceased to be a centrist party at that moment. And along with Buchanan came a steady stream of political misfits and malcontents, until the party had no idea what it stood for anymore.

But I'm not all that worried that he's going to get their nomination. It might not happen. I suspect Perot is going to jump into the race for a third time. He's going to try to put a noble spin on it, and come in like a knight in shining armor to save his party. And he'll probably get even fewer votes this time around than the 8.5 percent he got last time.

It's too bad. If Perot hadn't waffled during his first presidential run in 1992, he might have had a shot at it. I think he turned off a lot of voters when he ducked out of the race and then tried to come back. Voters probably saw him as a flake from then on out, and worried that if they elected him, he might waffle in his commitment to the White House too. I doubt that he'll ever be able to distance himself from the reputation he earned in the 1992 race. Add that to the fact that McCain is getting a pretty significant chunk of the reform vote because he's championing many of the same ideas that Perot did, and I think it's safe to say Perot won't have a snowball's chance this time around.

It's only come to the public's attention recently, but the Reform party has been hurting for quite some time because of the stagnation at its top and the infighting throughout. Unfortunately, because of its reputation for instability, the party has been losing out on some fabulous leadership in Minnesota. Just recently, former congressman Tim Penny, state auditor Judi Dutcher, and senator Dean Johnson, all powerful centrists who would fit right in politically, were offered an opportunity to join the party. But none of them would go near it because they know the party's in chaos.

The media have tried to pin the blame on me for causing all the discord within the party. They tried to paint me as a would-be national reform leader, butting heads with Perot in a bid to knock him off the party throne. But the truth is, I never had any intention of becoming a national leader. The whole issue is pure fiction. I never tried to take over the party. The party was in trouble long before I came on the scene. But of course, wars make good news stories, and so the fictional battle raged on.

Even the top people in the party seem to have bought into the notion that I was trying to steal power from Perot, because they were pretty eager to get rid of me. When Russ Verney was stepping down as party chairman, all the party members were allowed to vote on who would be his successor. I wasn't even there the day of the vote. We had bad weather in Minnesota that day, and my plane couldn't get off the ground. I participated only over the phone. They asked me who I supported and I told them I was behind Jack Gargan. Now, keep in mind that Gargan was already running long before that phone call; I had nothing to do with his decision to run. But the media decided that I had handpicked Gargan to run the party, in a bid to gain control over Ross Perot.

And now that I've moved my party affiliation back to Minnesota's Independence party, the media are at it again. Now they're trying to make it look like I want to control our state party. That's not true either. I want to be active in the party; I want to be a beneficial presence. But I've got enough on my plate right now, just doing the job I was elected to do. On the other hand, I don't mind advising them.

Minnesota's Independence Party: A Model for Others to Follow

I did recommend to the state Reform party here in Minnesota that they'd be better off disaffiliating from the National Reform party. But when they voted on March 4, 2000, I didn't participate in the vote at all, because I knew that if I did, the media would have said that Jesse Ventura was trying to take over the party. I wanted the committee members to look in the mirror and make the decision based on their own beliefs, without any pressure from me one way or the other.

Their vote came in 151 to 23 in favor of disaffiliating. But if they hadn't voted to disaffiliate, I would have been ready to say goodbye to them too. I would have become a man without a party, like Maine's governor, Angus King. That would have been nice, too. Then I would have been truly independent in my thinking. It would have given me an additional amount of freedom.

When the Minnesota Reform party split from the national party, we lost a few hard-core Perot supporters, but otherwise, we're doing just fine. We've got a bunch of good candidates running in this election. If a number of them get in, we'll become a major contender for Minnesota's political power. We'll be able to make a minor dent in the two traditional parties' power base.

A few other state reform parties are looking at the move the Minnesota party made and are considering doing the same. But we're not encouraging anybody one way or the other—it's really up to them. I'm sure they're frightened. They don't want to lose their power base or their national recognition. But if Pat Buchanan becomes a major power within the national party, I think you'll see more of them choosing to disaffiliate.

The media are trying to say that I want to dictate the Minnesota party's platform, which isn't true. If I did that it would only prove that I hadn't learned anything from Perot's mistake. Parties and the ideas they stand for shouldn't be dictated by a single personality.

Besides, the Minnesota Reform party already has a terrific platform of its own. It's still a work in progress, of course—every platform is. But it's very comprehensive and extremely well constructed. It deserves to stand as a model for other state reform parties.

The party's overarching philosophy is to be "socially inclusive, fiscally responsible," as our new official slogan puts it. We're not looking to court specific social groups, such as gays or pro-lifers or farmers. If we're going to stay true to our stance on independence, we need to keep our scope broader than that. The party is there for independent thinkers, regardless of any other group affiliation.

One of the party's fundamental principles is that political power belongs to the people; it's only entrusted to those who serve in public office. All policy making should be based on the public good. The platform requires that the government be open with the public about financial matters, it insists on accurate reporting of the national debt and an open fiscal reporting policy for all government agencies and departments. It supports the Balanced Budget Amendment. It calls for the simplification of the tax system, both here in Minnesota and nationally, and for replacing Minnesota's bicameral legislature with a unicameral legislature.

The party is very clear about its stand on campaign reform. It advocates eliminating campaign funding by PACs, unions, trade associations, and corporations, and it wants to make it so that every contribution to a candidate or to a political party must be publicly reported.

On the issue of social welfare, the platform favors social programs that encourage self-sufficiency. It supports affordable housing, and seeks to make medical costs and insurance premiums tax deductible. In addition, it advocates making a basic level of health care available to all Minnesotans, regardless of income.

The party doesn't take an official position about abortion or related issues, because it holds these issues to be a matter of personal choice, and none of government's business. It promotes legislation that would allow parents to raise their children according to their own conscience and beliefs without interference or government intrusion, unless there's abuse or neglect going on. It gives more power and autonomy to parents and local school districts, and cuts administration costs.

The party has a terrific system for keeping its platform clear and coherent, while still allowing room for its members to go with their conscience on any given issue. The platform is made up of "cornerstone planks," which require a 74 percent vote from the committee for passage, and "supporting planks," which have to get at least 60 percent. To get the party's endorsement, each candidate has to agree to support a majority or more of the supporting planks and at least 75 percent of the cornerstone planks. Each individual candidate decides which planks to support. Anything that isn't mentioned as a platform plank is left up to the individual candidates to decide in accordance with their own consciences. This system keeps the really divisive stuff out of the official platform, but still leaves room for candidates to go with their conscience.

The Third-Party Movement Falls Back to Regroup

The best thing the Minnesota party can do now is go back to what it was before Perot came along, which seems to be where they're headed. They recently voted to return to the name they had chosen for themselves at their inception in 1992: the Minnesota Independence party, so named by our state chairman, Rick McCluhan.

I'm happy with their choice. "Independence" reinforces the idea that our party members think for themselves. In the long run, I think "Independence" describes us better than "Reform." Imagine a few years from now, once we have accomplished our major goals for government reform, what would we call ourselves then? "Reform" describes a temporary goal, "Independence" describes a permanent one. And when it comes time to reaffiliate nationally, "Independence" may be the way to go. The New York reformer's party already goes by the name Independence party. The way is clear for us now to start getting the third-party movement back on track.

I'd like to see the Minnesota Independence party stand as a model for other centrist third parties. Minnesota has always been a leader in reform. Our party has a very thorough and well-written constitution and solid leadership. I'd like to see other new centrist parties look to us for an example of how it's done. Some day it will be the right time for us to start affiliating nationally again. I thoroughly expect to see another national-level centrist reform party in the future, after the Perot party has played itself out.

But for the time being, I think we're better off getting back to a grassroots level, strengthening ourselves at home, so that we don't make the same mistakes again. A number of state reform parties have said that now that we've disaffiliated, they want to join us. But for now, we're keeping in mind the rules of war: Take care of your own backyard before you venture into anybody else's. I trust we'll know when the time is right to go national again.

Beyond Two-Party Politics

One of the great strengths of the Reform party before it started to degenerate was that we were an extremely diverse bunch. On any given issue our members came down all over the political spectrum, but we were united by the common belief that that was the way it ought to be: Each issue should be evaluated, not by holding it up to the official party line, but on its own merits. Some issues are best handled with a conservative approach, others make more sense through a liberal view. Still others do best with a middle-of-the-road approach. The bottom line is that as moderates and centrists, we're not married to a preformulated ideology, which leaves us free to be open-minded in the way we approach our problems.

I'm no great fan of the bipartisan system, even if it were working ideally. If you think about it, a bipartisan system only gives us one party more than Communist countries have! A two-party system forces politicians to polemicize. Almost by default, they have to oppose whatever the other party's stance happens to be, and the resulting debates force either party further and further to the extremes, leaving nobody to argue the middle.

The bipartisan system was supposed to function as a moderating force; the two parties were supposed to create some kind of balance that would result in a government that was mostly centrist and moderate. But despite Bill Clinton's great personal success in governing from the center, it hasn't worked out that way. The two parties are concentrating too much on battling each other and not enough on tackling the issues of the day. And if one party or the other begins grabbing up power, it upsets the whole balance.

A multipartisan system frees us up to concentrate on the issues. Third parties tend to be much more centered around issues and ideologies than the two traditional parties are, at least in modern times. I think this would be a good time to examine other countries as models. We should look at democratic governments that have multiple parties, and weigh the pros and cons of their systems.

The two traditional parties love the chaos that's destroying the Perot party, because they think it means they won't have to worry about competition. But the irony is, as factionalized as the Democrats and Republicans have become, there's as much danger to the bipartisan system from within as there is from the outside. If they keep it up, I think we'll see people splitting away from the two parties and striking out on their own, pioneering new parties. The bipartisan system as we know it might some day soon be a thing of the past.

But before any third party could compete on anything like a level playing field with the two traditional parties, there's a hell of a lot of opposition to overcome. The two major parties aren't interested in competition, so they set up roadblocks to third-party participation wherever they can.

Neither the National Reform party nor any other third party will be a major concern in this election, both because of their internal disorganization and because of a new piece of legislation that was recently passed by the Commission on Presidential Debates. In January 2000 they passed a bill that mandated that only candidates with 15 percent of the vote or more would be allowed into the debates. Notice that until I won the election here in Minnesota, the standard had always been 5 percent. I entered the race with 10 percent, and won the election with 37. If that law had been in effect during the 1998 election, I wouldn't have won, because I would never have been heard.

That 15 percent law is clearly created to keep third parties out. The level for national party status is only 5 percent. Why should they raise the bar for debates? The group that put the law together called themselves nonpartisan, but one of the most prominent leaders is a former national leader of the Republican party, and currently one of the most entrenched lobbyists in Washington. How is that nonpartisan?

This is what really happened: Democrats and Republicans got together and decided how to keep the third parties out. Then they worked out a way to deflect the responsibility for it away from themselves. That's how gullible the American public can be: All the Democrats and Republicans had to do was call it nonpartisan, and the people believed them. That's the other major problem. In this dance, the apathetic public is the partner of the two corrupt parties.

This new law effectively silences millions of people. It reduces their choices. We should all be outraged. The media should be whipping themselves up into a frenzy. And to add insult to injury, once Democrats and Republicans drafted this new law, do you know who shepherded the legislation through? Washington lobbyists. If that doesn't tell you that lobbyists are controlling our political system!

Lenora Fulani, the former Socialist leader that has been called "the Communist," called me recently to ask if I would get on board with her to try to overturn the new 15 percent law. I'm all for seeing that law overturned, but I don't want to get involved with that right now, because my break from the party is too recent. We need time for things to settle a little. The timing's not right.

But I do believe that in spite of all the obstacles, the third-party movement is here to stay. There's a huge gap in our political system that's waiting to be filled. As long as the third-party movement has the presence of mind to fill that gap and provide the representation that's currently lacking, it will survive and thrive.

A third party must by necessity be a centrist party. We already have representation on the two political extremes. It's the middle of the road that's lacking representation. Any third-party platform that's truly going to give the public an alternative to the two major parties must be devoutly centrist and moderate.

A third party also needs to appeal to moderates in its stance toward the role of government in various aspects of our lives. Rather than being categorically for or against government's role on a given issue, it makes more sense to evaluate each issue on its own merits. Study after study has shown that the American public prefers practical solutions to its problems, rather than the ideological solutions the two major parties often promote. Since third-party members are usually not married to one political ideology or another, they're free to evaluate each issue on its own merits.

The great promise of the third-party movement is that it will free our government of narrow-minded, polarized thinking. It will generate a vast array of new choices for us. And it will allow us more opportunities to participate in the process of democracy. These are worthy goals for a nation of independent minds and free thinkers.

The true measure of the greatness of this country is that we can choose to do this if we wish. If some part of our government isn't working the way we want it to, we have all the tools we need to fix it. Nothing in government is written in stone. And no matter how powerful the media, the lobbyists, the party power brokers, and the career politicians seem to be, we are the ultimate authority behind our government. The Constitution has unequivocally declared it so.

It's still our government. We can shape it and focus it and reinvent it to better serve us all, simply by the power of our choices.

AFTERWORD

The first lady and I were down in San Diego recently. We stayed at the Lowe's hotel right next to the Coronado Cays. That's where you can take an Italian-style gondola ride: You get to drink wine and sample Italian cuisine while a guy rows you around. We decided we wanted to try it, so Terry and I and Captain Gary Bonelli and Captain Don Glasser, my old SEAL teammates, and their wives got onto this gondola. But of course, we had to have our security guys with us. So we ended up rowing along in this tiny, slender little boat, with a huge Harbor Patrol boat growling along, spewing diesel fumes, following right behind us.

Afterwards, we jumped into the Harbor Patrol boat and went around exploring the bay. We went out to where they park all those junk boats, and then we headed over toward the Navy shipyard. I said, "Hey, let's go up on one of the Navy ships." The Harbor Patrol called ahead to the USS *Pearl Harbor,* a gigantic troop-carrying ship. They said, "We've got the governor of Minnesota, requesting to come aboard." And they welcomed us.

We moved up to the pier to go aboard, but since it was low tide, and the boat we were in was so little, we had no way to get up to the pier. A lieutenant from the ship came down and said, "Sir, we welcome you aboard, but we have no way of getting you up there. The only thing we could do is drop the ladder on the other side." So I said, "Drop the ladder."

We went around to the other side of the boat, and they dropped the little skinny rope ladder the Navy calls the Jacob's ladder. And we all climbed up the side of the ship, which was probably 50 feet high. Higher than a house. And the minute you start climbing the ladder, the boat pulls away, so if you fall, you hit the water, not the boat. That makes it even more fun.

Our security was so excited. They even got Terry on film: "What other first lady would climb up the side of the ship like that!" Terry says she was terrified, but she did fine.

When we got up on deck, they sounded out six bells, and called out "Minnesota on board!" Everybody saluted. I'm third on the salute list: It goes President, Vice-President, and head of state. So anyone below president and VP in the military must salute me. They also announced Bonelli and Glasser, because they were retired captains. But they didn't get six bells!

The crew was great. They gave us a complete tour of the ship. We got to look through the infrared gun sights, where you can watch two people lighting a cigarette hundreds of yards away. And when we left they rang the six bells and said, "Minnesota departing."

But the real kicker is that before we left, the captain came up to me with a message from his crew: If I decided to run for president, I'd have their votes. All the branches of the service have told me, "We want you to be the president. We can guarantee you 800,000 military votes." And I've had people come up to me on the streets and literally beg me to run. I'm honored as hell that they would want me to be their president. But I still don't want the job.

I don't believe for a second that I'm the only person who could do what needs to be done. I'm absolutely certain that there are plenty of bright, talented people who would make outstanding leaders, at all levels of public service, if they would simply step forward and offer themselves for the job.

It's tough for me to see the apathy of people who complain about everything, but don't want to do anything to change it. I want to tell them, "Why are you complaining, when you won't work with me? Why won't you help me to change things?"

In many ways, the public is to blame for the political situation we're in, because of their apathy. They reelect incumbents over and over again because it's easier to stick with a known quantity, and because they don't want to give up the power that entrenched politicians have amassed.

And also, human nature is partly to blame. We just naturally fear change. When we get comfortable, it's hard for us to break out of that comfort level. But what's comfortable isn't necessarily what's right.

One of the greatest strengths of the American people is that we truly are a nation of individuals. One person's action can make a difference. It may take courage to face up to entrenched bureaucracy. But we Americans have never been short on courage, either.

The heart of American politics remains in that silent majority. Career politicians, partisan power brokers, and special interest bullies have only been able to "borrow" political power from the people because we've allowed them to. If we're going to become the masters of our own political process again, we have a decision to make. Because in the end, it all depends on whether or not that silent majority chooses to remain silent. Will you come forward and speak your mind, or do I truly stand alone?

SOURCES AND SUGGESTED READING

Anders, George. *Health Against Wealth: HMOs and the Breakdown of Medical Trust.* New York: Houghton Mifflin,1996.

Armey, Richard. *The Flat Tax: A Citizen's Guide to the Facts on What It Will Do for You, Your Country, and Your Pocketbook.* New York: Ballantine Books, 1996.

Bender, David L., Bruno Leone, and William Dudley. *Poverty: Opposing Viewpoints.* San Diego: Greenhaven Press , 1998.

Boliek, Brooks. "The Usual Suspects: How the Presidential Hopefuls Line Up with Hollywood." *Hollywood Reporter,* December 14–20, 1999, 18–19.

Carey, James W. "A Republic, If You Can Keep It: Liberty and Public Life in the Age of Glasnost." In *Crucible of Liberty: 200 Years of the Bill of Rights,* edited by Raymond Arsenault. New York: The Free Press, 1991.

Cooper, Matthew. "Keeping His Eye on the Ball." *Time,* December 27, 1999, 154(26): 128.

Davis, Lanny J. *Truth to Tell: Notes from My White House Education.* New York: The Free Press, 1999.

Douglas, Jack D. *The Myth of the Welfare State.* New Brunswick, N.J.: Transaction Publishers, 1989.

Drew, Elizabeth. *The Corruption of American Politics: What Went Wrong and Why.* Secaucus, N.J.: Birch Lane Press, 1999.

Drucker, Dan. *Abortion Decisions of the Supreme Court, 1973 Through 1989.* Jefferson, N.C.: McFarland & Co., 1990.

Fanning, Beverly J. *Workfare vs. Welfare.* Hudson, Wis.: Gary E. McCuen Publications, 1989.

Finley, M. I. *Democracy Ancient and Modern.* New Brunswick, N.J.: Rutgers University Press, 1973.

Grobel, Laurent. "Jesse Ventura." *Playboy,* November 1999, 55–56, 60–64, 66.

————."Jesse II." *Playboy,* March 2000, 116–17, 158–60, 162, 164–67.

Hall, Kermit. "The Bill of Rights, Liberty and Original Intent." In *Crucible of Liberty: 200 Years of the Bill of Rights,* edited by Raymond Arsenault. New York: The Free Press, 1991.

Holder, Angela Roddey. *The Meaning of the Constitution.* Hauppage, N. Y.: Barron's Educational Series, 1987.

Huff, Darrell. *How to Lie with Statistics.* New York: W. W. Norton, 1954.

McWhirter, Darien A. Exploring the Constitution Series: *Freedom of Speech, Press, and Assembly.* Phoenix, Ariz.: Oryx Press, 1994.

————. Exploring the Constitution Series: *The Separation of Church and State.* Phoenix, Ariz.: Oryx Press, 1994.

Paine, Thomas. *Common Sense.* Mineola, N.Y.: Dover Publications, 1997.

Smiley, Tavis. *Hard Left: Straight Talk About the Wrongs of the Right.* New York: Anchor Books, 1996.

Tannen, Deborah. *The Argument Culture: Moving from Debate to Dialogue.* New York: Random House, 1998.

Von Hoffman, Nicholas. "God Was Present at the Founding." *Civilization,* April/May 1998, 39–42.

Welton, K. B. *Abortion Is Not a Sin: A New-Age Look at an Age-Old Problem.* Costa Mesa, Calif.: Pandit Press, 1987.

Weston, Anthony. *A Rulebook for Arguments.* Indianapolis: Hackett Publishing, 1987.